SOUP

SOUP

foreword by eric schlosser

London, New York, Melbourne,
Munich, and Delhi

Photography William Reavell

Editor Michael Fullalove
Designer John Round

Project Editor Robert Sharman
Designer Kathryn Wilding
Senior Jacket Creative Nicola Powling
Managing Editor Dawn Henderson
Managing Art Editor Christine Keilty
Production Editor Kelly Salih
Production Controller Alice Holloway
Creative Technical Support Sonia Charbonnier

Published in the United States by
DK Publishing
375 Hudson Street
New York, New York 10014

12 13 10 9 8 7 6 5 4 3 2 1

001-186930-Sept/12
This paperback edition published in 2012.

Published in Great Britain
by Dorling Kindersley Limited

A catalog record for this book is available
from the Library of Congress.

ISBN 978-0-7566-9832-4

DK books are available at special discounts when
purchased in bulk for sales promotions, premiums,
fund-raising, or educational use. For details,
contact: DK Publishing Special Markets,
375 Hudson Street, New York, New York 10014
or specialsales@dk.com

Colour reproduction by Colourscan, Singapore
Printed and bound in China by South China Printing Co.Ltd

**Discover more at
www.dk.com**

contents

foreword by **eric schlosser**

Some wonderful chefs have donated their favorite soup recipes to this cookbook for a simple reason. Proceeds from the book will support the work of the Soil Association, a nonprofit based in Bristol, England. Few Americans have heard of the Soil Association. But almost everyone has heard of organic food and sustainable agriculture, two of the causes that the Soil Association has been promoting for more than 60 years. Indeed, the modern organic movement was launched during the 1940s by a pair of British iconoclasts, Lady Eve Balfour and Sir Albert Howard. At a time when herbicides and pesticides and synthetic fertilizers were first being introduced on a wide scale, Balfour and Howard began to question whether these were good things. They rebelled against a mindset that viewed the land as just one more economic commodity, to be doused with chemicals for a short-term profit. They rebelled against a mentality that worshipped technology for its own sake, that eagerly sought to control and dominate nature. They embraced a much more holistic view of how we should treat livestock, the land, and the rural communities dependent upon farming.

The "Soil Association" seems like an odd name for an organization devoted to producing food that's healthy, nutritious, and environmentally sound. But the soil plays a central role in the thinking behind sustainable agriculture—both as a literal concern and as a metaphor for the interconnectedness of all things. What you put in the soil winds up in the crops that grow in the soil, winds up in the animals that eat those crops, winds up in the people who eat those animals. And every living thing, and every one of us, ultimately returns to the soil. You cannot mistreat one of these elements without harming the others. This is a deeply humble philosophy, founded upon a reverence for nature and a skepticism about some of mankind's latest inventions. It is a belief that we must try to work with nature, not seek to conquer nature. And it is the guiding spirit of many groups today, like the Soil Association, that are fighting against Global Warming, genetically modified food, and the toxic chemicals that are poisoning the earth.

We need to reduce the power of agribusiness and reclaim our government from the corrupt grip of special interests. But unlike many social movements, the battle for sustainable agriculture doesn't always have to be grim, hard work. As the great chef Alice Waters likes to say, this revolution tastes good. It's about shopping at farmers' markets or growing your own, eating food that's local and organic, educating yourself about the issues and learning how to cook. Every little bit helps. That's why a book like this can make a difference. Buy it, read it, use it often. I can't think of a better way to make friends and influence people.

Eric Schlosser

Eric Schlosser
Author of *Fast Food Nation*

introduction

What does a book about soup have to do with the global food crisis and building a more sustainable and organic food and farming future?

Actually, everything! In preparing a simple bowl of soup for your family and loved ones sourced from fresh, organic, in season, and ideally local ingredients, you are taking powerful direct action to prepare the earth for a more resilient and sustainable future, both for yourself and for future generations. Whether your ingredients are coming freshly grown from your own backyard or you've bought them directly from a real person at the farmers' market, making the connection between the food you eat and the place it comes from is crucial to a healthy sense of cultural identity.

In a world where the problems we face seem so enormous and intractable, making the food connection is coined perfectly by poet and philosopher Wendell Berry when he wrote "Eating is an agricultural act." By eating food—in this case soup—with a good story, you are contributing to the solution at a local level, which, scaled up, has global implications.

This book has been planned with real food enthusiasts in mind. It is organized by produce, so you can look up whatever seasonal produce you've come across and find a range of different, wholesome recipes for it. The Soil Association, a UK-based organization that works internationally, has been working for over sixty years to promote a healthier food culture that puts the health and welfare of our environment, our farm animals, and people at center stage. We believe in the power of individual citizens to "be the change" and this soup book is a part of that revolution in our food culture.

Patrick Holden

Patrick Holden
Director of the Soil Association

techniques

The cornerstone of many soups is a well-made stock, and although the ingredients for it may seem humble and the preparation simple, the contribution it makes is vital.

making stock

The four stocks most commonly called for in soup-making are chicken stock, brown meat stock, fish stock, and vegetable stock. Made from bones and/or common vegetables and flavorings, they are easy to prepare and freeze well for up to three months. If produced from meat bones, stock is clear and relatively fat-free, although it will be gelatinous enough to set when cold. Vegetable stock is lighter and requires a careful balance of ingredients to make it flavorsome. Stocks should not be seasoned with salt—they are one of the building blocks for a soup, not a dish in their own right.

selection of stocks

brown meat stock is so called because it is produced from meat bones that have been "browned" by cooking in fat. It jellies when cold.

vegetable stock can be given extra depth by the addition of mushrooms, potatoes, and tomatoes that will offset the sweetness of the other veggies.

fish stock is quick to make, ideally from the bones and heads of salmon or mild-flavored white fish, especially flatfish like sole and plaice.

chicken stock serves as the base for many fine soups. Some raw or cooked chicken bones and a few standard aromatics are all that's required to produce a rich, gelatinous stock.

This recipe gives an ideal list of ingredients, but as long as you have the chicken carcass, onion, carrot, and one or two of the herbs, you can turn out a fine stock.

chicken stock

⊘ **MAKES** 1.5 QT (1.5 L)   🕐 **PREP** 5 MINS **COOK** 3 HRS   ❄ **FREEZE** 3 MONTHS

1 raw or cooked chicken carcass,
   roughly broken into pieces
1 onion, quartered
1 carrot, quartered
1 leek, quartered
1 celery rib, quartered

1 bay leaf
2 parsley stems
1 sprig of thyme
8 black peppercorns
1.7 quarts (1.7 liters) cold water

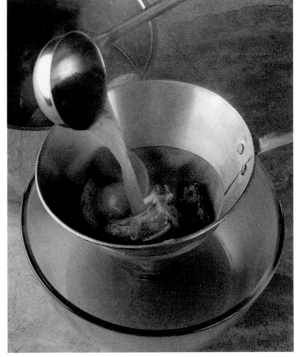

1 Put the chicken, vegetables, and all the seasonings into a large pan, cover with the water, and bring to a boil. Cover with a lid, lower the heat, and simmer for 2–3 hours, skimming off any foam from time to time.

2 Ladle the stock through a sieve into a bowl, pressing the ingredients well against the side of the sieve with the back of the ladle to extract as much liquid as possible.

3 If you're using the stock immediately, remove any globules of fat from the surface by skimming the top of the stock with a paper towel folded in two.

4 Otherwise, let the stock cool before chilling it in a covered container for up to 3 days. A layer of congealed fat will form on the surface. Scoop this off before use.

microwave chicken stock
If you are short on time, you can also make chicken stock in a microwave. Put the broken-up chicken carcass into a large microwaveable bowl along with the onion, carrot, leek, and celery. Add the bay leaf, parsley, thyme, and peppercorns, then cover with boiling water. Cover the bowl with plastic wrap (roll it back at one edge to allow the steam to escape) and microwave on high for 25 minutes. Let stand for 25 minutes longer, then strain.

For a rich meat-based stock, use either beef or lamb bones, but never a mixture of the two. If you have any bacon rinds or vegetable trimmings on hand, pop them in the pot too.

brown meat stock

MAKES 2.5 QT (2.5 L)　　**PREP** 10 MINS **COOK** 3½–4½ HRS　　**FREEZE** 3 MONTHS

3lb (1.35kg) raw or cooked beef or lamb bones
2–3 onions, halved
2–3 carrots, halved

a bouquet garni (see p24)
2.5–3 quarts (2.5–3 liters) cold water
1 tsp black peppercorns

1 If you're using raw bones, roast them with the onions and carrots in an oven preheated to 400°F (200°C), turning them frequently, for 30 minutes or until browned. If you're using cooked bones, start the stock from step 2.

2 Put all the ingredients into a large pan, bring to a boil, then skim off any foam that rises to the surface with a slotted spoon. Lower the heat, cover with a lid, and simmer for 3–4 hours. Strain the stock through a sieve, pressing the ingredients against the sides of the sieve to extract all the liquid. Cool, then chill in a covered container for up to 3 days. Before use, remove any solidified fat from the surface, then bring the stock to a boil.

hale and hearty
A meaty stock based on beef or lamb makes a world of difference to hearty broth-based soups like French onion soup.

This is an excellent stock, with a good balance of flavors. The potato means it will not be clear, but since it is being used in a soup, that doesn't matter.

vegetable stock

⊘ MAKES 1 QT (1 L)   **⏱ PREP** 5 MINS **COOK** 35 MINS   **❄ FREEZE** 3 MONTHS

1 leek, thickly sliced
1 large carrot, thickly sliced
2 celery ribs, thickly sliced
1 onion, coarsely chopped
2½oz (75g) button or cremini
 mushrooms, quartered

1 medium potato, thickly sliced
1 tomato, quartered
3 parsley stems
2 bay leaves
4 sprigs of thyme
1.5 quarts (1.5 liters) cold water

1 Put all the ingredients into a large pot. Bring to a boil, then lower the heat, cover with a lid, and simmer very gently for 30 minutes.

2 Strain the stock through a fine sieve, pressing the ingredients well against the sides of the sieve to extract all the liquid. Let cool completely, then chill in a covered container for up to 3 days before use.

light and fragrant
A flavorful vegetable stock makes a good alternative to chicken stock, whether you are vegetarian or not.

Ask the fishmonger for the bones when getting fish filleted, and check to see if they have any extra they can give you. Fish bones will freeze, well-wrapped, for up to two months.

fish stock

◗ MAKES 1.5 QT (1.5 L)   **◗ PREP** 5 MINS **COOK** 30 MINS   **✸ FREEZE** 2 MONTHS

1½–2¼lb (675g–1kg) salmon or white fish bones, heads, and skin (don't use those from dark, oily fish such as mackerel, herring, and sardines—they will give an unpleasant flavor)
6 black peppercorns
1 sprig of thyme

1 bay leaf
2 parsley stems
2 small carrots, coarsely chopped
1 onion, coarsely chopped
2 celery ribs, coarsely chopped
1 cup dry white wine
1.7 quarts (1.7 liters) cold water

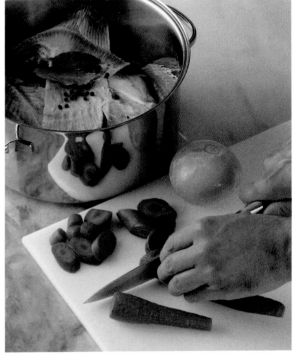

1 Put the fish heads and bones into a large pan, breaking or cutting them up with a knife to fit. Add the black peppercorns, thyme, bay leaf, and parsley.

2 Add the vegetables to the pot with the wine. Place the pan over medium-high heat and let the wine bubble for 3 minutes. Add the water and bring to a boil.

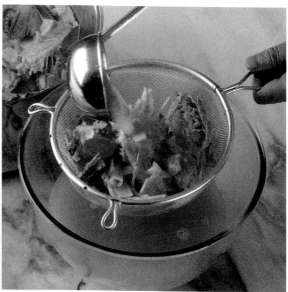

3 Lower the heat and simmer, uncovered, for 20–25 minutes—but no longer, or the stock may begin to develop a bitter taste. Skim off any white foam from time to time with a slotted spoon.

4 Strain the stock through a fine sieve into a bowl, pressing the solids against the side of the sieve to extract all the liquid. Allow to cool completely, then chill in a covered container for up to 3 days.

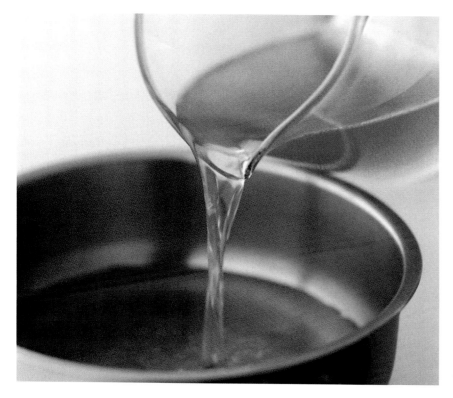

5 The finished stock should be thin in texture, with a delicate flavor. It will make an excellent base for all kinds of fish soup.

Careful preparation of vegetables is essential—not only do properly cut vegetables contribute to the finished appearance of a soup, they cook more evenly too.

preparing vegetables

Vegetables are best prepared just before cooking: washed, peeled, and cut ahead of time, they are left exposed to air and moisture, which can lead them to deteriorate and lose their vitamins. Most often vegetables can be cut by hand, so a good sharp knife is vital. Use a large or small knife depending on the vegetable you're cutting. Here's how to prepare those most commonly used in soups.

chopping or crushing garlic

1 Lay the clove of garlic on a cutting board with the blade of a large knife on top of it. Strike the blade with the heel of your hand to break the skin of the clove, but don't press down so hard that you smash the garlic.

2 Peel off the skin, then chop the ends off of the garlic. Chop the garlic coarsely, then sprinkle it with a little salt to keep it from sticking to the blade. You can then chop it finely or crush smooth with the flat blade.

chopping onions

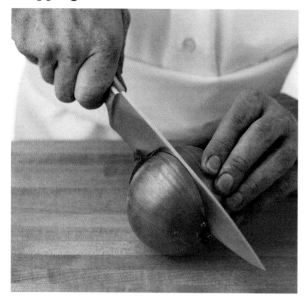

1 Cut the onion in half lengthwise with a chef's knife. Peel away the skin, but leave the root intact—it will help keep the halves together as you chop.

2 With the onion flat side down on the cutting board, make two or three horizontal slices, cutting up to—but not through—the root.

3 Now, vertically slice the onion finely, being careful once again to cut up to but not through the root.

4 Turn the onion 90 degrees and slice across to make even-sized dice. Discard the root when you get to it.

peeling and seeding tomatoes

1 With a sharp knife, cut an "X" in the base of the tomato.

2 Immerse it in boiling water for 20 seconds, or until the skin begins to split.

3 Remove the tomato with a slotted spoon and plunge it into ice water to cool it.

4 When it's cool enough to handle, use a paring knife to peel off the skin.

5 Slice the tomato in half, then squeeze the seeds into a bowl and discard.

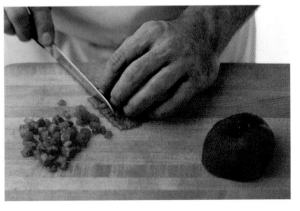

6 Slice the tomato half first into strips and then into dice.

cleaning and chopping leeks

1 With a large knife, trim off the root and some of the dark green leaf at the top, then slice the leek lengthwise in two and fan it open.

2 Rinse the leek under cold running water to remove the soil that tends to collect between the layers, then pat it dry with paper towels.

3 Sit the halved leek on the cutting board and slice it into thick or thin strips, according to the recipe.

chopping carrots

Peel the carrot, then slice it lengthwise. Cut the lengths crosswise, then stack them and cut into batons. Slice across the batons to make even-sized dice.

sweating vegetables

Sweating chopped vegetables in oil or butter gives a soup a more pronounced flavor. Heat a little fat over low heat, stir in the vegetables, then add a pinch of salt, cover, and cook for 5–10 minutes or until soft but not brown.

Chopped herbs release more of their flavor than whole, but before the leaves of some herbs like rosemary can be chopped, they need to be stripped from their stalks.

preparing herbs

chopping herbs with tender stalks

1 To chop the leaves of herbs with tender stalks like basil, roll them together into a tight bunch.

2 Holding the bunch of leaves steady with one hand, slice across them with a chef's knife.

3 Using the knife in a rocking motion, chop the leaves finely, turning them 90 degrees halfway through.

using a mezzaluna

removing stalks

making a bouquet garni

A mezzaluna makes light work of chopping herbs. Rock it from side to side across them until they're chopped to your liking.

To strip the leaves off herbs with stalks, run the thumb and forefinger of one hand along the stalk.

For a classic soup flavoring, tie a sprig of thyme and parsley with a bay leaf. You could also include sage or rosemary.

Spices lend an extra dimension to many soups and, whether you're using them fresh or dried, they usually require a little straightforward preparation.

preparing spices

bruising whole spices

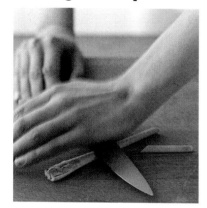

Before use, whole fresh spices like lemongrass are usually bruised with the blade of a heavy knife and your hand.

grating roots

Roots like ginger can be finely chopped by hand, but it's often easiest to grate them. Peel off the skin beforehand.

seeding chiles

Scraping out the seeds from chiles lessens their heat. Wear a pair of rubber or plastic gloves to do it.

frying in oil

When spices are cooked until lightly colored, their flavor gets trapped in the oil. Use the oil along with the spices.

dry-roasting

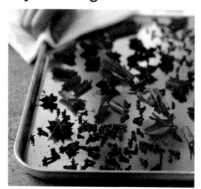

To dry-roast spices, place them in an oven preheated to 325°F (160°C), or cook them in a dry pan until lightly browned.

crushing

Dried or dry-roasted spices can be crushed by hand in a pestle and mortar or by machine in a spice mill.

Dried beans, peas, and lentils are perfect for soup-making. Little effort is required to prepare them—all you need to do is think ahead.

preparing legumes

The basic preparation of legumes is simple: first, you need to sort and rinse them; then (in nearly all cases) you need to soak them; finally, the legumes have to be cooked until tender. This can take anywhere from around half an hour to 3 hours. Once cooked, legumes are well-suited to puréeing, but they also work well left whole in soups.

sorting and rinsing

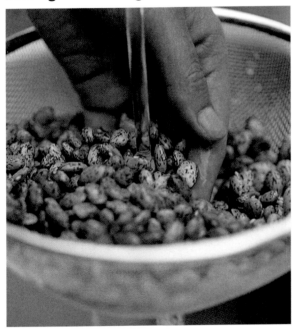

Whatever kind of legume you're using, start by sorting and rinsing them. Place the legumes in a colander and carefully pick out any husks or pieces of grit, then rinse the legumes well under cold running water.

soaking

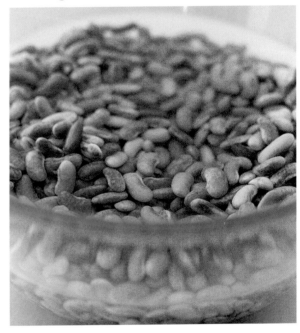

Apart from lentils and split peas, all legumes need to be soaked for at least 8 hours, and preferably overnight. Place them in a bowl, add three times their volume of cold water, then cover and place in the refrigerator.

adding flavor

The flavor of legumes can be rather bland, so it's usually a good idea to add some aromatics. A bouquet garni (see p24) or a sprig of herbs will do the trick: bay leaves, parsley, rosemary, or thyme all work well. A pinch of cumin, cilantro, hot red pepper flakes, or caraway is another option, but you could also pop a carrot into the pan or an onion studded with cloves. Alternatively, you can cook legumes in a well-seasoned stock, but never season it with salt—it will prevent them from softening.

cooking legumes

Drain the soaked legumes, then place them in a large pan along with any seasonings. Pour in four times their volume of cold water and add 1 tbsp vegetable oil to keep them from sticking. Bring rapidly to a boil, and boil hard for 10 minutes, skimming away any foam with a slotted spoon. Lower the heat, partially cover with a lid, and simmer until tender. The cooking time will depend on the variety of legume (see right).

COOKING TIMES

Here are approximate cooking times for the legumes most commonly used in soups.

black beans	1 hour
black-eyed peas	1–1½ hours
borlotti beans	1–1½ hours
fava beans	1–1½ hours
cannellini beans	1–1½ hours
chickpeas	2–3 hours
navy beans	1½ hours
green beans	1–1½ hours
lentils (split)	25 minutes
lentils (whole)	45 minutes
pinto beans	1–1½ hours
red kidney beans	1–1½ hours
split peas	45 minutes

Among the easiest soups to prepare are those you process to a purée in a blender. The alternative is to use a food mill—this requires a little more effort, but the results are smoother.

puréeing

The secret to success with puréed soups is thorough cooking, so that the starchy ingredients that give the soup its body can be blended to a smooth purée. For that reason, always cook root vegetables and dried beans till they are extremely tender, but never overcook potatoes, or they will become glutinous and gluey. There is also a range of semi-puréed soups, in which some of the ingredients are blended to thicken the broth, while the rest are left whole for interest.

in a blender

1 Before blending, test the ingredients are really tender with a knife—they are only ready to purée when completely soft.

2 Blend the soup until you have a smooth consistency with no lumps. Do it in batches so you don't overload the machine.

3 The consistency of a puréed soup will vary according to the ingredients used and the way in which they're processed. But, in general, it should be totally smooth and lump-free. To remove all traces of skins, seeds, and fibers, you may need to push the purée through a fine sieve.

using a food mill

Working the ingredients through a food mill is particularly successful for soups that contain ingredients with skins and seeds, which blenders sometimes can't cope with.

semi-puréed soups

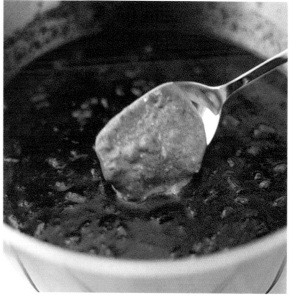

To thicken a soup but keep some texture for interest, purée about half of it and then return it to the pan. Gently reheat the soup before serving.

A little butter or cream stirred into a soup just before serving will enrich it (see pp32–33), but there will be times when you want to thicken a soup a bit more. Here's how to do it.

thickening

There are several quick and easy ways you can give body to a soup at the end of cooking. You could whisk egg yolk or a mixture of egg yolk and cream into the hot liquid. Another option is to use starch, in the form of rice flour, all-purpose flour, or cornstarch. Or you could make a paste from flour and butter and stir this into the soup before serving. But perhaps the oldest method of thickening a soup is with bread, either stirred into the broth at the last minute or incorporated into it earlier in the cooking process.

with starch

Mix a little cornstarch, rice flour, or all-purpose flour to a thin paste with some cold water. Stir the mixture into the pot of hot soup, bring back to a boil, and simmer, stirring all the time, for 1–2 minutes until the soup thickens.

with flour and butter

Combine two parts softened butter to one part flour. Gradually whisk small pieces of the paste into the hot soup at the end of cooking. Allow the flour to cook for 1–2 minutes, stirring all the time.

with egg

Added toward the end of cooking, egg yolk or a mixture of egg yolk and cream will thicken a hot soup and make it velvety. Remove the pan from the heat to incorporate the mixture, then reheat the soup gently, whisking until thick. Do not allow it to boil or it will curdle.

with bread

Bread has long been used to thicken country soups. For gazpacho (left), bread crumbs are blended into the soup at an early stage. But bread can also be added to a broth at the last minute, and stirred until it breaks up and thickens the soup.

Butter or cream stirred into a soup at the last minute will greatly improve its character, adding body and shine. For interest, you can flavor the butter and serve it at the table.

enriching

Both cream and butter make a quick and simple garnish for individual servings of soup (see pp36–39), but if you have another garnish in mind, you can add them to the soup to enrich it while it's still in the pan. Butters flavored with herbs, nuts, or smoked fish are another way of enriching a soup, although these are best served separately, to be added to the soup by your guests.

with cream

with butter

Add the cream at the end of cooking and, in a puréed soup, after blending. Stir it in well, then check the seasoning. If you've added a substantial amount of cream, you may want to reheat the soup gently before serving.

Cut 1 tbsp of chilled unsalted butter into cubes. Remove the pan from the heat and whisk it in a cube at a time—the soup should become glossy and smooth. Do not reheat the soup or the butter will separate.

with a flavored butter

Flavored butters are an ideal accompaniment to puréed soups and bisques. They are also easy to prepare and work well with a variety of ingredients. Blend the flavorings of your choice into the butter, then place the butter on a sheet of wax paper and roll it tightly into a cylindrical shape. Chill it in the refrigerator or freezer until you're ready to serve the soup, then simply slice it into rounds. You could also serve the butter at the table and allow your guests to help themselves. Here are recipes for two flavored butters that are great with a whole range of soups.

herb butter Mix 2oz (60g) softened butter with 6 blanched and finely chopped spinach leaves, 1 chopped shallot, 1 tsp each chopped parsley, chervil, and tarragon, and some salt and pepper. Roll in wax paper and chill until needed.

lemon and hot pepper butter Combine 2oz (60g) softened butter with 1 tsp finely grated lemon zest and ¼ tsp crushed hot red pepper flakes (or more if you like your food quite spicy). Season to taste with salt.

There's no need to worry if your soup hasn't turned out quite as you had intended—even the most accomplished cook occasionally produces a dish that's less than perfect.

rescuing

Whether you are unhappy with the finished consistency or think the soup is too highly seasoned, here are some quick fixes to set things right.

too thin

There are a number of ways you can thicken a soup that's too thin. You could whisk in a paste of butter and flour or a mixture of eggs and cream (as here). Or, you could add some starch in the form of rice flour, all-purpose flour, or cornstarch blended with water (for more details, turn to pp30–1). Another option is to stir in a few instant potato flakes or a little instant oat cereal.

too thick

Depending on the liquid you've used to produce the soup, thin it with a little stock, milk, or water. Once the soup has reached the desired consistency, taste it, season, and reheat gently.

stringy or lumpy

Even a soup you've processed in a blender can turn out lumpy or stringy. Ladle it into a fine sieve, then use the back of the ladle, a wooden spoon, or a pestle to push the ingredients through. Reheat gently before serving.

too salty

If you only ever add salt toward the end of cooking and use homemade stock that's unseasoned, the chances of your soup being too salty are slim. But, if it is, there are a couple of things you can do. Add a couple of raw potatoes cut in half and simmer the soup gently until they're cooked, then remove and discard them before serving. Alternatively, add a little sugar and, if the soup is also too thick, some cream, milk, or water.

From a single piece of seafood to a simple swirl of cream, a well-chosen garnish transforms a soup, adding extra color, as well as texture and flavor.

garnishing

For some soups, a garnish is an essential component—the sour cream stirred into Borscht, for instance, or the cheese-topped croûtes served with French onion soup. For others, a garnish is a way of introducing contrasting textures and flavors. Many ingredients can act as a garnish if they also complement the flavors of the soup, but here is a selection to suit almost every type.

with cream

Dolloped, swirled, or drizzled, cream makes an excellent garnish for thick puréed soups. Use heavy cream, whipped cream, sour cream, or crème fraîche. Yogurt is also a good alternative if you're counting calories.

with herbs

Fresh sage or parsley leaves fried in olive oil until crisp make a flavorful garnish for gutsy soups, but a sprinkling of chopped parsley, chervil, or cilantro instantly adds interest, fragrance, and color to almost any soup.

with shellfish

A whole shrimp, crab claw, grilled scallop, or (as here) an oyster poached and served in its shell makes a spectacular garnish for a seafood soup. A wild garlic flower provides the finishing touch for this dish.

with olive oil

As much a condiment as a garnish, a drizzle of fragrant, full-bodied extra virgin olive oil brings a Mediterranean flavor to soups, while looking appetizing and glossy on the surface.

with vegetables

Raw or cooked, vegetables make eye-catching and healthy garnishes. If small, like peas, they can be served whole. Otherwise, slice them into decorative strips, dice, or rings.

with bacon

Cooked until crisp and then crumbled, bacon makes a tasty garnish that looks attractive floating on the surface of a pale puréed soup. Here it is accompanied by pieces of pan-fried scallop.

with seeds or nuts

Toasted seeds or nuts not only look pretty, they also lend a satisfying crunch. Served with a vegetable soup, they are a good source of protein too.

with croûtons

Small dice of fried bread are a classic garnish. For about 40 croûtons, cut 4 slices of day-old white bread (crusts removed) into ½in (1cm) dice. Heat 2 tbsp olive oil and 2 tbsp unsalted butter in a large frying pan until hot, then cook the bread, stirring constantly, for 10 minutes or until golden. Drain on paper towels before serving. For extra flavor, stir in a finely chopped garlic clove a few minutes before the croûtons are through cooking.

with croûtes

Large croûtons are known as croûtes. To make them, cut a day-old baguette into ½in (1cm) slices, and toast until golden. Alternatively, place on a baking sheet and bake in an oven preheated to 350°F (180°C) for 15 minutes.

ways of serving croûtes

Croûtes are a versatile garnish. Rubbed with garlic, then topped with cheese and popped under the broiler, they are perfect for French onion soup (above). For fish soups, spread them thickly with a garlicky rouille sauce.

A well-stocked pantry will save you time and help you rustle up soups even on short notice. With the right ingredients, it will also be a source of inspiration.

pantry essentials

Putting together soups from the contents of your cupboards or pantry is a satisfying experience. Whether you're cooking for unannounced guests or whipping up a quick supper, with a few well-chosen basics on hand, you'll always have the ability to make a tasty soup. Here are the required items.

onions

basic vegetables

Onions, garlic, carrots, and leeks are the basis for countless soups, so it makes sense to have them available at all times. Obviously, they are perishable—store them in a cool, dark place.

frozen stock and bouillon cubes

A supply of homemade stock is a must. Make it in advance and store it in the freezer. For those days when you're in a real hurry, have some good-quality chicken, beef, or vegetable stock cubes on hand, too.

a selection of oils

From the best-quality olive oil for garnishing to the more work-a-day varieties such as sunflower oil used for cooking and frying, a good selection of oils is invaluable. The more unusual, like sesame oil, are available in small bottles—a blessing when space is at a premium.

garlic

flavorings

Salt and whole black peppercorns are indispensable in the kitchen, but there are other flavorings worth having in your kitchen cupboard, too. Wine vinegars, sherry vinegar, Worcestershire sauce, soy sauce, and fish sauce are frequently used in soups.

dried or canned legumes

Whether canned or dried, beans, peas, and lentils are among the staples of soup-making. Dried legumes do not keep indefinitely, so buy them from stores with a healthy turnover, and be sure to use them within a year—no amount of cooking will soften them after that. Canned legumes need almost nothing in the way of preparation—simply drain, rinse, then drain them again.

dried legumes

dried spices

You don't need a taste for particularly spicy food to make use of a wide range of spices—a pinch of hot red pepper flakes or a tablespoon of crushed coriander seeds may be all that's required to give a soup that extra dimension. Among the dried spices most often called for are cumin, coriander, caraway, nutmeg, fenugreek, star anise, cinnamon, and ginger.

herbs—fresh and dried

For the rounded flavor and complexity they give to soups, herbs are invaluable. The more popular, such as parsley and chives, are available fresh all year round, but it's handy to keep dried and frozen herbs on hand as well. They are generally more pungent than fresh, so use them sparingly. And keep an eye on expiration dates: frozen herbs will keep well for up to six months; dried for up to four. If you grow your own herbs, try drying or freezing them for use during the winter.

fresh herbs

canned ingredients

Canned tomatoes are excellent in soups, and in winter are likely to be more flavorful than fresh tomatoes. They even come already chopped. Make some shelf space for a can of tomato purée, too, and a can of sweet corn. Some coconut milk might also be handy.

dried pasta and noodles

Dried pasta and noodles are at the heart of many comforting soups, so it's worth making them a permanent feature in your cupboards. If space is an issue, a small supply of vermicelli, rice noodles, and udon noodles will serve you well.

dried pasta

However well we plan, we all have food left over at times. Cooked chicken and ham are obvious candidates for soup, but you can make good use of many other leftovers, too.

making use of leftovers

The ideal home for leftovers is in comforting rustic-style soups. Add the ingredient sparingly to begin with, then use your discrimination to decide on balance, texture, and seasoning. Recycling food calls for ingenuity and skill, so never give in to temptation and use your soup pot as a receptacle, or your soup-making skills will acquire a poor reputation. Here are some thrifty ideas for using leftovers.

stale bread

stale bread

Stale white bread is the perfect starting point for making croûtons and croûtes (see p39), which are a welcome addition to a wide range of soups. Processed in a blender or food processor to form bread crumbs, stale bread is also an essential ingredient in the chilled Spanish soup Gazpacho (see p107).

cooked meat

Cooked chicken, turkey, and game are all excellent in soups, as is cooked ham. Cured meats such as chorizo and salami work equally well. In general, leftovers of red meats are not suitable for making soup, although the bones from cooked beef or lamb can go straight into the cooking pot for stock.

**egg yolks
and whites**

eggs yolks and egg whites

Making use of leftover egg yolks is never a problem. Whisk them into a hot soup toward the end of cooking—they will thicken it and give a velvety texture. Although less versatile, leftover egg whites are useful for clarifying consommé.

cooked vegetables

Cut into dice, shredded, or left whole if small like sweet corn and peas, cooked vegetables can be added to a soup just before serving and heated through. Alternatively, they can be popped in the blender along with the other ingredients and puréed.

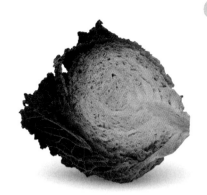

leftover cabbage

homemade gravy

Capitalize on gravy's richness and depth of flavor by stirring it into meaty soups just before serving. If the sauce has acquired a skin since you first prepared it, carefully remove this beforehand with a slotted spoon.

boiled pasta

Small pasta shapes that have been cooked but not covered in sauce can turn a simple soup into a square meal. Add leftover pasta at the last minute and then heat it through gently.

chunks of cheese

scraps of cheese

Small chunks of Cheddar, Parmesan, and Gruyère never need go to waste when you make your own soups. Grate the cheese finely and use it to top croûtes. Broiled until golden brown and bubbling, these make a hearty topping for soups.

red or white wine

A small glass of white wine splashed into a fish soup will help bring out the flavor of the seafood, while a little red wine added to a rich meaty soup will lend body and depth.

cold potatoes

Cooked potatoes are a boon when making soups, since they give extra substance. Process them in the blender with the other ingredients or dice and add them to the pan just before serving and heat gently through.

leftover potatoes

recipe planners

vegetarian

mango and curry leaf soup
🕐 35 mins **page 325**

creamy pistachio soup
🕐 1 hr **page 229**

beet and apple soup
🕐 1 hr 20 mins **page 78**

jerusalem artichoke soup
🕐 50–60 mins **page 164**

creamy kidney bean soup
🕐 3 hrs 35 mins **page 209**

tuscan bean soup
🕐 1 hr 35 mins **page 204**

sweet corn chowder
🕐 40 mins **page 96**

chilled

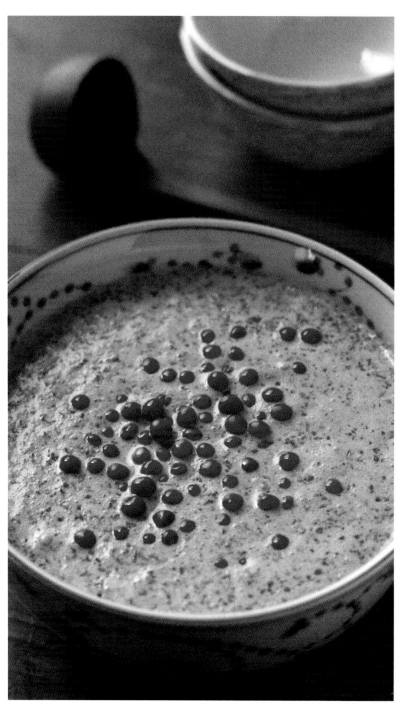

lettuce soup with peas

mango, cilantro, and pomegranate soup

rose hip soup

cherry soup

chilled melon and ginger soup

vichyssoise

hearty

pistou soup
🕐 2 hrs page 86

porcini mushroom soup
🕐 35–45 mins (plus standing) **page 195**

white bean soup
🕐 2 hrs 30 mins **page 212**

minted pea and ham soup
🕐 35–40 mins **page 93**

mexican chili bean soup
🕐 50 mins **page 207**

creamy kidney bean soup
🕐 3 hrs 35 mins **page 209**

cannellini bean and carrot soup
🕐 1 hr 10 mins **page 211**

rosemary's bean soup with italian cheese crisps
🕐 25–30 mins (plus soaking) **page 214**

lentil soup
🕐 55 mins **page 217**

harissa and chickpea soup
🕐 1 hr 10 mins **page 221**

split pea and bacon soup
🕐 1 hr 40 mins **page 225**

soupe de poissons
🕐 1 hr 20 mins **page 239**

creamy smoked trout soup
🕐 25 mins **page 251**

italian wedding soup
🕐 1 hr 50 mins **page 314**

pichelsteiner
🕐 1 hr 30 mins **page 315**

tuscan bean soup
🕐 1 hr 35 mins **page 204**

healthy

spicy

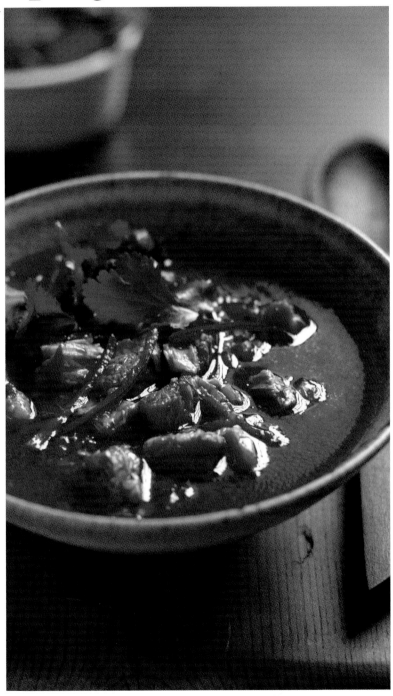

pork vindaloo broth
3 hrs 35 mins (plus chilling) **page 312**

keralan shrimp soup
🕐 1 hr page 277

sopa de tortilla
🕐 1hr 5 mins page 109

mussels in ginger and chile broth
🕐 50–55 mins page 265

spicy turnip soup with pimento and noodles
🕐 40 mins page 167

african sweet potato soup
🕐 45 mins page 172

bigos
🕐 2 hrs 40 mins page 184

cuban black bean soup
🕐 2 hrs 5 mins (plus soaking) page 202

mexican chili bean soup
🕐 50 mins page 207

kichidi
🕐 1 hr 5 mins page 219

harissa and chickpea soup
🕐 1 hr 10 mins page 221

hot and sour chicken broth
🕐 30 mins page 295

beef chili
🕐 45 mins page 307

spiced lamb broth
🕐 3 hrs page 316

thai chicken soup
🕐 55 mins page 292

main meals

sopa seca de fideos

fish soup with fennel

quick

chilled melon and ginger soup
🕐 15 mins page 320

summer vegetables

This warming recipe is based on a French country soup and is delicious topped with a spoonful of pesto, some chopped fresh parsley or tarragon, or some grated Parmesan.

allotment soup

⊘ SERVES 6   **⏱ PREP** 20 MINS   **❄ FREEZE** UP TO 3 MONTHS
                 COOK 1 HR 20 MINS   WITHOUT THE GREEN BEANS

3oz (85g) French beans
2 tbsp olive oil
1 medium leek, finely sliced
1 small turnip, cut into ½in (1cm) dice
2 medium carrots, cut into ½in (1cm) dice
1 large zucchini, cut into ½in (1cm) dice
1 celery rib, cut into ½in (1cm) dice
1 large potato, cut into ½in (1cm) dice

2 tomatoes, peeled and cut into
  ½in (1cm) dice
2 garlic cloves, finely chopped
2 quarts (2 liters) cold water
sea salt and freshly ground
  black pepper
6oz (175g) green beans, cut into
  ¾in (2cm) lengths

1 Put the French beans in a saucepan with plenty of cold unsalted water. Bring to a boil, cover with a lid, and boil for 15 minutes. Lower the heat, then simmer until tender and drain.

2 Meanwhile, heat the oil in a large saucepan, add the leek, turnip, carrots, zucchini, celery, potato, tomatoes, and garlic, and cook, stirring often, for 10–15 minutes or until they are soft but not brown. Add the water, season with salt and freshly ground black pepper, then bring to a boil, cover with a lid, and simmer for 45 minutes or until all the vegetables are tender.

3 Add the cooked French beans to the pan along with the green beans, and cook for 5 minutes or until tender. Divide the soup among six bowls and serve with some crusty bread.

Raymond Blanc, Chef Patron of Le Manoir aux Quat' Saisons, Oxfordshire (UK), says, "This soup offers a multitude of flavors which can vary with the seasons."

vegetable and chervil soup

⊘ **SERVES** 4–6   🕐 **PREP** 20 MINS **COOK** 10–12 MINS   ❄ **FREEZE** UP TO 3 MONTHS
AT THE END OF STEP 2

1 tbsp unsalted butter
1 onion, finely chopped
1 garlic clove, finely chopped
2 large carrots, finely sliced
3 celery ribs, sliced into ¼in (½cm) pieces
2 medium leeks, sliced into ¾in
  (1cm) chunks
salt and freshly ground white pepper

1 large zucchini, halved lengthwise and
  cut into ¼in (½cm) slices
2 ripe tomatoes, quartered and
  coarsely chopped
1 tbsp unsalted butter or sour cream
1 tbsp chervil, finely chopped
crème fraîche, to serve (optional)

1 Melt the butter in a pan and cook the onion, garlic, carrots, celery, and leeks for 5 minutes (do not allow them to color). Season with salt and freshly ground white pepper.

2 Add 1 quart (1 liter) boiling water, the zucchini, and tomatoes (using boiling water will reduce the cooking time and also keep the lively colors). Fast boil for another 5 minutes only—it is vital that you do not spoil the fresh, clean flavors of your vegetables by overcooking.

3 Whisk in the butter or sour cream (or both) and add the chervil. Taste and correct the seasoning if required, and blend the soup if you would like a finer texture. Pour into a large tureen and serve to your guests. A spoon of crème fraîche would always be welcome.

A Maltese tale tells of a poor widow, who had only home-grown vegetables, a few eggs from her chickens, and a little soft, local cheese. She made this simple, but delicious soup.

widow's soup

SERVES 4–6   **PREP** 7 MINS **COOK** 40 MINS   **FREEZE** NOT SUITABLE

1 tbsp olive oil
1 large onion, chopped
1 large potato, chopped
6oz (175g) cauliflower florets, quartered
6oz (175g) carrots, sliced
1 small lettuce head, shredded
6oz (175g) shelled fresh peas or thawed
   frozen peas
9oz (250g) tomatoes, peeled and coarsely
   chopped, or half a 14oz (400g)
   can chopped tomatoes

1½ tbsp tomato purée
1 tsp sugar
1 tsp red wine vinegar
salt and freshly ground black pepper
6 eggs
9oz (250g) ricotta cheese or firm young
   goat cheese

1 Heat the oil in a large pan and cook the onion until soft, but not colored. Add the potato, cauliflower, carrots, lettuce, and fresh peas, if using. Stir, then add the tomatoes, tomato purée, sugar, vinegar, salt and pepper, and enough water (or stock) to cover generously. Bring to a boil and simmer until the vegetables are almost tender. If using thawed frozen peas, add them now. Taste and adjust the seasoning.

2 Reduce the heat so that the surface of the water is barely simmering. Break the eggs one at a time onto a saucer or ramekin, and slide them into the soup. Poach the eggs until the white has just set, about 8–10 minutes.

3 Cut the cheese into 4–6 portions, according to the number of serving bowls, and place one in each bowl. Carefully place one egg in each bowl, and ladle the soup around the eggs and cheese before serving.

This spicy, exotically flavored carrot soup makes an elegant starter. Serve it with lime wedges so that guests can adjust the flavor to their liking.

carrot soup with coconut and lemongrass

⊙ **SERVES** 4   ⏱ **PREP** 15 MINS **COOK** 35 MINS   ❄ **FREEZE** UP TO 3 MONTHS

2 tbsp vegetable oil or sunflower oil
1 onion, chopped
1 lemongrass stalk, trimmed and tough
   outer layer discarded
2 garlic cloves, chopped
2 tsp finely grated ginger
1 tbsp red Thai curry paste

1lb (450g) carrots, sliced
1 quart (1 liter) hot vegetable stock
3 kaffir lime leaves
1 x 6oz (165ml) can coconut milk
salt and freshly ground black pepper
lime wedges, to serve

1 Heat the oil in a large saucepan, add the onion, and cook for 3–4 minutes or until starting to soften. Meanwhile, finely chop the lemongrass, then add to the pan along with the garlic and ginger, and cook for 2 minutes. Add the curry paste and cook for 1 minute, stirring all the time, then add the carrots and cook for 2 minutes. Pour in the stock, add the lime leaves, and simmer for 20–25 minutes or until the carrots are tender.

2 Remove from the heat and take out and discard the lime leaves. Pour in the coconut milk, then process in a blender or food processor until smooth. The soup shouldn't be too thick—dilute with more stock if it is. Season to taste with salt, then serve with a grinding of black pepper and lime wedges.

The maple syrup helps the carrot to caramelize in the oven, giving this soup its deep, rich flavor. If you cannot find lovage, use chopped chives to finish.

maple-roasted carrot and ginger soup

SERVES 8   **PREP** 20 MINS **COOK** 55–65 MINS   **FREEZE** UP TO 3 MONTHS

4½lb (2kg) carrots, cut roughly into
   little-finger-sized pieces
2 onions, cut into eighths
1¾in (4cm) piece of ginger, cut
   into matchsticks
4 garlic cloves, peeled
3 tbsp sunflower oil

4 tbsp maple syrup
1½ quarts (1½ liters) chicken
   or vegetable stock
salt and freshly ground black pepper
a couple of squeezes of lemon juice
   (optional)
chopped lovage, to serve

1 Preheat the oven to 425°F (220°C). Place the carrots in a roasting pan with onion, ginger, garlic, sunflower oil, and maple syrup. Mix thoroughly with your hands, then smooth down lightly. Roast for about 45–60 minutes, turning occasionally, until the vegetables are very tender and patched here and there with brown.

2 Cool slightly, then scrape into a blender, including as much of the brown sticky residue at the bottom of the pan as you can scrape off. Add half the stock and process until smooth, adding more stock if necessary. You may need to do this in batches.

3 Pour into a saucepan and stir in the last of the stock, adding extra if necessary to thin the soup. Season with salt and pepper and taste. Add a couple of squeezes of lemon juice if you find the sweetness too intense. Heat thoroughly just before serving, and sprinkle each bowlful with chopped lovage or chives.

A light, refreshing soup with a hint of spice, this is the perfect start to a summer meal. Try adding a swirl of cream or a spoonful of low-fat plain yogurt before serving.

carrot and orange soup

⚙ **SERVES** 4   🕐 **PREP** 10 MINS **COOK** 40 MINS   ❄ **FREEZE** UP TO 3 MONTHS

2 tsp extra-virgin olive oil or sunflower oil
1 leek, sliced
1lb 2oz (500g) carrots, sliced
1 potato, about 4oz (115g), chopped
½ tsp ground coriander
pinch of ground cumin

1¼ cups orange juice
2 cups vegetable or chicken stock
1 bay leaf
salt and freshly ground black pepper
2 tbsp chopped cilantro, to garnish

1 Put the oil, leek, and carrots in a large saucepan and cook over low heat for 5 minutes, stirring frequently, or until the leek has softened. Add the potato, coriander, and cumin, then pour in the orange juice and stock. Add the bay leaf and stir occasionally.

2 Increase the heat, bring the soup to a boil, then lower the heat, cover, and simmer for 40 minutes, or until the vegetables are very tender.

3 Let the soup cool slightly, then transfer to a blender or food processor and process until smooth, working in batches if necessary.

4 Return to the saucepan and add a little extra stock or water if the soup is too thick. Bring back to a simmer, then transfer to heated serving bowls and sprinkle with chopped cilantro.

Pressing this colorful, zingy soup through a strainer may seem tedious, but it does wonders for the texture and is worth the effort.

carrot cream with onion and cumin

⊘ SERVES 4   **⏲ PREP** 20 MINS **COOK** 30 MINS   **❄ FREEZE** UP TO 3 MONTHS
BEFORE HALF-AND-HALF IS ADDED

2 tbsp sunflower or olive oil
2 large Spanish onions, peeled
 and coarsely chopped
1 tsp cumin seeds
1 tsp ground cumin
2¼lb (1kg) carrots, peeled and
 coarsely chopped

sea salt and freshly ground black pepper
juice and grated zest of 1 small
 unwaxed orange
½ cup half-and-half
1 tbsp finely chopped flat-leaf parsley

1 Place a large sauté pan over medium-high heat. Add the oil and stir in the onion and cumin. Cook for 3–5 minutes, or until softened, stirring frequently. Add the carrots and 1½ quarts (1½ liters) water, then season lightly with salt and pepper. Bring to a boil, reduce the heat, cover, and simmer gently for 20 minutes, or until the carrots are very tender. Turn off the heat and let cool a little.

2 Pour into a blender or food processor and process until smooth. Place a strainer over a saucepan (or the sauté pan if possible). Pour the soup into the strainer and press it through with the back of a wooden spoon.

3 Taste and adjust the seasoning. Stir in the orange juice and zest. Reheat until piping hot and stir in the half-and-half, then the parsley. Season with a little extra pepper. Serve hot.

This chilled soup will always go down well on a hot summer's day. Fresh-tasting and with just the right amount of acidity, it can be enjoyed for lunch or dinner.

beet and tomato soup

⊘ **SERVES** 6   🕐 **PREP** 20 MINS, PLUS 3 HRS CHILLING
COOK 55 MINS   ❄ **FREEZE** UP TO 3 MONTHS
AT THE END OF STEP 2

6 tbsp olive oil, plus extra to garnish
½ head garlic, coarsely chopped
1 large onion, coarsely chopped
4 celery ribs, coarsely chopped
1 bulb fennel, coarsely chopped
1lb 2oz (500g) very ripe plum tomatoes, coarsely chopped
1lb 2oz (500g) very ripe beefsteak tomatoes, coarsely chopped
9oz (250g) cooked beets, coarsely chopped

2 tbsp freshly chopped basil (stems reserved), plus 6 sprigs, to garnish
salt and freshly ground black pepper
1¾oz (50g) red, yellow, or pink baby beets, to garnish
1 tbsp chives, with blossoms if available, to garnish
4oz (115g) red, yellow, or orange cherry tomatoes, to garnish
crème fraîche, to garnish (optional)

1 Preheat the oven to 400°F (200°C). In a large, heavy saucepan over low heat, cook the garlic, onion, celery, and fennel in the oil, stirring, for 6–8 minutes. Add the tomatoes, beets, and basil stems and season. Barely cover with water, bring to a boil, then place, uncovered, in the oven for 40 minutes.

2 Transfer to a blender and process until smooth, adding a little water if necessary. Pass through a strainer, pushing as much as you can through with the back of the ladle. Season, then chill in the fridge for at least 3 hours.

3 Cook the baby beets in boiling salted water for 20–25 minutes or until tender, then drain, cool, and peel. Trim the ends, then halve or quarter, depending on size. Season and stir in half the chopped basil, half the chives, and a drizzle of oil. Halve and season the cherry tomatoes.

4 Stir the soup well, check the seasoning, and half-fill six chilled bowls. Spoon the baby beets and cherry tomatoes into the center of each bowl, then garnish with a drizzle of olive oil or a generous scoop of crème fraîche, the basil sprigs, and the rest of the chives, snipped.

This thickly textured, satisfying soup is a Russian classic to enjoy at any time of year and on any occasion. Try it with grated carrots piled on top and chunks of dark rye bread.

borscht

SERVES 4   **PREP** 15 MINS **COOK** 1½ HRS   **FREEZE** UP TO 3 MONTHS

3 tbsp butter
2 large beets, coarsely grated
1 onion, coarsely grated
1 carrot, coarsely grated
1 celery rib, coarsely grated
1 x 14oz (400g) can chopped tomatoes
1 garlic clove, crushed (optional)

1¾ quarts (1¾ liters) hot vegetable stock
2 bay leaves
4 cloves
2 tbsp lemon juice
salt and freshly ground black pepper
¾ cup sour cream

1 Melt the butter in a large saucepan over medium heat. Add the beets, onion, carrot, and celery, and cook, stirring, for 5 minutes or until just softened. Add the tomatoes and garlic, if using, and cook for 2–3 minutes, stirring frequently, then stir in the stock.

2 Tie the bay leaves and cloves in a small piece of muslin or cheesecloth and add to the pan. Bring the soup to a boil, then lower the heat, cover, and simmer for 1 hour 20 minutes. Discard the muslin bag, stir in the lemon juice, and season to taste with salt and pepper. Ladle the soup into warm bowls and add a swirl of sour cream to each one.

BEETS
You can find a variety of types of beets at your local farmers' market—red has the richest flavor. Be gentle when washing because heavy scrubbing may damage the skin and cause "bleeding."

For adults only, with a finishing kick of gin, this dramatic-looking dark pink dish carries distinct eastern European flavors of dill, caraway, and sour cream.

beet and gin soup

🍲 **SERVES** 4–6   🕐 **PREP** 10 MINS **COOK** 50 MINS   ❄ **FREEZE** UP TO 3 MONTHS
WITHOUT THE GIN

2 stems of fresh parsley
1 bay leaf
2 large sprigs of fresh dill or fennel
2 tbsp sunflower oil
1 onion, chopped
½ tbsp caraway seeds
3 tbsp arborio rice
1½lb (650g) beets, peeled and grated

1 tbsp lemon juice
1 quart (1 liter) beef stock, chicken stock,
   or vegetable stock
salt and freshly ground black pepper
2 tbsp gin or vodka
sour cream or crème fraîche, to serve
chopped fresh dill or chives, to serve

1 Make a bouquet garni (see p24) using the parsley, bay leaf, and sprigs of dill or fennel. Heat the oil in a saucepan and cook the onion, caraway, and bouquet garni over low heat, covered, for 10 minutes.

2 Add the rice to the pan, and stir for about 1 minute to coat it in the juices. Add the beets and lemon juice (to set the color), and continue cooking, stirring constantly, for another 2–3 minutes.

3 Pour in the stock, season with salt and pepper, and bring to a boil. Simmer for 25–30 minutes, until both the beets and rice are tender. Remove and discard the bouquet garni. Add ½ cup of water to the pan.

4 Using a blender, process the soup until smooth, in batches if necessary. Return to the pan, adjust the seasoning, and stir in the gin. Reheat thoroughly, without letting the soup boil. Serve steaming hot, with a generous swirl of sour cream in each and a sprinkling of dill or chives.

in praise of...

beets

The underrated and under-used, yet vastly versatile beet is good to eat all year round, as one of its many virtues is that it stores so well. A sweet-sour, ruby-colored soup is guaranteed to convert even the most beet-averse of diners.

This soup should be sharp, sweet, and spiced—the juice of a whole lemon, one or two tablespoons of sugar, and quite a generous seasoning of salt and pepper are recommended.

beet and apple soup

⚙ **SERVES** 6–8 🕐 **PREP** 20 MINS **COOK** 1 HR   ❄ **FREEZE** UP TO 3 MONTHS
WITHOUT THE HERB CREAM

1 onion, halved
2 garlic cloves
3 tbsp olive oil
salt and freshly ground black pepper
12oz (350g) raw beets, peeled and halved
1 potato, halved
4 eating apples, peeled and cored
1½ quarts (1½ liters) hot vegetable stock
    or chicken stock

1–2 tbsp brown sugar
juice of 1 lemon
2 tbsp finely chopped parsley, chives,
    dill, or cilantro, or a mixture
7oz (200g) crème fraîche, sour cream,
    or thick creamy yogurt

1 Briefly process the onion and garlic in a food processor. Heat the oil in a large pan over low heat, add the onion, garlic, and a pinch of salt, and cook gently, stirring once or twice, for 5 minutes or until soft. Meanwhile, process the beets, potato, and apples in the food processor.

2 Add the beets, potato, and apples to the pan and stew gently for 10 minutes, stirring occasionally. Pour in the stock, bring to a boil, then cover with a lid and simmer gently for 45 minutes or until the beets are cooked through.

3 Transfer the mixture to a blender and process until smooth. You may need to do this in batches. Season with the sugar, lemon juice, and some salt and freshly ground black pepper.

4 Stir the chopped herbs into the cream or yogurt, then ladle the soup into warm bowls and drop a big spoonful of green-speckled cream into the middle of the deep pink soup.

This is a fantastic way to cook beets. The distinctive flavor of the goat cheese complements the round sweetness of the beets.

beet soup with tomatoes and goat cheese

SERVES 4   **PREP** 20 MINS **COOK** 45 MINS   **FREEZE** UP TO 3 MONTHS
AT THE END OF STEP 2

1lb 2oz–1lb 5oz (500–600g) beets
1lb 2oz (500g) ripe tomatoes, halved
9oz (250g) apples, diced
2 tbsp olive or sunflower oil

1 medium onion, peeled and finely chopped
2 cups strong beef stock
salt and freshly ground black pepper
4½oz (125g) goat cheese

1 Preheat the oven to 375°F (190°C). Wearing gloves to keep from staining your hands, peel, and coarsely grate the beets and set aside, then place the tomatoes and apples in an ovenproof dish and drizzle with half the oil. Roast for 25–30 minutes, or until soft and pulpy, then press them through a sieve to remove the skin and seeds.

2 Heat the remaining oil in a pan and cook the onion for 6–8 minutes until soft. Add the beets and stock and bring to a boil, then season with salt and pepper and simmer gently for 10 minutes, or until the beets are tender. Stir in the tomato and apple mixture, transfer to a blender, and process until completely smooth. Taste and adjust the seasoning.

3 To serve cold, chill the soup in the refrigerator then divide between six bowls. To serve hot, reheat until piping hot but not boiling. In either case, crumble the cheese over each bowl and serve with crusty bread.

This is a wonderful sweet, earthy soup that can be enjoyed all year round. For the best flavor, serve it warm rather than piping hot.

swiss chard and coconut soup

SERVES 6   **PREP** 10 MINS **COOK** 20 MINS   **FREEZE** UP TO 3 MONTHS

9oz (250g) Swiss chard (or spinach)
4½oz (125g) Red Giant mustard, kale, or more chard
2 medium onions, finely chopped
1 garlic clove, finely chopped

2 tbsp olive oil
3¼ cups vegetable stock
2 x 14oz (400ml) cans coconut milk
salt and freshly ground black pepper

1 Prepare the chard and/or Red Giant mustard or kale, stripping the green leaves from the stems and shredding it into ribbons.

2 Cook the onion and garlic gently in the oil for about 10 minutes, or until soft. Add the shredded greens, stock, and coconut milk and bring to a boil. Simmer for 10 minutes, then process everything together in a food processor or blender. Season to taste with salt and pepper and serve.

SWISS CHARD
Now a familiar sight at the farmers' market or supermarket. The leaves should be firm and green, not limp or yellowing. Do not wash it before storing in the fridge as it may wilt, and use it quickly for maximum nutritional value.

If you are a fan of puréed soups, you can process the mixture in a blender at the end of cooking, then pass it though a fine sieve and reheat gently before serving.

cream of asparagus soup

SERVES 4   **PREP** 10 MINS **COOK** 40 MINS   ❄ **FREEZE** UP TO 3 MONTHS
AT THE END OF STEP 3

1 quart (1 liter) water
salt and freshly ground black pepper
4 tbsp butter
1lb 2oz (500g) white or green asparagus,
   trimmed, peeled (reserve the trimmings),
   and cut into 1in (2.5cm) lengths
1¼ cups milk

4 tbsp flour
pinch of sugar
pinch of freshly grated nutmeg
2 medium egg yolks
2 tbsp heavy (whipping) cream
1½ tbsp chopped flat-leaf parsley

1 Put the water into a saucepan with 1 level tsp salt and 1½ tbsp of the butter. Add the asparagus trimmings, bring to a boil, then cover and simmer for 15 minutes over medium heat. Strain through a sieve (reserving the cooking liquid) and discard the trimmings.

2 Bring the cooking liquid to a boil and add the trimmed asparagus. Return to a boil, cover, and cook for 10–12 minutes or until *al dente*, then drain, reserving the cooking liquid. Add enough of the milk to the cooking liquid to make 4 cups in all.

3 Melt the remaining butter in a pan, add the flour, and cook over low heat, stirring, for 2–3 minutes or until smooth. Gradually add the milk mixture, stirring vigorously with a whisk to make sure there are no lumps. Bring to a boil and cook, uncovered, over low heat for 5 minutes, stirring occasionally. Add the sugar and nutmeg and season with salt and freshly ground black pepper.

4 Stir the egg yolks into the cream and slowly add the mixture to the soup, stirring carefully to get a smooth texture. Add the asparagus and reheat gently. Do not let the soup boil. Serve garnished with the parsley.

This soup is for early summer when asparagus first appears and when fresh morel mushrooms are in season. It should taste fresh and light, so cooking times are brief.

asparagus and morel soup

SERVES 4   **PREP** 15 MINS **COOK** 20 MINS   **FREEZE** NOT SUITABLE

1½ quarts (1½ liters) chicken stock
1 small potato, cut into ¾in (2cm) dice
1 small leek, rinsed, trimmed, and cut into
    ¾in (2cm) lengths
14oz (400g) asparagus, trimmed and
    cut into 2in (5cm) lengths

1 tbsp olive oil
1 tbsp crème fraîche
2 tbsp unsalted butter
salt and freshly ground black pepper
4 large fresh morels (or 4 dried morels soaked
    in lukewarm water for 30 minutes)

1 Heat the stock in a large saucepan, add the potato, and bring to a boil. Lower the heat and simmer for 5 minutes. Add the leek and asparagus and cook, uncovered, for 7–8 minutes. Pick out four attractive asparagus tips and reserve for garnishing. Transfer the contents of the pan to a blender and process until smooth. Add the olive oil, crème fraîche, and 1½ tbsp of the butter, then season with salt and freshly ground black pepper.

2 Halve the morels lengthwise and brush clean inside and out. Cook gently in a pan with the remaining butter for a few minutes until cooked. Meanwhile, reheat the soup. Serve garnished with the morels and reserved asparagus tips.

ASPARAGUS
Buy spears with plump, firm stems and tight buds. Organic asparagus is expensive to produce (keeping the beds weeded is a labor of love) but, for its subtle flavor of freshly cut grass, it is well worth the indulgence.

Fennel will store better in the refrigerator if you remove the feathery fronds, but be sure to save a good handful for this soup as a garnish.

fennel and apple soup

⊘ SERVES 4   **🕐 PREP** 10 MINS **COOK** 30 MINS   **❄ FREEZE** UP TO 3 MONTHS

HOT OR COLD

2 tbsp extra virgin olive oil
4 scallions, sliced
2 cloves garlic, chopped
1lb 5oz (600g) fennel (trimmed weight),
    coarsely chopped
1 celery heart with leaves, or 3 celery
    ribs, chopped

1 cooking apple, peeled, cored
    and coarsely chopped
sea salt
3¼ cups vegetable stock
fennel fronds, to serve

1 Heat the oil in a large pan over medium heat and add the scallions. Soften for 3 minutes, then add the garlic. Cook for 1–2 minutes until fragrant, then add the fennel, celery, and apple with a little salt. Stir, cover, and sweat for 10 minutes, stirring frequently.

2 Pour in the stock and bring to a boil. Simmer for 15 minutes, until the fennel is tender. Cool briefly, then purée with a hand blender. Taste and adjust the seasoning. Serve hot, or allow to cool, chill for several hours, and serve cold. Serve each bowl scattered with torn fennel fronds.

FENNEL
In the market, look for firm, unblemished bulbs that are heavy for their size with bright green fronds. If you are considering growing your own, keep in mind that fennel thrives in warm conditions.

The last-minute addition of paprika-flavored chorizo gives spice to this hearty soup. Keep the texture chunky by processing only briefly.

fennel soup with beans, thyme, and chorizo

SERVES 4   **PREP** 15 MINS PLUS SOAKING OVERNIGHT   **FREEZE** UP TO 3 MONTHS
COOK 1 HOUR   WITHOUT THE CHORIZO

9oz (250g) dried haricot beans
1 tbsp sunflower or olive oil
1 Spanish onion, finely chopped
2 cloves garlic, crushed
1 head fennel, cored and finely chopped

2 tsp dried fennel seeds
1 tbsp finely chopped fresh parsley
2 tsp thyme leaves
salt and pepper
3½oz (100g) diced cubed chorizo

1 Soak the beans overnight in plenty of cold water, then drain and rinse. Put a heavy pot over medium heat. Add the oil, then the onion, and stir for 2 minutes. Add the garlic, fennel and fennel seeds, parsley, and half the thyme and cook for 3–5 minutes until slightly softened. Add the beans. Stir, pour in 2 quarts (2 liters) water and season lightly with salt and pepper.

2 Bring to a simmer and cook for 40 minutes, or until the beans are tender, skimming from time to time. Remove from the heat and let cool slightly. Transfer to a food processor or blender and process briefly until partly puréed. Return to the pot, adjust the seasoning, then gently reheat.

3 Meanwhile, place a small non-stick frying pan over medium-high heat and cook the chorizo for 2–3 minutes until crisp and colored, stirring frequently. Drain on a plate lined with paper towels.

4 Ladle the soup into bowls, add a little chorizo to each, and finish with a scattering of thyme. Serve immediately.

This rustic soup owes its substance to the beans. Buy fresh beans when they are available in early summer—they are quicker to cook and easier to digest.

pistou soup

◉ SERVES 6–8   **◔ PREP** 30 MINS **COOK** 1½ HOURS   **❄ FREEZE** UP TO 3 MONTHS
WITHOUT THE PISTOU

for the pistou
3 garlic cloves, smashed and peeled
coarse sea salt, to taste
leaves from a large handful of fresh basil
2 small tomatoes, peeled, seeds removed
  and chopped (see p22)
freshly ground black pepper
1oz (25g) Parmesan cheese, grated
3 tbsp olive oil

1 ham hock, or a thick piece of smoked
  bacon, about 5½oz (150g)

7oz (200g) fresh white beans,
  such as cannellini, shelled
3½oz (100g) fresh red beans,
  such as borlotti, shelled
9oz (250g) flat green beans, sliced
2 medium floury potatoes, diced
3 tomatoes, peeled, seeds removed
  and chopped (see p22)
4 medium zucchini, chopped
salt and freshly ground black pepper
3½oz (100g) small macaroni noodles

1 To make the pistou, pound the garlic in a large mortar and pestle, then add a little salt and the basil and pound to a paste. Add the tomatoes and continue pounding and mixing until you have a thick sauce. Add pepper, the cheese, and the oil, mixing well, and adjust the seasoning.

2 For the soup, put 2 quarts (2 liters) cold water in a large stewing pot. Add the ham hock. Bring to a simmer, then partially cover and simmer gently for 30 minutes, skimming occasionally.

3 Meanwhile, put the white and red beans in a saucepan, cover with plenty of cold water, and bring to a boil. Simmer for 10 minutes, drain, and refresh. Add all the vegetables to the stewing pot. Season lightly. Return to a simmer, then partially cover and simmer for 1 hour, skimming occasionally.

4 Remove the ham hock and shred the meat. Remove half the ingredients out of the pan, mash with a fork, then return to the soup with the ham. Add the macaroni and cook until just tender. Stir in the pistou, and serve.

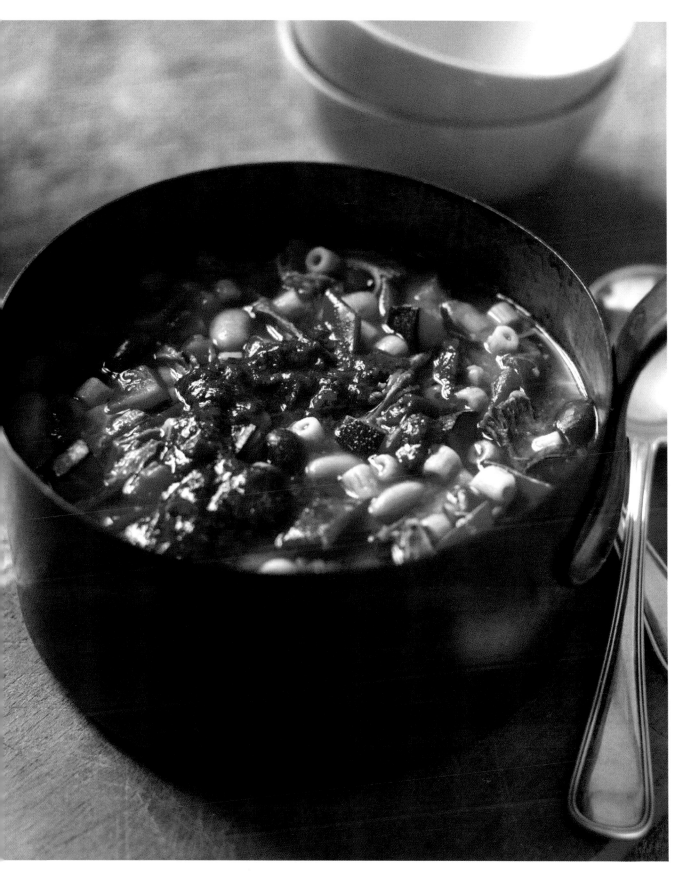

Edamame, or fresh soy beans, are widely available as frozen whole pods from Asian supermarkets—thaw them slightly before using.

edamame noodle soup

◉ SERVES 4   **🕐 PREP** 10 MINS **COOK** 10 MINS   **❄ FREEZE** NOT SUITABLE

1lb 2oz (500g) edamame in the pod or
  8oz (225g) shelled weight
4 tbsp white miso paste
14oz (400g) cooked udon noodles
1 tbsp brown sugar, or to taste
juice of 1 lemon

for the hot garlic oil
1 small hot red chile, snipped
1 clove garlic
½ tsp coarse sea salt
2 tbsp sesame oil

1 Remove the edamame from the pod, if necessary, and set aside. Bring 1 quart (1 liter) of water to a boil in a large pot. Meanwhile, make the hot garlic oil. With a mortar and pestle, pound the chile, garlic, and salt together until smooth, then stir in the sesame oil.

2 Place the miso in a small bowl and mix with 2–3 tbsp of boiling water from the pan, stirring until you have a pourable paste. Add the edamame, noodles, and sugar to the water in the pan and cook for 3 minutes, or until the edamame are tender but still bright green.

3 Turn off the heat and stir in the diluted miso paste, then add lemon juice to taste. Ladle into warm bowls and drizzle with the hot garlic oil before serving.

This soup is a beautiful cool, pale green, flecked with mint and bright, skinned beans. Do not reheat once you have mixed in the yogurt, as it may curdle.

fava bean and mint soup

◉ SERVES 4   **🕐 PREP** 30 MINS **COOK** 25 MINS   **❄ FREEZE** UP TO 3 MONTHS
AT THE END OF STEP 2

1lb (450g) fava beans (shelled weight), thawed if frozen
1 onion, chopped
1 rib celery, thinly sliced
2 tbsp butter
2 tbsp short-grain rice
1 generous sprig summer savory or thyme

1 quart (1 liter) chicken or vegetable stock
salt and pepper
4oz (110g) Greek yogurt
handful of fresh mint leaves, chopped
4 small sprigs of mint
paprika or cayenne pepper, to serve

1 If the beans are fresh, drop them into a pot of boiling water and simmer for 1 minute. Drain and run under the cold tap. Then, whether using fresh or frozen, skin each bean by slitting the tough outer skin with a fingernail or a small sharp knife and squeezing out the bright green beanlet inside. Take about one-eighth, chop coarsely, and set aside.

2 Over low heat in a covered pan, sweat the onion and celery gently in the butter for 10 minutes, or until very tender. Add the rice and savory or thyme and cook for another minute, uncovered. Now add the unchopped beans, 3¾ cups of the stock, salt, and pepper; bring to a boil and simmer for 10 minutes, or until the rice is tender. Remove the herbs then blend in batches, adding more stock if you want a looser consistency.

3 Shortly before serving, reheat thoroughly, then remove from the heat. Stir a tablespoonful of the yogurt into the reserved chopped beans and the mint. Mix in the remaining yogurt, a tablespoon at a time, until it is all added. Taste and adjust the seasoning and serve while still warm, floating a sprig of mint and a light dusting of paprika or cayenne on the surface of each bowl.

This soup is a perfect spring starter. Try serving it topped with a splash of extra virgin olive oil and cubes of bread fried in olive oil.

fava bean soup

⊘ SERVES 4–6 **⏱ PREP** 20 MINS **COOK** 1 HOUR **❄ FREEZE** UP TO 3 MONTHS
WITHOUT THE CROÛTONS

3 slices slightly stale bread, for croûtons
6 tbsp olive oil
3 large mild onions, sliced
1 leek, sliced
3lb 3oz (1.5kg) fava beans, shelled

4 garlic cloves, crushed
a small handful of fresh chives, chopped
4 new potatoes, peeled and chopped
salt and freshly ground black pepper
leaves from a bunch of fresh radishes

1 To make the croûtons, cut the bread into ½in (1.5cm) cubes. Heat 3 tbsp oil in a large frying pan over fairly high heat. Add the bread cubes and spread them out. Fry for a minute, then stir and turn them over. Fry for another minute. Spread the croûtons over a plate lined with paper towels. Pat with more paper towels to drain off excess oil. Set aside.

2 In a big stewing pot or flameproof casserole, heat the remaining oil over medium heat. Add the onions and leek. Soften for 10 minutes, stirring frequently.

3 Add the fava beans to the pot with the garlic, chives, and potatoes. Stir, then pour in about 3 quarts (3 liters) water. Season lightly with salt and pepper and stir in the radish leaves. Turn up the heat a little and bring to a boil, then let simmer gently for 15–20 minutes.

4 Let cool a little, then work through a food mill. Alternatively, process briefly in a blender, then press through a sieve. (If you prefer, you can omit the sieving, in which case the soup will serve 6–8 people.) Reheat until piping hot before serving, topped with the croûtons.

Quick to make, this soup transforms everyday ingredients into a splendid light lunch. Frozen peas, with their natural sweetness, make a good match for the fresh mint.

minted pea and ham soup

SERVES 4–6   **PREP** 15 MINS **COOK** 20–25 MINS   **FREEZE** UP TO 2 MONTHS
BEFORE CRÈME FRAÎCHE IS ADDED

2 shallots, finely chopped
2 tbsp butter
1 potato, peeled and chopped
1¼ cups hot vegetable stock
1lb (500g) frozen peas, defrosted

2 handfuls of fresh mint leaves, plus 2 tbsp
   extra for garnishing
5oz (150g) cooked ham, diced
salt and freshly ground black pepper
2–3 tbsp crème fraîche, to serve

1 Cook the shallots in the butter in a pot over low heat for 2–3 minutes until soft. Add the potato and continue cooking, covered, for another 7–10 minutes or until the potato is tender. Pour in the stock and simmer for 10–15 minutes.

2 In a separate pot, boil 1¾ cups water and cook the peas for 2–3 minutes. Add the mint leaves for the last 20 seconds of cooking. Put the peas and mint into a sieve placed over a bowl, reserving the cooking liquid in the bowl. Add the peas and mint to the stock and process the soup using a blender until smooth, pouring in enough cooking liquid from the peas to loosen the consistency. Stir in the diced ham.

3 For the garnish, stretch a sheet of plastic wrap tightly over a dinner plate. Brush with olive oil and press the extra mint leaves onto the surface. Cover with another layer of plastic wrap and cook in the microwave for 2 minutes, until crisp. Reheat the soup, seasoning with salt and pepper to taste. Serve with a dollop of crème fraîche in the center, garnished with the dried mint leaves.

Try this hearty soup with slices of dark German rye bread and a glass of white wine or wheat beer. It is warming and perfect for a cold winter's day.

pea and sausage soup

SERVES 6   **PREP** 20 MINS **COOK** 20 MINS   **FREEZE** NOT SUITABLE

2 tbsp butter
1 large carrot, peeled and diced
1 small leek, diced
2 celery ribs, diced
1 medium potato, peeled and diced
½ bunch fresh parsley, chopped

½ cup dry white wine
1¼ quarts (1¼ liters) hot chicken stock
3 Toulouse sausages or kielbasa
1lb 10oz (750g) peas (frozen or fresh)
salt and pepper

1 Preheat the oven to 350°F (180°C). In a large saucepan, melt the butter and add the carrot, leek, celery, and potato and cook, stirring, until softened. Add the parsley, wine, and stock and simmer for 15 minutes.

2 Place the sausages on a baking sheet and cook, turning occasionally, for 15–20 minutes, or until cooked through and golden brown on all sides, then slice and set aside.

3 Add the peas to the pot and cook for 3–4 minutes, or until just *al dente*. Season and process to a puree in a blender. Return to the pot and heat through. Serve in 6 bowls, garnished with the sliced cooked sausage.

If you don't have chili-flavored olive oil, stir a little bit of piquant pimenton, harissa, or smoked paprika into fruity olive oil and drizzle over the servings.

mexican sweet corn soup

SERVES 4   **PREP** 15 MINS **COOK** 20 MINS   **FREEZE** UP TO 3 MONTHS

3 tbsp olive oil
1 Spanish onion, finely chopped
1 red bell pepper, halved, cored, seeded
  and finely chopped
1 clove garlic, crushed
1 tsp fennel seeds

1 tsp fresh thyme leaves
14oz (400g) sweet corn kernels
  (drained and rinsed, if canned)
salt and pepper
½ cup half-and-half
1½ tbsp chili-flavored olive oil, to serve

1 Heat the oil in a large sauté pan over medium heat, add the onion, bell pepper (reserve a scant tablespoon to finish), garlic, fennel seeds, and thyme, and stir-fry for 3 minutes. Add the sweet corn and season lightly. Continue stirring and cooking for 2 minutes, then pour in 2 cups hot water, stir, and bring to a simmer. Lower the heat, cover, and simmer for 15 minutes or until the vegetables are tender and cooked through. Stir in the half-and-half and let cool for a few minutes.

2 Process the soup until smooth in a blender (you may need to do this in batches). Return to the pan and reheat gently, stirring occasionally. Taste and adjust the seasoning. Ladle into bowls and add the reserved red pepper. Drizzle a little chili-flavored olive oil over the top and serve at once.

SWEET CORN
A seasonal delight. Look for locally grown cobs with the squeaky, stiff leaves that are a sign of freshness. The grains should be firm and bright yellow, not wrinkled. Use as soon as possible, as the corn will quickly lose its sweetness.

If you have grown your own sweet corn, wait until the very last minute to harvest it—the quicker you get it from the plot to the pan, the sweeter it will be.

sweet corn chowder

⊘ SERVES 4–6   **◕ PREP** 10 MINS **COOK** 30 MINS   **✽ FREEZE** UP TO 1 MONTH
WITHOUT MILK OR CREAM CHEESE

4 fresh corn on the cob
2 cups water
sea salt
2 bay leaves
2 tbsp olive oil
1 large onion, chopped
4 fresh sage leaves, chopped,
  or ½ tsp dried sage, crushed
1 tsp fresh thyme leaves,
  or ½ tsp dried thyme

1 medium carrot, chopped
2 celery ribs, chopped
1 large potato, chopped
7oz (200g) cream cheese
½ cup milk
salt and freshly ground black pepper
half-and-half or heavy cream, to serve
dusting of paprika, to serve

1 Stand each corn cob upright in a large bowl, and strip the kernels by cutting downward with a sharp knife. Set the kernels aside. Place the cobs in a large saucepan and add the water, a generous dose of salt, and the bay leaves. Bring to a boil and simmer, covered, for 15 minutes. Remove and discard the cobs and bay leaves.

2 Heat the oil in a saucepan and cook the onions until translucent. Add the sage, thyme, carrot, celery, and potatoes. Cook for about 5 minutes, until softened. Add the corn cob stock and simmer until the potato softens. Meanwhile, place the corn kernels in a saucepan and barely cover with cold water. Bring to a boil and cook for 2 minutes. Set aside.

3 Add the cream cheese and milk to the soup mixture, then purée until smooth. Stir in the corn kernels with their cooking liquid. Give the chowder one more process if desired, to break up corn kernels slightly. Reheat, seasoning with salt and pepper to taste. Ladle into warm bowls. Drizzle with streaks of half-and-half and dust with paprika.

Nutmeg and saffron bring out the delicate, nutty taste of the artichoke. Fresh is best, but canned and drained, or frozen and defrosted, artichoke hearts also work well.

globe artichoke soup

SERVES 4   **PREP** 20 MINS **COOK** 20 MINS   ❄ **FREEZE** UP TO 3 MONTHS
WITHOUT THE HALF-AND-HALF

1 tbsp olive oil
2 tbsp butter
½ Spanish onion, finely chopped
1 shallot, finely chopped
1 clove garlic, crushed
¼ tsp ground nutmeg
a few saffron strands

1¾lb (800g) artichoke hearts, chopped
salt and pepper
½ cup half-and-half
4 pieces of bacon or pancetta
a large handful of baby spinach
   leaves, chopped

1 Bring a full teapot to a boil. Put a sauté pan over medium heat and add the oil and butter. Add in the onion, shallot, garlic, nutmeg, and saffron, and stir for 3 minutes. Add the artichoke hearts and season lightly. Continue stirring and cooking for 3 minutes. Pour 1 quart (1 liter) of hot water from the teapot into the sauté pan and stir to mix. Bring to a simmer. Reduce the heat, cover, and simmer for 10 minutes, or until the vegetables are tender and cooked through. Let cool for several minutes.

2 Pour the soup into a blender and process until smooth, then pour back into the pan. Reheat gently, stirring occasionally. Meanwhile, heat the half-and-half until simmering in a small saucepan over medium heat.

3 Place a nonstick frying pan over medium-high heat. Once the pan is hot, add the bacon or pancetta. Sizzle for 2 minutes, until crisp and colored. Turn over with tongs and cook the other side until crisp. Drain on a plate lined with paper towels. Add the spinach to the same pan and stir until wilted. Turn off the heat.

4 Stir the simmering half-and-half into the soup. Taste and adjust the seasoning. Ladle the soup into bowls and add the spinach, stir lightly, then float the bacon or pancetta in the middle of each bowl. Serve at once.

Jeff Cox was an editor on one of America's first organic gardening magazines, and now writes on cooking and gardening from his home in Sonoma, California.

broccoli soup

SERVES 4–6   **PREP** 10 MINS **COOK** 40 MINS   **FREEZE** UP TO 3 MONTHS
AT THE END OF STEP 3

1 tbsp lemon juice
1½lb (675g) broccoli florets
3 tbsp butter
2–3 celery ribs, finely chopped
2 leeks (white parts only), chopped

4 tbsp plain flour
1½ quarts (1½ liters) hot chicken stock
salt and pepper
½ cup heavy cream
2 tbsp snipped chives, to serve

1 Bring a large pot of salted water to a boil and add ½ tbsp of the lemon juice. Add half the florets and cook for 3 minutes, or until just tender. Remove to a colander and run cold water over them to stop the cooking. Let them drain and set aside.

2 In a large saucepan, melt the butter over medium-low heat. Add the celery and leeks and cook, stirring, for 5–7 minutes or until the vegetables are tender. Add the flour and stir it in thoroughly, then whisk in the stock until the flour is entirely absorbed. Turn the heat to high and bring to a vigorous boil, then reduce the heat to low and simmer for 5 minutes.

3 Chop the uncooked broccoli into small pieces and add to the soup. Simmer for 15 minutes, or until very tender. Process in a blender until almost smooth—you want to retain a slightly grainy texture.

4 Return the purée to the saucepan, season to taste with salt and pepper and the rest of the lemon juice, then add the cream and the reserved broccoli. Reheat and serve, sprinkled with chives.

This is a two-in-one soup, a mild and gentle eggplant cream yanked into high gear with a swirl of the sweeter, hotter red pepper.

eggplant and red pepper soup

SERVES 6 · **PREP** 25 MINS **COOK** 40 MINS · **FREEZE** UP TO 3 MONTHS
THE TWO SOUPS SEPARATELY

for the eggplant soup
2 tbsp extra virgin olive oil
1 onion, chopped
1 carrot, coarsely sliced
2 tbsp chopped parsley
1 tbsp crushed coriander seeds
2 large eggplants, diced
1 tbsp risotto or short-grain rice
3¼ cups chicken or vegetable stock
salt and pepper

for the pepper soup
2 tbsp extra virgin olive oil
2 cloves garlic, chopped
1–2 fresh red chiles, seeded and chopped
2 red bell peppers, seeded and cut into strips
9oz (250g) tomatoes
1 tbsp tomato purée
1 tbsp sugar
salt and pepper
2½ cups chicken or vegetable stock
handful of fresh basil leaves

1 To make the eggplant soup, put the oil, onion, carrot, parsley, coriander, eggplant, and rice in a pan, cover, and sweat over low heat for 15 minutes. Add the stock and season with salt and pepper. Bring to a boil and simmer for 15 minutes until the carrots and rice are tender. Process in a blender.

2 To make the red pepper soup, place the olive oil, garlic, chile, and red pepper in a deep pan, and sauté until the peppers are very tender. Blanch and peel the tomatoes (see p22), then quarter, seed, and coarsely chop before adding to the pan along with the tomato purée, sugar, salt, and pepper. Cook for another 5–10 minutes until very thick. Stir in the stock and bring to a boil, then cool slightly and process to a puree in a blender.

3 Reheat both soups in separate pans, then taste and adjust seasonings. Divide the eggplant soup between 6 soup bowls and add a ladle of the pepper soup, swirling it in lightly. Sprinkle with basil and serve at once.

Easy to make from kitchen pantry ingredients, using canned tomatoes, this delicious soup can be enjoyed all year round to brighten the dullest day.

classic tomato soup

◎ **SERVES** 4   🕒 **PREP** 20 MINS **COOK** 55 MINS   ❄ **FREEZE** UP TO 3 MONTHS

1 tbsp olive oil
1 onion, chopped
1 garlic clove, sliced
2 celery ribs, sliced
1 carrot, sliced
1 potato, chopped

2 x 14oz (400g) cans tomatoes
3¼ cups vegetable or chicken stock
1 bay leaf
1 tsp sugar
salt and pepper

1 Heat the oil in a large saucepan over medium-low heat, add the onion, garlic, and celery and cook, stirring frequently, until softened but not colored.

2 Add the carrot and potato and stir for 1 minute, then add the tomatoes with their juices, the stock, bay leaf, and sugar. Season to taste, bring to a boil, then reduce the heat, cover, and simmer for 45 minutes, or until the vegetables are very soft.

3 Remove from the heat and let cool slightly, then process in a blender or food processor until smooth, working in batches if necessary. Taste and adjust the seasoning, then reheat and serve.

This extra-special version of the old standard uses fresh, sun-dried, and roasted tomatoes, and takes the humble tomato to new heights.

cream of tomato soup

◉ SERVES 4–6 **🕐 PREP** 30 MINS **COOK** 40 MINS **❄ FREEZE** UP TO 3 MONTHS
BEFORE CREAM IS ADDED

3½ tbsp butter
1 tbsp olive oil
2 onions, finely chopped
2 celery ribs, finely chopped
2 carrots, finely diced
2 garlic cloves, minced
12 plum tomatoes, about 2¼lb (1kg),
   quartered, roasted, and coarsely chopped

8 plum tomatoes, about 1¼–1½lb (600–720g),
   peeled and finely chopped
6 sun-dried tomatoes, finely chopped
1 quart (1 liter) hot vegetable stock
2–3 tbsp heavy cream
salt and freshly ground black pepper

1 Heat the butter and olive oil in a heavy saucepan over medium heat. Add the onions and sauté for 8–10 minutes, stirring frequently, until very soft but not colored. Next, add the celery and carrots, and continue cooking gently without burning for another 10 minutes, stirring from time to time. Add the garlic and sauté for another 2 minutes, stirring.

2 Mix together the roasted plum tomatoes, fresh tomatoes, and sun-dried tomatoes. Add them into the pan with any juices, and cook, stirring, for 5 minutes to allow the flavors to combine; if the sauce looks too thick or starts sticking to the bottom of the pan, add a little of the hot vegetable stock. Pour in the remaining vegetable stock and simmer the soup for 15–20 minutes.

3 Blend the soup to a smooth purée using a food processor or hand-held blender. Pass through a sieve or mouli into a clean pan, unless you prefer to make a peasant-style soup. Add the heavy cream a teaspoon at a time until you are happy with the taste and texture. Season with salt and pepper, reheat very gently if needed, and serve.

In Russia and the Ukraine, borscht often includes tomatoes as well as beets. This version may seem unusual, but you will love its rich color and fantastic taste.

tomato borscht

SERVES 4   **PREP** 25 MINS **COOK** 25 MINS   **FREEZE** UP TO 3 MONTHS
AT THE END OF STEP 2

HOT OR COLD

2 tbsp olive oil
1 small onion, finely chopped
1 garlic clove, chopped
8oz (225g) raw beets, peeled
  and finely grated
1 tsp freshly ground toasted cumin seeds
¼ tsp ground cinnamon
8oz (225g) ripe fresh tomatoes, peeled
  and coarsely chopped
1 cup tomato juice

1 tbsp sun-dried tomatoes,
  very finely chopped
2½ cups vegetable stock
1 tbsp soy sauce
salt and freshly ground black pepper
toasted cumin seeds, to serve
sour cream or crème fraîche,
  to serve

1 Heat the oil in a heavy pan over low heat. Gently cook the onion and garlic for about 5 minutes, then add the beets. Cook gently for another 10 minutes, stirring from time to time, until softened but not browned.

2 Add the ground spices, tomatoes, tomato juice, and sun-dried tomatoes, then pour in the stock. Bring to a boil. Reduce the heat slightly, cover, and simmer very gently for 15 minutes or until all the vegetables are soft. Remove from the heat. Blend or process until velvety smooth.

3 Check the seasoning, adding the soy sauce, salt, and pepper to taste. Serve chilled, at room temperature, or slightly warm. If you do reheat the soup, do so gently over low heat. To serve, spoon into bowls, and garnish with toasted cumin seeds and a spoonful of sour cream or crème fraîche.

For homemade food in a jiffy, roast the vegetables up to three days in advance and keep them in the fridge. This soup then takes just minutes to prepare.

roasted tomato soup

SERVES 4   **PREP** 10 MINS **COOK** 30 MINS   **FREEZE** UP TO 3 MONTHS

8 plum tomatoes, about 1½lb (675g) in total, quartered
1 red onion, cut into 8 wedges
2 garlic cloves, unpeeled

3 tbsp olive oil
sea salt and freshly ground black pepper
1 quart (1 liter) hot vegetable stock
3 tbsp sun-dried tomato paste

1 Preheat the oven to 350°F (180°C). Put the tomatoes, onion, and garlic on baking sheets covered with parchment paper. Drizzle with the oil, and season well with salt and freshly ground black pepper. Roast until they are soft, caramelized, and slightly browned—allow 10–15 minutes for the garlic, 15–20 minutes for the onion, and 25 minutes for the tomatoes. Squeeze the garlic from their skins once they have cooled slightly.

2 Transfer to a blender, add the stock and tomato paste, then process until smooth but still slightly chunky. Season with salt and freshly ground black pepper, reheat gently, and serve hot.

CHOOSING TOMATOES
Pick out firm tomatoes that smell of the vine. Go organic for the best flavor, but also because organic tomatoes contain more health-promoting antioxidants than those cultivated by conventional means.

Wonderfully refreshing, this perfect hot summer's day lunch is fantastically quick to make and is superbly healthy. Serve it up with garlic-rubbed toast.

gazpacho

◉ SERVES 6–8   **🕐 PREP** 30 MINS   **❄ FREEZE** UP TO 3 MONTHS

1 red bell pepper, seeded and chopped
10 scallions, trimmed and chopped,
   or 1 red onion, finely chopped
5 garlic cloves, chopped
1 cucumber, finely chopped
2¼lb (1kg) ripe tomatoes, finely chopped
1 tbsp fresh thyme, marjoram, parsley,
   mint, or basil, chopped

3–4 pieces stale bread
1 fresh chile, seeded and finely chopped, or
   ½ tsp cayenne pepper (optional)
2 tbsp red wine vinegar
3 tbsp olive oil, plus extra to serve
½ cup cold water
salt and freshly ground black pepper

1 Place a serving bowl in the refrigerator. Put the pepper, scallions or onion, garlic, cucumber, and tomatoes in a mixing bowl, then add the herbs.

2 Process the bread in a blender to make breadcrumbs, then add to the mixing bowl along with the chile, if using, the vinegar, and oil. Gradually add the water. ½ cup will give a good thick consistency but you can use more if you prefer.

3 Transfer to the blender and process briefly—you can blend until smooth, or so it still contains the odd chunk of cucumber. Season generously with salt and freshly ground black pepper. Transfer to the chilled serving bowl, add a few ice cubes, and drizzle with olive oil before serving.

Fresh lime juice, cilantro, and dried poblano chiles—not to mention the corn tortillas—give a Mexican flavor to this spicy tomato soup.

sopa de tortilla

SERVES 4   **PREP** 15 MINS **COOK** 50 MINS   **FREEZE** UP TO 3 MONTHS
AT THE END OF STEP 2

5 tbsp sunflower oil
½ onion, finely chopped
2 large garlic cloves, finely chopped
1lb (450g) tomatoes, peeled
1.5 quarts (1.5 liters) chicken stock
  or vegetable stock
1 or 2 dried poblano chiles, seeded

2 soft corn tortillas, cut into strips
3 tbsp chopped fresh cilantro
2 tbsp fresh lime juice
salt and freshly ground black pepper
3oz (85g) Gruyère cheese, grated
2 limes, cut into wedges, to serve

1 Heat 1 tbsp of the oil in a large saucepan over medium heat. Add the onion and cook, stirring, for 5 minutes, until softened. Add the garlic and stir for 30 seconds. Using a blender, process with the tomatoes until smooth.

2 Add the tomato-onion purée to the pan and simmer for 8–10 minutes, stirring constantly. Stir in the stock and bring to a boil. Reduce the heat, partially cover the pan, and simmer for 15 minutes or until thickened.

3 Place a nonstick frying pan over medium heat. Add the chiles and press them flat against the pan with a spatula until they blister, then repeat on the other side. Remove from the pan, cut into small pieces, and set aside.

4 Heat the remaining oil in the frying pan until sizzling hot. Add the tortilla strips in batches and fry until just crisp. Remove with a slotted spoon and drain on paper towels.

5 When ready to serve, add the chiles to the soup, bring to a boil, and simmer for 3 minutes, or until the chiles are soft. Stir in the cilantro and lime juice and season with salt and pepper. Divide the toasted tortilla strips between 4 soup bowls. Ladle in the soup and top with a sprinkling of cheese. Serve with wedges of lime.

Dan Barber, the top chef with a Blue Hill restaurant in Manhattan and another on a farm outside New York, teaches all his staff the principles of good farming.

smoked tomato soup

 SERVES 4   **PREP** 15 MINS **COOK** 30 MINS   **FREEZE** UP TO 3 MONTHS

10 large plum tomatoes, about 2½lb (1.1kg) total in weight, 2 halved and seeded, 8 coarsely chopped
4 tbsp extra virgin olive oil
1 large onion, finely chopped
1 large leek, cut in half lengthwise and then thinly sliced crosswise
1½ tsp coriander seeds
2 garlic cloves, crushed

2 bay leaves
1 tsp finely grated fresh horseradish or drained bottled horseradish
1 cup hot chicken stock
pinch of sugar
4 tbsp unsalted butter, softened
salt and freshly ground black pepper
basil leaves, to garnish

1 Scatter a handful of apple, pecan, or hickory wood barbecue chips in a medium-sized, cast-iron frying pan or wok, cover tightly with a lid, and place over medium heat. When the chips start to smoke, put the 4 tomato halves on a rack, and set the rack in the pan. Replace the lid and smoke the tomatoes for 2–3 minutes or until barely softened. Transfer to a plate and let cool slightly, then peel.

2 Heat the oil in a large pan, add the onion and leek, and cook over medium heat, stirring frequently, for 10 minutes or until softened but not browned. Add the coriander, garlic, bay leaves, and horseradish and cook for 2 minutes or until fragrant. Add the chopped tomatoes, stock, and sugar, cover with a lid, and cook over medium heat for 10 minutes or until the tomatoes are soft. Pick out and discard the bay leaves.

3 Transfer to a blender, add the butter and smoked tomatoes, and process until smooth. You may need to do this in batches. Strain through a sieve into a clean pot and season with salt and freshly ground black pepper. Serve garnished with basil leaves.

This fragrant soup is seasoned with a blend of spices often used to give Indian pickles and preserves their distinctive tang. It is best enjoyed with hot naan.

curried broth with peppers

⊘ SERVES 4   **⏱ PREP** 15 MINS **COOK** 25 MINS   **❄ FREEZE** UP TO 3 MONTHS

2 tbsp vegetable oil
1 star anise
½ tsp hot red pepper flakes
½ tsp nigella seeds
1½ tsp fennel seeds
¼ tsp fenugreek seeds
2 onions, diced
1½in (4cm) piece of ginger, peeled and grated
1 orange bell pepper, diced

1 yellow bell pepper, diced
2 tbsp basmati rice
¾ tsp turmeric
½ tsp garam masala
1 quart (1 liter) hot vegetable stock
1 tbsp palm sugar
grated zest and juice of 1 large lemon
salt and freshly ground black pepper
2 tbsp cilantro, coarsely chopped

1 Heat the oil in a large saucepan over medium heat, add the star anise, pepper flakes, nigella, fennel, and fenugreek, and stir-fry for 30 seconds. Lower the heat, add the onions and ginger, then cover and cook for 5 minutes or until the onions have softened. Stir in the peppers and fry for 2–3 minutes.

2 Add the rice, turmeric, and garam masala, stir well, and cook for 1 minute. Pour in the stock, then add the sugar and lemon zest. Season with salt and freshly ground black pepper, and simmer for 15 minutes or until the soup has thickened slightly and the peppers and rice are tender. Sharpen with the lemon juice and serve garnished with cilantro.

PEPPERS
Look for bright, shiny peppers that feel firm, and avoid any that have soft spots or are pale or shriveled. Yellow and orange bell peppers are ripe versions of green peppers. Because of this, they are sweeter.

Make this soup toward the end of the summer when tomatoes and peppers are plentiful. It freezes well and will be a treat when defrosted for winter meals.

roasted red pepper, fennel, and tomato soup

⊘ SERVES 4–6   **⏱ PREP** 25 MINS **COOK** 2 HRS   **❄ FREEZE** UP TO 2 MONTHS

1 large fennel bulb, peeled
1 red onion
2 red bell peppers, halved and seeded
1lb (500g) tomatoes
4 garlic cloves, in their skins
1½ tsp sugar
2 tbsp olive oil
1 large sprig of fresh rosemary, leaves only

1–2 tbsp vegetable oil
1½ tsp fennel seeds
½ tsp nigella seeds
14fl oz (400ml) passata
1 quart (1 liter) vegetable stock
1 red chile pepper, split and seeded
salt and freshly ground black pepper
handful of fennel leaves

1 Preheat the oven to 400°F (200°C). Cut the fennel and onion into wedges. Slice a cross into the base of each tomato and squeeze the juice and seeds into a bowl. Strain the juice and set aside.

2 Line a roasting pan with parchment paper and add the fennel, onion, peppers, tomatoes, and garlic cloves. Sprinkle over the sugar, drizzle with the olive oil, and scatter the rosemary on top. Roast the vegetables for 1 hour, or until the tomatoes are soft. Cool the vegetables before peeling the blackened skin from the peppers. Peel the garlic and discard the skins.

3 Heat the vegetable oil in a large pan and toss in the fennel and nigella seeds, swirling them around for a few seconds. Pour over the passata, the stock, and the reserved tomato juice, and bring to a boil. Add the roasted vegetables, pop the chile pepper into the pan, and season with salt and pepper to taste. Half cover with a lid and simmer for about 45 minutes.

4 Using a blender, process the soup until smooth and press through a sieve. Reheat, re-season, and finish with a sprinkling of fennel leaves.

Rich, slightly nutty avocado works well with arugula. Hass avocados are particularly good, but always buy extra in case one turns out to be blemished.

avocado and arugula soup

◎ SERVES 4   **🕑 PREP** 15 MINS PLUS 1 HR CHILLING   **❄ FREEZE** NOT SUITABLE
COOK NONE

3 large (or 4 medium) ripe avocados
juice of 1 lemon
5½oz (150g) wild arugula
3¼ cups cold chicken
   or vegetable stock

¼ tsp harissa
salt and freshly ground black pepper

1 Peel the avocados and remove their pits, then chop the flesh and put it in a blender or food processor with the lemon juice. Coarsely chop the arugula (save a few sprigs to decorate) and add to the avocado mixture. Pour in the stock. Add the harissa and season with salt and pepper, then blend until smooth. Transfer to a bowl, cover and refrigerate for 1 hour.

2 Before serving, taste and adjust the seasoning. Pour into bowls or glasses, add an ice cube or two to each and decorate with sprigs of arugula. Serve chilled.

This lovely, cool summer soup is just perfect when it's too hot to cook. If you can't find sorrel, try substituting spinach seasoned with lemon juice or zest.

avocado, cucumber, and sorrel soup

SERVES 4–6   **PREP** 5–10 MINS   **FREEZE** NOT SUITABLE

CHILLED

1 ripe, buttery avocado, pitted and peeled
a generous handful of sorrel leaves (discard any tough stems)
¼ large cucumber, coarsely diced but not peeled

7oz (200g) Greek yogurt
1–2 cloves of garlic, peeled and chopped
salt and freshly ground black pepper
avocado oil, to serve

1 Place the avocado in a blender with the sorrel, cucumber, yogurt, garlic, salt and pepper. Add about ½ cup of water, and then process. As soon as it is smoothly blended, taste and adjust the seasoning, adding more sorrel if desired. Thin down with a little more water as needed.

2 Once you are happy with the taste and consistency, divide between 6 serving bowls or cups and drizzle a bit of avocado oil on the surface. Serve at once, or at least within the next hour while it is fresh and vivid.

PITTING AND PEELING AN AVOCADO

Slice the avocado in two, cutting all the way around, then separate the two halves by twisting gently.

Strike the pit with the blade of a large knife, then lift the knife to remove the pit.

Cut the avocado in half again and carefully remove the skin with a paring knife.

This refreshing soup can be prepared ahead and makes an elegant starter for a summer meal. For a lunch or dinner party, try serving it with smoked salmon.

cucumber and dill soup

◉ SERVES 4   **◷ PREP** 30 MINS PLUS 3HRS CHILLING   **❄ FREEZE** NOT SUITABLE

2 medium cucumbers
salt and pepper
1 quart (1 liter) whole or low-fat milk

small bunch of fresh dill
¼ cup plain yogurt

1 Peel the cucumbers, leaving one or two strips of skin on for color. Slice, put into a colander, and sprinkle with a teaspoon of salt. Toss and set it over a bowl for one hour. Meanwhile, put the milk in another bowl, add a few whole dill fronds, stir, and refrigerate for an hour to allow the flavors to infuse slightly.

2 Rinse the cucumber under cold running water, pressing down to extract as much moisture as possible. Remove the dill fronds from the milk. Put the milk and cucumber in a blender or food processor. Add a few more fronds of dill and some pepper and blend well. Pour into a bowl and refrigerate for 3 hours.

3 Place a sieve over a second bowl, pour in the chilled soup, and push through with the back of a wooden spoon, adding ½ cup–⅔ cup cold water, and return to the refrigerator until ready to serve.

4 Stir in the yogurt, taste, and adjust the seasoning if necessary. Whisk until frothy with a handheld or balloon whisk then pour into cups, bowls, or glasses. Decorate with a little more dill and serve immediately.

This is delicious in the fall, when it will use up any particularly mature cucumbers, although you may need to remove any hard seeds and bitter skin.

cucumber and walnut soup

◉ **SERVES** 4–6   ⏱ **PREP** 10–15 MINS PLUS 30 MINS CHILLING   ❄ **FREEZE** NOT SUITABLE

2 medium cucumbers, about 1lb 9oz (700g) in total
1lb 2oz (500g) Greek or thick and creamy yogurt
1 clove garlic
coarse sea salt

1¾oz (50g) walnuts, plus more chopped walnuts for garnish
handful of fresh mint leaves, finely chopped
2 tbsp fresh lemon juice
freshly ground black pepper
extra virgin olive oil, to serve

1 Peel, seed, and finely dice the cucumbers. Be diligent about this to ensure your soup is delicately flavored without any bitterness.

2 In a medium bowl or large measuring jug, mix together the yogurt and 1 cup cold water until combined. Pound the garlic with a large pinch of coarse sea salt in a mortar until smooth. Scrape it into the yogurt. Pound the walnuts in the garlicky mortar to a coarse paste; do not crush them too fine. Add to the yogurt mixture with the cucumber, mint, lemon juice, and a good grinding of pepper and stir well. Taste and adjust the seasoning.

3 Cover and chill for 30 minutes or more. Pour into bowls and garnish with a drizzle of olive oil and a few chopped walnuts.

CUCUMBERS
Go for locally grown cucumbers that feel firm and avoid any with soggy, limp ends. Be sure to store them in the refrigerator for no longer than a week, as they contain mostly water and will quickly lose their vibrancy.

Cooked cucumber has a subtle flavor which combines particularly well with the more assertive but still delicate tarragon in this light soup.

hot cucumber and tarragon soup

◎ SERVES 4   **● PREP** 15 MINS **COOK** 20 MINS   **❋ FREEZE** NOT SUITABLE

2 medium-large or 3 small cucumbers
1 tbsp sunflower oil
3 tbsp chilled butter, diced
2 tbsp chopped fresh tarragon
3⅓ cups light vegetable or
   chicken stock

salt and freshly ground black pepper
2 tbsp cornstarch
4 heaped tsp cream cheese (optional)

1 Peel the cucumbers, cut crosswise in half, then cut each half lengthwise. With a pointed teaspoon, scoop out and discard all the seeds and chop the flesh coarsely.

2 Place a sauté pan over medium heat. Add the oil and 1 tbsp of the butter. Once the butter has melted, add the cucumber and half the tarragon. Stir for 2 minutes, then pour in the stock and season lightly with salt and pepper.

3 Bring to a simmer, reduce the heat a little, then cover and simmer gently for 10–15 minutes. Stir in the cornstarch. Cook for 2 minutes. Take off the heat and set aside to cool a little.

4 Transfer to a blender or food processor and blend until smooth. Return to the pan and whisk in the remaining butter. Taste and adjust the seasoning, stir in the rest of the tarragon, and serve hot. If you like, add a dollop of cream cheese (if using) to each serving at the last minute.

For absolute decadence, omit the poached eggs and top each bowl with a little chopped hard-boiled egg and a shucked oyster in its half shell.

wakame soup with poached eggs

SERVES 4　　**PREP** 10 MINS **COOK** 30 MINS　　**FREEZE** UP TO 3 MONTHS

7oz (200g) fresh or dried wakame
2–3 tbsp unsalted butter
1 large leek, washed thoroughly and sliced
1 large potato, diced
1 thick slice of lemon
small handful of fresh parsley

1 quart (1 liter) light vegetable
  or chicken stock
pepper
2–3 tbsp milk (optional)
1 tbsp white wine vinegar
4 eggs

1 Rinse the wakame (or soak, if dried), then boil in a little water over medium-high heat for 3–5 minutes or until tender. Drain, rinse with cold water, and drain again.

2 Melt the butter in a large saucepan. Add the leek and potato and cook gently, stirring, for 2 minutes or until soft but not browned. Add the lemon, parsley, stock, and pepper—it's unlikely to need salt as wakame is salty. Bring to a boil, reduce the heat, cover, and simmer gently for 20 minutes, or until the vegetables are really soft. Discard the lemon and process in a blender with the wakame. Return to the pan, taste, and add more pepper if necessary. If freezing, cool and freeze at this point, then defrost and continue. Thin with the milk, if desired, then reheat gently.

3 Meanwhile, bring a large pan of water to a boil and add the vinegar. Swirl around to make an eddy and break in the eggs one at a time. Poach until cooked to your liking, then remove with a slotted spoon. Ladle into wide, shallow soup plates then rest a poached egg in the center of each.

This spin on a popular Indian curry makes an innovative first course. The crackling curry leaves, toasted spices, and tangy tamarind work well with the yogurt base.

whipped yogurt soup with sautéed zucchini

SERVES 4   **PREP** 30 MINS, PLUS 20 MINS STANDING **COOK** 25 MINS   **FREEZE** NOT SUITABLE

3 tbsp vegetable oil
2 dried red chiles
1 tsp mustard seeds
¼ tsp fenugreek seeds
1 tsp cumin seeds
12 curry leaves
3 tbsp gram flour
½ tsp turmeric
1¾ cups Greek yogurt
1¾ cups cold water

2 tbsp tamarind pulp
2 tbsp chopped cilantro, to garnish

for the sautéed zucchini topping
2 tbsp vegetable oil
1 small red onion, diced
1 zucchini, finely diced
1 green chile, seeded and finely chopped
sea salt flakes, to season

1 Heat the oil in a wok over medium heat. Toss in the chiles and mustard seeds and swirl around for a few seconds before adding the fenugreek, cumin, and curry leaves. Lower the heat and stir-fry for a few seconds. Sprinkle in half the flour and stir-fry for 2–3 minutes or until lightly toasted. Remove from the heat, add the turmeric, and let cool slightly.

2 Whisk the remaining flour with the yogurt and water and add to the wok. Return to the heat and, whisking all the time, bring to a simmer and cook for 3–4 minutes. Add more water, if needed, to loosen the consistency. I like to leave the whole spices in, but you can sieve the soup at this stage. Season with salt and enough tamarind to sharpen.

3 For the sautéed zucchini topping, heat the oil in a frying pan and soften the onion for 3–4 minutes over low heat. Turn the heat up, add the zucchini and green chile, and continue cooking for another minute. Season with salt and add to the hot soup. Finish with the chopped cilantro.

A very simple soup, easy to make and with very few ingredients, this is lifted out of the ordinary by the gentle anise-tang of dill.

zucchini and potato soup

◎ SERVES 4 **🕐 PREP** 10 MINS **COOK** 15 MINS **❄ FREEZE** UP TO 3 MONTHS

2 large potatoes, peeled and diced
2 cups hot chicken stock
1 tsp salt
1 tbsp olive oil
3 medium zucchini, peeled, finely diced, or grated

1 onion, peeled, finely diced, or grated
white pepper
½ cup heavy cream
1¼ cups milk
small bunch of fresh dill, chopped

1 Place the potatoes into a large, deep saucepan with the hot stock and salt, bring to a boil, and simmer for about 5 minutes, or until tender. Blend with an immersion blender until smooth and return to the saucepan.

2 In another saucepan, heat the olive oil, add the zucchini and onion, and cook over low heat for 2–3 minutes or until slightly softened but not colored. Stir in a dash of the pepper, the cream, milk, and puréed potato broth and simmer gently for 5 minutes, or until the zucchini has softened. Add dill and season to taste. Serve hot.

ZUCCHINI
A welcome addition to many soups, zucchini should be firm, unblemished, feel heavy, and have glossy skin. Avoid purchasing those that are shriveling and soft. Smaller zucchini have the best flavor.

Make sure you add the greens at the last minute, otherwise they will overcook and the soup will lose its fresh taste and bright green color.

spinach and rosemary soup

⊘ SERVES 6   **⏱ PREP** 15 MINS **COOK** 25 MINS   **❄ FREEZE** UP TO 3 MONTHS

3½ tbsp butter
4oz (115g) finely chopped onion
5½oz (150g) diced potato
salt and freshly ground black pepper
2 cups hot vegetable stock,
   chicken stock, or water
2 cups creamy milk (¼ cream
   and ¾ milk)

12oz (350g) spinach, stalks removed
   and chopped
1 tbsp chopped fresh rosemary
2 tbsp half-and-half, to garnish
sprig of rosemary or rosemary
   flowers, to garnish

1 Melt the butter in a heavy-bottomed saucepan. When it is starting to foam, add the onion and potato, and stir to coat well. Season with salt and freshly ground black pepper, then cover the pan with a lid and cook the vegetables over low heat for 10 minutes.

2 Add the stock and milk, bring to a boil, then simmer for 5 minutes or until the potato and onion are completely cooked. Add the spinach and boil the soup with the lid off for 2–3 minutes or until tender. Do not overcook. Add the chopped rosemary, then process the soup in a blender until smooth. You may need to do this in batches. Return to the pan and reheat gently.

3 Serve in warm bowls garnished with a swirl of half-and-half and a sprig of rosemary. If you have a rosemary bush in bloom, sprinkle a few flowers over the top for extra pizzazz. This is good with crusty bread.

This verdant spinach soup is so simple; it takes no more than a few minutes to make, yet sings of the garden. It is beautiful served warm or at room temperature.

spinach and parmesan soup with crème fraîche

⊘ **SERVES** 4 ● **PREP** 10 MINS **COOK** 15–20 MINS ❄ **FREEZE** UP TO 3 MONTHS
BEFORE PARMESAN IS ADDED

10oz (300g) baby spinach leaves
2 tbsp unsalted butter
2 large shallots, finely sliced
1 garlic clove, finely chopped
sea salt and freshly ground black pepper

1 quart (1 liter) chicken stock
5 tbsp crème fraîche
3½oz (100g) Parmesan cheese, grated
grated lemon zest, to garnish

1 Wash the spinach thoroughly, drain, and shake until almost dry. Place a large pan over medium heat. Add the spinach, cover, and cook until it just wilts. Drain in a colander and set aside.

2 Rinse and dry the saucepan. Add the butter to the pan and melt over low heat, then add the shallots and sweat for five minutes, or until softened and translucent. Add the garlic and cook for 1–2 minutes, then season with a little salt and some pepper.

3 Add the cooked spinach and stir once or twice. Pour in the stock and turn up the heat. Bring to a simmer then immediately remove from the heat. Purée the soup in a blender until smooth. Return it to the saucepan and stir in the crème fraîche. Add the grated Parmesan cheese and check the seasoning. Then either reheat gently and serve warm, or allow to cool and enjoy at room temperature. Add a sprinkling of grated lemon zest before serving.

Here, the astringent bite of green chiles and ginger is tempered by the subtlety of herbs and delicate spinach leaves. Add a dollop of cream just before serving.

spicy spinach soup

SERVES 4   **PREP** 12 MINS PLUS 90 MINS MARINATING   **FREEZE** UP TO 2 MONTHS
COOK 40 MINS   BEFORE CUMIN SEEDS ARE ADDED

for the chicken
2 garlic cloves, finely chopped
1¼in (3cm) piece of ginger,
    finely chopped
¾ tsp garam masala
juice of 2 limes
3 tbsp Greek-style yogurt
salt to season
2 boneless chicken thighs, without skin
1 tsp vegetable oil

for the soup
3 tbsp vegetable oil

1 onion, finely chopped
2 green chiles, seeded and finely chopped
1 garlic clove, finely chopped
2 tbsp ground almonds
1 quart (1 liter) hot chicken stock
1¼in (3cm) piece of ginger, peeled
1lb (2oz 500g) baby spinach leaves
large handful cilantro
handful mint leaves
1 tsp sugar
salt and freshly ground black pepper
1 tsp roasted and ground cumin seeds,
    to garnish

1 Mix the garlic, ginger, and garam masala with the lime juice, yogurt, and salt. Add the chicken and coat. After 1–2 hours, heat the vegetable oil in a pan. Drain any excess yogurt off the chicken, drizzle with vegetable oil, and cook for 5–7 minutes on each side. Cool, then cut into small pieces. Pour any cooking juices over the chicken and set aside.

2 Heat the oil in a large saucepan over low heat. Add the onions, chiles, and garlic and cover. Cook for about 10 minutes, stirring occasionally. Add the ground almonds and cook for another minute, stirring. Add the chicken stock and ginger. Season well and simmer for 10 minutes.

3 Bring to a boil and add the spinach. When it wilts, add the herbs and sugar. Turn the heat off and remove the ginger. Blend until smooth. Pour the soup into a clean pan. Add the chicken and reheat gently. Check the seasoning and serve sprinkled with roasted ground cumin seeds.

in praise of...
lettuce
If you grow your own vegetables, it is easy to end up with an abundance of lettuces, and soup is a great way to use them for something delicious and different.

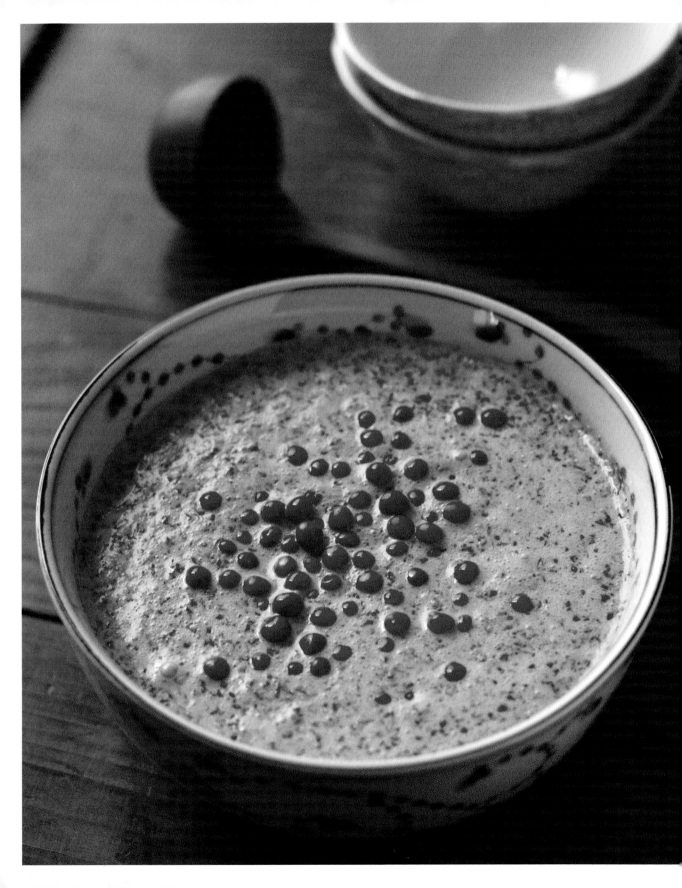

Don't used lettuces that have bolted for this—they will have bitter cores. Some of the leaves may still be good to use, though. Taste before using.

lettuce soup with peas

⊘ **SERVES** 4   🕐 **PREP** 30 MINS, PLUS 30 MINS CHILLING   ❄ **FREEZE** NOT SUITABLE

4½oz (125g) peas (shelled weight)
1 small garlic clove
pinch of coarse salt
2 medium heads lettuce (about 1lb 2oz/
500g in total), cleaned, torn into
pieces, and solid cores discarded

1 cup plain yogurt
¾in (2cm) piece fresh ginger, peeled
and finely grated
handful of mint leaves
juice of ½ lemon
salt and freshly ground black pepper

1 Bring a small amount of water to a boil in a pan, add the peas, and cook for 1 minute. Drain (reserving the cooking water), cool under cold running water, and refrigerate. Cut the garlic in half, remove any green at the center, and discard. Crush the halves along with a pinch of coarse salt.

2 Combine the garlic with all the other ingredients (except the peas) in a food processor or blender, adding just enough of the reserved cooking water to get the blades moving or until the desired consistency is achieved—this will vary according to the type of lettuce and the kind of machine you are using, but it is nice if you can get it fairly smooth, with a bit of texture.

3 Transfer the soup to a large bowl and chill for 30 minutes. When ready to serve, stir through the cooked peas, leaving a few to garnish.

CHOOSING AND PREPARING LETTUCE
Search your farmers' market for lettuces with fresh-looking leaves and a silky, slightly firm heart. Avoid any that are wilted or bruised. To clean, pat the leaves with damp paper towels, then tear them—rather than cut—to size.

Serve this velvety smooth soup hot, topped with shavings of Parmesan cheese, or chilled with an extra swirl of cream or crème fraîche.

watercress soup

🥄 **SERVES** 4   ⏱ **PREP** 10 MINS **COOK** 15 MINS   ❄ **FREEZE** 3 MONTHS

2 tbsp butter
1 onion, finely chopped
6oz (175g) watercress
3 ripe pears, cored and coarsely chopped
1 quart (1 liter) vegetable stock

salt and freshly ground black pepper
¾ cup heavy cream
juice of ½ lemon
Parmesan cheese, shaved, to serve
olive oil, to drizzle

1 Melt the butter in a saucepan and cook the onion for 10 minutes, or until soft, stirring occasionally to prevent burning. Meanwhile, trim the watercress and pick off the leaves. Add the watercress stalks to the onion with the pears and stock, and season with salt and pepper.

2 Bring to a boil, cover, and simmer gently for 15 minutes. Remove from the heat and pour into a blender along with the watercress leaves. Process until the soup has a very smooth texture.

3 Stir in the cream and lemon juice, adjust the seasoning, and serve sprinkled with Parmesan shavings and drizzled with a little oil. The soup can be made up to 4 hours in advance and refrigerated until ready to use. To serve chilled, pour the soup into chilled bowls, top with crushed ice, and drizzle with a little olive oil.

CHOOSING WATERCRESS
Locally produced watercress with fresh, round leaves and thick stalks are best. Unwashed leaves will keep in the fridge for several days, but ready-washed ones must be eaten quickly.

Peppery watercress, curry leaf oil, and caramelized pear make a marvelous melange of flavors. The oil can be made a few days before and kept refrigerated.

spicy watercress soup

◉ **SERVES** 4–6   🕐 **PREP** 20 MINS **COOK** 30 MINS   ❄ **FREEZE** UP TO 1 MONTH
AT THE END OF STEP 2

3 tbsp fresh curry leaves
⅔ cup plus 2 tbsp olive oil
1 onion, chopped
2 medium potatoes, such as
   russet, chopped
1 quart (1 liter) hot vegetable stock
9oz (250g) watercress

salt and freshly ground black pepper
2 tbsp crème fraîche

for the garnish
1 pear, peeled and finely diced
2 tbsp confectioner's sugar
pinch of coarsely ground black peppercorns
1 tbsp crème fraiche

1 First make the curry leaf oil. Drop the leaves into a pan of boiling water and cook for about 30 seconds. Remove and refresh with cold water. Pat dry with paper towels and transfer to a blender. Warm the ⅔ cup oil and gradually pour into the blender as the leaves are being processed. Blend to a smooth paste. Line a sieve with a thin paper towel and pour the curry leaf mixture into it—the oil will slowly drip through.

2 For the soup, heat the 2 tbsp olive oil in a large pan and add the onion and potato. Cover and cook over low heat, stirring frequently, until softened but not colored. Pour in the stock and simmer for another 10 minutes, until the potatoes are cooked. Add the watercress and cook for another minute. Season with salt and pepper, and stir in 2–3 tsp of the curry leaf oil. Blend with a stick blender until smooth and sieve to remove any tough fibers.

3 For the garnish, toss the pear in confectioner's sugar seasoned with pepper. Cook in a heated frying pan until caramelized.

4 Reheat and re-season the soup and whisk in 2 tbsp of crème fraiche. Ladle into bowls, and top with an extra dollop of crème fraiche. Scatter the pears over the top and finish with an extra drizzle of curry leaf oil.

This makes good use of peppery late-season arugula which may have become a bit leathery. If your arugula is in bloom, the flowers have a distinctive savory flavor.

arugula and parmesan soup

⊘ SERVES 4   **⏱ PREP** 11 MINS **COOK** 30 MINS   **❄ FREEZE** UP TO 3 MONTHS

2 tbsp olive oil
2 medium onions, chopped
1lb 7oz (650g) potatoes, washed but not peeled, cut into ¾in (2cm) cubes
sea salt
4 small or 2 large garlic cloves, crushed

1 quart (1 liter) vegetable stock
1 Parmesan rind, about 1¼ x 3½in (3 x 9cm), cut into tiny dice
4½oz (125g) arugula leaves, coarsely chopped
fresh Parmesan, to serve
arugula flowers, to serve (optional)

1 Heat the oil in a soup pan over medium heat. Add the onions and cook, stirring frequently, until soft and translucent. Add the potatoes with a little salt, stir, cover, and cook for 5 minutes, stirring frequently.

2 Add the garlic and stir for a few seconds until fragrant, then pour in the stock. Bring to a boil, add the Parmesan rind, then simmer for about 10 minutes, stirring occasionally, until the potato is soft.

3 Add the arugula, stir, and cook for 3–5 minutes, until tender but still bright green. Cool briefly, then purée the soup with a hand blender until smooth. Taste for seasoning. Serve each bowl with grated or shaved fresh Parmesan, and a few arugula flowers if you have them.

ARUGULA
A versatile ingredient with a pronounced peppery flavor. Go for locally grown arugula, choosing fresh leaves and firm stems. You can store unwashed arugula in the fridge for several days. Pre-washed leaves will only last a day.

A real tonic on a chilly spring day, this soup, with its bright sorrel sharpness, is always welcome. Later in the summer, when the temperature rises, serve it chilled.

sorrel soup

SERVES 6 **PREP** 15 MINS **COOK** 30–35 MINS **FREEZE** UP TO 3 MONTHS
WITHOUT CREAM

HOT OR COLD

3 big handfuls of sorrel (or substitute
    spinach seasoned with lemon juice)
2 tbsp extra virgin olive oil
1 onion, chopped
14oz (400g) potatoes, peeled and diced
1 bay leaf
2 sprigs of parsley

2 sprigs of thyme
1½ quarts (1½ liters) chicken or
    vegetable stock
salt and freshly ground black pepper
6 tbsp heavy cream (optional) or 3 tbsp
    Greek yogurt

1 Cut out and discard the larger tougher stems of the sorrel, then shred the leaves coarsely. Warm the oil in a large saucepan and add the onion, potatoes, bay leaf, parsley, and thyme, tied together with string to form a bouquet garni. Stir to coat in oil, then cover and cook over low heat for 10 minutes or so.

2 Uncover and pour in the stock, then season with salt and pepper. Bring to a boil and simmer for 15 minutes or so until the potato is very tender. Take off the heat, remove the bouquet garni, then stir in the sorrel. Process in a blender in batches and return to the pan. Reheat, stir in the cream if using, then taste and adjust the seasoning. Serve immediately. Alternatively, when the weather is warm, chill the soup for a few hours in the refrigerator, then serve with a teaspoonful of Greek yogurt floating in each bowlful.

SORREL
Look for sorrel at farmers' markets. If you're lucky, you might even be able to forage for it. Look for firm stems and fresh, green, spear-shaped leaves. Mature leaves are best in soups and sauces, but be careful not to overcook.

If you don't grow this old-fashioned herb yourself, ask around among your gardening friends or head down to the nearest organic foods market to see if they sell it.

lovage soup

⊚ SERVES 4–6   **🕐 PREP** 10 MINS **COOK** 30 MINS   **❄ FREEZE** UP TO 3 MONTHS
                                                                      BEFORE CREAM IS ADDED

4 tbsp butter
1 onion, chopped
9–10oz (250–300g) floury potatoes,
    peeled and diced
1 large carrot, diced
a large handful of fresh lovage leaves

1¼ quarts (1¼ liters) chicken or
    vegetable stock
salt and freshly ground black pepper
6 tbsp heavy cream
cayenne pepper

1 Melt the butter in a large pan and add the onion, potato, carrot, and lovage. Stir, then cover and cook over low heat for 10 minutes.

2 Add the stock and a little salt and pepper. Bring to a boil and simmer for 15 minutes until all the vegetables are very tender. Cool slightly, process in a blender, and, if you would like a smoother soup, pass through a sieve. Taste and adjust the seasoning if necessary. Reheat when needed and stir in the cream. Serve with a dusting of cayenne pepper.

LOVAGE
When buying cut leaves, choose strong stems and yellow-green leaves, but remember that they don't keep for long. If you choose to grow your own, you will find that lovage can grow to a considerable height.

This is a favorite soup in Portugal, where fresh cilantro is used enthusiastically. It is essentially a potato and onion soup, blended with lots of fresh cilantro.

potato and cilantro soup

⊘ SERVES 4–6   **⏱ PREP** 10–15 MINS **COOK** 30 MINS   **❄ FREEZE** UP TO 3 MONTHS

1 small bunch of fresh cilantro
2 onions, chopped
2 cloves garlic, chopped
3 tbsp olive oil

2lb (900g) potatoes, peeled and cubed
2 pints (1.2 litres) chicken stock, vegetable
   stock or water
salt and pepper

1 Cut the stems from the cilantro and tie them in a bundle with string. Chop the leaves finely and reserve.

2 Cook the onion and garlic gently in the oil until tender without browning. Add the potatoes and cilantro stems, stir, then cover and cook over low heat for 5 minutes.

3 Now add the stock, salt, and pepper and bring to a boil. Simmer until the potatoes are very tender. Remove the bundle of cilantro stems. Process in a blender, adding a little more stock or water if the soup is too thick. Stir in the cilantro leaves and reheat gently without boiling. Taste and adjust the seasoning. Serve immediately.

USING CILANTRO
You can easily grow hardy cilantro in a pot on your windowsill. Cook it, eat it raw, or use it as a garnish. Cut bunches should be kept in water or in a sealed pack in the refrigerator, but make sure you use them within a week.

A fantastic way to use this much maligned, fragrant weed—choose young and tender specimens and wear a double layer of latex gloves to pick them.

nettle soup

◎ SERVES 4   **🕐 PREP** 10 MINS **COOK** 20 MINS   **❄ FREEZE** UP TO 3 MONTHS

2 tbsp canola oil or olive oil
4 scallions, sliced
3 leeks, coarsely chopped
1lb 7oz (650g) potatoes, washed but not
   peeled, cut into ¾in (2cm) cubes
sea salt

1 quart (1 liter) vegetable stock
3½oz (100g) young nettles or nettle tips
   (about ¼ bag full), washed
juice of half a lemon
freshly ground black pepper
plain thick yogurt, to serve

1 Heat the oil in a heavy soup pan over medium heat. Add the scallions, leeks, and potatoes with a little sea salt. Stir, cover, and cook for about 5 minutes, stirring frequently.

2 Add the stock and bring to a boil. Add the nettles, stir, and simmer for 10 minutes, or until the potatoes are soft. Cool briefly, then purée with a hand blender until completely smooth. Taste for seasoning, then squeeze in a little lemon juice and grind in some pepper. Serve each bowl with a dollop of thick yogurt and more pepper.

PICKING NETTLES
Because they grow everywhere, nettles are generally easy to find. When fresh, the stems are firm and the young leaves are green, but ones with wilted or yellowing leaves should be avoided. Cooked nettles lose their sting.

In Provence, they say *aïgo boulido sauvo la vido*—"garlic broth saves your life." Ten cloves of garlic go into this dish, yet it is not terrifyingly garlicky.

garlic broth

🍶 **SERVES** 4   🕐 **PREP** 15 MINS **COOK** 20 MINS   ❄️ **FREEZE** NOT SUITABLE

10 garlic cloves, crushed
6 sage leaves
1 bay leaf
1 large sprig of thyme
2 tbsp extra virgin olive oil, plus extra
　to drizzle

1 quart (1 liter) water or light chicken stock
salt and freshly ground black pepper
8 croûtes (see p39)
1 garlic clove, halved (optional)
3 egg yolks
grated Gruyère, to serve

1 Put the garlic into a saucepan with the sage, bay leaf, thyme, oil, water or stock, and some salt and freshly ground black pepper. Bring to a boil, then simmer gently for 15 minutes. Meanwhile, rub one side of each croûte with the cut clove of garlic, if using, and place two in each bowl. Drizzle a little oil over each one.

2 Turn off the heat and pick out and discard the bay leaf and thyme (but not the sage). Whisk 3 tbsp of the hot soup into the egg yolks, then pour everything back into the pan and stir. Taste and adjust the seasoning, then transfer the soup to a hot tureen. Ladle the soup into the bowls and serve at once, passing around the Gruyère for topping.

GARLIC
The flavor of garlic differs according to how you prepare it. Left whole and boiled, it tastes mild and sweet. When you chop it, its flavor intensifies, and the more finely it's chopped, the more pungent it becomes.

A great way to use up potatoes, and celebrate Spring.
If you can't find wild garlic leaves, use spinach instead and
add a couple of garlic cloves with the potato and onion.

wild garlic soup

SERVES 4–6   **PREP** 10 MINS **COOK** 35 MINS   **FREEZE** UP TO 3 MONTHS

6 large handfuls of wild garlic leaves
2 tbsp butter
3 medium potatoes, diced

1 large onion, diced
2½ cups hot vegetable stock
sea salt and freshly ground black pepper

1 Bring 3 cups of water to a boil and immerse the garlic leaves for 30 seconds. Remove with a slotted spoon (reserving the cooking liquid) and plunge into a bowl of cold water. Let cool, then drain and set aside.

2 Meanwhile, melt the butter in a saucepan over medium heat. Add the potatoes and onion and cook gently for 15 minutes. Add the stock and 2½ cups of the reserved cooking liquid, bring to a boil, then lower the heat and simmer for 15 minutes or until the potatoes are soft.

3 Remove the pan from the heat and add the garlic leaves. Process the mixture in a blender until smooth, then return to the pan and reheat gently. Season with salt and freshly ground black pepper and serve.

winter vegetables

Simple, affordable, and immensely satisfying, this hearty soup makes a warming meal when accompanied with some freshly baked crusty bread.

cream of vegetable soup

SERVES 6   **PREP** 15 MINS **COOK** 40–55 MINS   **FREEZE** UP TO 3 MONTHS
WITHOUT HALF-AND-HALF OR MILK

3 tbsp butter
2 carrots, sliced
1 leek (white part only), sliced
2 parsnips, sliced
1 onion, sliced
1 small turnip, sliced
3 celery ribs, sliced
1 potato, sliced

5 cups hot vegetable stock
2 tsp fresh thyme leaves
1 bay leaf
pinch of grated nutmeg
salt and freshly ground black pepper
3 tbsp half-and-half
3 tbsp milk
bunch of chives, snipped, to garnish

1 Melt the butter in a large pan, add the carrots, leek, parsnips, onion, turnip, celery, and potato, and stir to coat well. Cover the pan with a lid and cook for 10–15 minutes or until the vegetables have softened.

2 Add the stock, thyme, bay leaf, and nutmeg, then season with salt and freshly ground black pepper. Bring to a boil and simmer, uncovered, for 30–40 minutes or until the vegetables are meltingly soft. Scoop out the bay leaf and discard.

3 Process the soup in a blender until smooth. You may need to do this in batches. If you like the texture of your soups very smooth, strain it through a fine sieve; otherwise, leave it as it is. Stir in the half-and-half and milk, adding more milk if the consistency is still too thick. Season with salt and freshly ground black pepper, then reheat gently. Garnish with the chives and serve immediately.

This is a substantial soup that is a meal in itself. Mix and match whatever vegetables are in season—zucchini, cabbage, and leeks are all excellent in a minestrone.

minestrone soup

SERVES 4–6   **PREP** 20 MINS, PLUS 8 HOURS SOAKING   **FREEZE** UP TO 1 MONTH
COOK 1¾ HRS   AT THE END OF STEP 2

3½oz (100g) dried white cannellini beans
2 tbsp olive oil
2 celery ribs, finely chopped
2 carrots, finely chopped
1 onion, finely chopped
1 x 14½oz (400g) can chopped tomatoes

2½ cups hot vegetable stock
  or chicken stock
salt and freshly ground black pepper
2oz (60g) small short-cut pasta
4 tbsp chopped flat-leaf parsley
1½oz (40g) Parmesan, finely grated

1 Put the dried beans in a large bowl, cover with cold water, and leave to soak in the fridge for at least 8 hours or overnight. Drain the beans, then place them in a large saucepan and cover with cold water. Bring to a boil, then boil hard for 10 minutes, skimming the surface of any foam with a slotted spoon. Lower the heat, partially cover the pan, and simmer for 1 hour or until the beans are tender. Drain and set aside.

2 Heat the oil in the rinsed-out pan over medium heat. Add the celery, carrots, and onion, and cook, stirring occasionally, for 5 minutes or until tender. Stir in the cooked beans, then add the tomatoes and their juice, the stock, and some salt and freshly ground black pepper. Bring to a boil, stirring all the time, then cover with a lid and simmer for 20 minutes.

3 Add the pasta and simmer for 10–15 minutes or until it is cooked but still firm to the bite. Stir in the parsley and half the Parmesan, then adjust the seasoning. Serve hot, sprinkled with the remaining Parmesan.

Mounded together in the center of the bowl, the vegetables in this soup resemble coins—which is one of the reasons it got its name. The other is that it is very inexpensive to make.

"penny" soup

◉ SERVES 4   **◷ PREP** 15 MINS **COOK** 30 MINS   **❄ FREEZE** UP TO 3 MONTHS
WITH ALL VEGETABLES BLENDED

1 leek, rinsed well
11oz (300g) potatoes
9oz (250g) large carrots
6oz (175g) small sweet potatoes
1 tbsp olive oil

1 tbsp butter
2 cups hot vegetable stock
1 tbsp chopped flat-leaf parsley
salt and freshly ground black pepper

1 Slice the vegetables into ⅛in (3mm) rounds. Heat the oil and butter in a large saucepan, add the leeks, and cook over medium heat, stirring frequently, for 3–4 minutes or until soft. Add the potatoes, carrots, and sweet potatoes and cook, stirring, for 1 minute.

2 Pour in the stock, then bring to a boil, cover with a lid, and simmer for 20 minutes or until the vegetables are tender but not soft. Transfer about one-third of the vegetables to a blender or food processor with a little of the liquid and blend to a smooth purée, then return to the pan. Stir in the parsley, season to taste with salt and freshly ground black pepper, and serve, with the vegetables in a little mound in the center.

Leftovers of this big warming soup from Tuscany are never thrown away, but used to make the sturdy Ribollita (see right). Both are frugally filling and very good.

zuppa di verdure

◎ SERVES 6 **⏱ PREP** 25 MINS, PLUS OVERNIGHT SOAKING **❄ FREEZE** UP TO 3 MONTHS
COOK 2–3 HRS BEFORE CAVOLO NERO IS ADDED

7oz (200g) dried cannellini beans, soaked overnight in water, or 1 x 14oz (400g) can cannellini beans, drained and rinsed

bouquet garni made from a sprig of rosemary, a sprig of thyme, and 2 bay leaves (see p24)

4 tbsp extra virgin olive oil, plus extra to serve

1 onion, chopped

3 carrots, diced

2 celery ribs, diced

2 leeks, very thinly sliced

3 garlic cloves, chopped

1 dried red chile pepper, finely chopped

3 tomatoes, peeled, seeded, and chopped

2 tbsp tomato purée

salt and freshly ground black pepper

4 cavolo nero or curly kale leaves, or the outer leaves of a Savoy cabbage, tough stalks removed and the leaves coarsely chopped

6 slices stale bread

1 garlic clove, cut in half

1 Drain the beans and place them in a large pan with the bouquet garni and twice their volume of cold water. Bring to a boil, then boil hard for 10 minutes. Lower the heat, and simmer gently for 1–2 hours or until tender, adding more water if needed. Remove the pan from the heat, discard the bouquet garni, and leave the beans to cool in their cooking water.

2 Heat the oil in a large heavy pot, then add the onion, carrots, celery, leeks, garlic, and chile. Cover with a lid and sweat over low heat for 10 minutes, stirring once or twice. Add the tomatoes and tomato purée and cook over a moderate heat for 3–4 minutes. Add the beans, their cooking water, and enough water to cover the vegetables generously. Season well with salt and pepper. Bring to a boil and simmer gently for 20 minutes or until the vegetables are tender. Purée half the soup in a blender, then return to the pan. Add the cavolo nero and simmer for 10 minutes or until tender. Adjust the seasonings.

3 Rub the bread with the garlic and arrange in a warm shallow casserole dish. Spoon in the soup and serve with a bottle of high-quality olive oil out on the table for people to help themselves.

Ribollita means "reboiled" in Italian, and that is more or less what this soup is—reboiled Zuppa di verdure (see left). It is wonderful, heart-warming comfort food.

ribollita

SERVES 4–6 **PREP** 10 MINS **COOK** 40 MINS **FREEZE** NOT SUITABLE

1 quantity day-old Zuppa di verdure, made up to the point just before the cavolo nero is added

6 cavolo nero or curly kale leaves, or the outer leaves of a Savoy cabbage, tough stalks removed and the leaves coarsely chopped

6 slices good-quality stale bread

1 garlic clove, halved

2–3 tbsp extra virgin olive oil, plus extra to serve

½–1 red onion, very finely sliced

4 tbsp freshly grated Parmesan (optional)

1 Preheat the oven to 375°F (190°C). Bring the soup to a boil in a large pan, stir in the cavolo nero, and simmer for 10 minutes or until tender. Meanwhile, rub the stale bread with garlic.

2 Oil a large gratin dish or similar ovenproof dish with olive oil, then spoon about a quarter of the soup into the dish, spreading it over the base. Now, lay half the slices of bread over the soup, then spoon over half the remaining soup. Repeat these two layers one more time. Lay the red onion over the top, then scatter with the Parmesan, if using. Drizzle over a little olive oil, then bake for 30 minutes. Serve sizzling hot, with extra olive oil out on the table for those that want it.

This one-pot meal of slowly cooked vegetables flavored with pork and confit of duck comes from southwest France. It is best made the day before and reheated.

garbure

◎ SERVES 4–6   **◔ PREP** 40 MINS **COOK** 1 HR   **❄ FREEZE** UP TO 3 MONTHS

3½oz (100g) diced bacon or pancetta
1 Spanish onion, finely chopped
3 garlic cloves, crushed
1 leg confit of duck
1½ quarts (1½ liters) chicken stock
1 small Savoy cabbage, core removed and leaves cut into 1 x 3in (2.5 x 7.5cm) strips
1 large carrot, sliced
1 celery rib, diced
1 leek, cleaned and sliced
1 large floury potato, cubed

sea salt and freshly ground black pepper
1 tsp pimentón picante or hot smoked paprika
½ tsp ground cumin
2–3 sprigs of fresh thyme
2–3 sprigs of flat-leaf parsley, plus 1 tbsp finely chopped parsley to garnish
1 x 9oz (250g) can white beans, drained, rinsed, and drained again
8–12 croûtes (see p39), rubbed with garlic and brushed with olive oil, to serve

1 Put a large, deep, heavy-based soup pot over medium heat, add the bacon or pancetta, and cook, stirring frequently, for 2–3 minutes or until crisp and cooked through. Remove with a slotted spoon and drain on paper towels. Add the onion and garlic to the pot, reduce the heat a little, and cook, stirring frequently, for 5–8 minutes or until softened.

2 Pick the meat from the duck leg, discarding the skin and bones but reserving the fat, and cut into shreds. Stir the meat into the onion and garlic, then add the stock, cabbage, carrot, celery, leek, and potato. Season lightly with salt and more generously with freshly ground black pepper, then add the pimentón or paprika, cumin, thyme, and parsley. Bring to a simmer, cover, reduce the heat a little, and cook, stirring occasionally, for 30 minutes.

3 Lift out the thyme and parsley. Lightly mash the beans in a bowl, then stir them into the soup and continue cooking until the vegetables are tender. Taste and adjust the seasoning. To serve, stir in the reserved bacon or pancetta along with 1 tbsp of the duck fat, then sprinkle with the parsley. Place a croûte in each bowl and ladle the piping hot soup on top.

A mixed vegetable potage (soup) like this is traditional French family fare. It is ladled out of a tureen into wide shallow bowls as a starter all over the country.

french country soup

🍲 **SERVES** 4   🕐 **PREP** 15 MINS **COOK** 45 MINS   ❄ **FREEZE** UP TO 3 MONTHS
AT THE END OF STEP 2

1 tbsp sunflower oil or peanut oil
2 tbsp butter
3 large leeks, cleaned and chopped
1 large floury potato, coarsely cubed
2 large carrots, chopped

3¼ cups vegetable stock or chicken stock
2 bay leaves
sea salt and freshly ground black pepper
½ cup hot water

1 Put the oil and half the butter in a large sauté pan over medium-low heat. Add the leeks, potato, and carrots and cook, stirring frequently, for 5 minutes. Reduce the heat a little, add the stock and bay leaves, then season lightly with salt and freshly ground black pepper. Cover and cook gently, stirring occasionally, for 30 minutes or until the vegetables are very soft.

2 Let cool for several minutes, then lift out the bay leaves. Transfer the soup to a blender and process until smooth. Strain back into the pan through a sieve, using the back of a wooden spoon to push through as much as possible. Pour the hot water through the sieve to extract as much as you can from the vegetables.

3 Reheat gently, stirring frequently. Taste and adjust the seasoning, then stir in the remaining butter and serve very hot.

POTATOES
Getting some of the less common varieties of potato is one of the great benefits of shopping at farmers' markets or belonging to a co-op or CSA. The same goes for many other kinds of vegetable, too.

Despite its French name, this silky-smooth, cold soup actually comes from the US. It is also delicious served hot—simply add the cream and chives at the end of cooking.

vichyssoise

◎ **SERVES** 4   🕐 **PREP** 15 MINS, PLUS 3 HRS CHILLING   ❄ **FREEZE** UP TO 3 MONTHS
COOK 45 MINS   BEFORE THE CREAM IS ADDED

2 tbsp butter
3 large leeks (white parts only), finely sliced
2 potatoes, about 6oz (175g) in total, chopped
1 celery rib, coarsely chopped
4 cups hot vegetable stock

salt and freshly ground black pepper
5fl oz (150ml) heavy cream, plus extra
 to garnish
2 tbsp finely chopped chives

1 Melt the butter in a heavy pan over medium heat, add the leeks, and stir to coat well. Press a circle of damp wax paper on top of them, cover with a lid, and cook, shaking the pan gently from time to time, for 15 minutes or until they are soft and golden. Discard the wax paper.

2 Stir in the potatoes, celery, and stock, then season with salt and freshly ground black pepper. Bring to a boil, stirring all the time, then cover with a lid and simmer for 30 minutes or until the vegetables are tender.

3 Remove the pan from the heat and leave to cool slightly, then process the soup in a blender until very smooth. You may need to do this in batches. Season to taste with salt and freshly ground black pepper, then chill for at least 3 hours. To serve, pour into bowls, stir a little cream into each, then sprinkle with the chives and more freshly ground black pepper.

CHOOSING LEEKS
Although it means trimming and cleaning them, go for leeks with roots and plenty of green leaves rather than the neat cylinders you see in pre-prepared packs—it's hard to tell how fresh these are. For more information, see p23.

in praise of...
leeks

Leeks are regularly among the supporting cast in recipes, but on center stage, they are a revelation. Choose for tenderness and taste, then cook until they are soft; they are especially wonderful in soups.

A teaspoon of saffron is all that's required for this soup, as its flavor is overpowering if used in greater quantity. Also, it's the most expensive spice in the world.

saffron soup

◉ SERVES 4 **🕐 PREP** 15 MINS **COOK** 20 MINS **❄ FREEZE** UP TO 3 MONTHS
WITHOUT CREAM AND LEMON JUICE

1 tbsp olive oil
1 large onion, sliced
7oz (200g) leeks, cut into 1in (2.5cm) lengths
5½oz (150g) potatoes, diced
1 tsp saffron
1 tsp ground cumin

1 quart (1 liter) hot chicken stock
salt and freshly ground black pepper
2 tbsp dry white wine
2 tbsp heavy cream
1 tbsp lemon juice
snipped chives, to garnish

1 Heat the oil in a heavy-based pan and cook the onion for 6–8 minutes or until soft. Add the leeks, potatoes, saffron, cumin, and stock, then season with salt and freshly ground black pepper. Cover with a lid and bring to a boil, then lower the heat and simmer for 10 minutes or until the potatoes are tender. Do not let them disintegrate into the soup.

2 Transfer to a blender, add the wine, and process until smooth. Stir in the cream and lemon juice and season again with salt and freshly ground black pepper. If the soup is too thick, dilute it with more stock or water. If it is too thin, add more olive oil. Garnish with the snipped chives and serve at once.

This is excellent with croûtes (see p39). Top them with grated Gruyère or Cheddar and some freshly ground black pepper, then put them under the broiler until bubbling.

onion and garlic soup

🌀 **SERVES** 4　　🕐 **PREP** 20 MINS **COOK** 40 MINS　　❄ **FREEZE** NOT SUITABLE

1 tbsp olive oil
1 tbsp butter
1 Spanish onion, finely chopped
1 large shallot, very finely chopped
sea salt and freshly ground black pepper
½ cup hot water
1 small head of garlic, broken up into
　individual cloves but left unpeeled

⅔ cup dry white wine
2½ cups hot vegetable stock
　or chicken stock
½ cup whole or skim milk
2 egg yolks
4 heaped tbsp heavy cream
1 heaped tsp Dijon mustard

1 Heat the oil and butter in a large sauté pan or other heavy-based pan over medium heat. Add the onion and shallot, season lightly with salt and ground black pepper, and cook for 3 minutes, stirring constantly. Lower the heat, add the hot water, and cook gently, stirring frequently, for 20 minutes or until the water has evaporated and the onion mixture is very soft.

2 Meanwhile, bring some lightly salted water to a boil in a small pan. Add the garlic and bring back to a boil, then lower the heat and simmer for 10–15 minutes or until very soft. Drain, then refresh under cold running water. Pour the wine, stock, and milk into the onion mixture and bring to a simmer over medium heat, stirring occasionally.

3 Working over a bowl, squeeze each garlic clove between your thumb and forefinger until the flesh pops out. Add the egg yolks, then mash the garlic, stirring to make a smooth mix. Gradually whisk in the cream. Pour in 3 tbsp of the simmering soup and whisk well. Season lightly with salt and freshly ground black pepper. Whisking vigorously, pour or spoon the garlic mixture into the soup, keeping the pan over low heat. Stir in the mustard, adjust the seasoning, and serve.

This Parisian classic is given extra punch with a spoonful of brandy in every bowl. Serve it the moment you've made it—French onion soup is best piping hot.

french onion soup

⊘ SERVES 4   **◷ PREP** 10 MINS **COOK** 1 HR 20 MINS   **✷ FREEZE** UP TO 1 MONTH
WITHOUT THE CROÛTES AND CHEESE

2 tbsp butter
1 tbsp sunflower oil
1½lb (675g) onions, thinly sliced
1 tsp sugar
salt and freshly ground black pepper
½ cup red wine

2 tbsp plain flour
1½ quarts (1½ liters) hot beef stock
4 tbsp brandy
8 croûtes (see p39)
1 garlic clove, cut in half
4oz (115g) Gruyère or Emmental, grated

1 Melt the butter with the oil in a large, heavy pan over low heat. Add the onions and sugar and turn to coat well. Season with salt and freshly ground black pepper, then press a piece of damp wax paper on top of the onions. Cook, uncovered, stirring occasionally, for 40 minutes or until they are a rich dark brown color. Make sure that they do not stick and burn.

2 Remove the wax paper and stir in the wine. Increase the heat to medium and stir for 5 minutes while the onions glaze. Sprinkle in the flour and stir for 2 minutes, then pour in the stock and bring to a boil. Reduce the heat to low, cover with a lid, and let simmer for 30 minutes. Taste and season with salt and freshly ground black pepper, if necessary.

3 Preheat the grill to its highest setting. Divide the soup among flameproof bowls and stir 1 tbsp of the brandy into each. Rub the croûtes with the cut garlic and place one in each bowl. Sprinkle with the cheese and grill for 2–3 minutes or until the cheese is bubbling and golden. Serve at once.

Meltingly soft onions make a flavorful base for this lightly spiced soup enriched with almonds and sweetened with a hint of caramel.

onion and almond soup

SERVES 4   **PREP** 20 MINS, PLUS 2 HOURS SALTING   **FREEZE** UP TO 2 MONTHS
                 COOK 1 HR   BEFORE HALF-AND-HALF IS ADDED

1 onion, very finely sliced
½ tsp sea salt
vegetable oil, to deep-fry
3½oz (100g) almonds (with skins on)
3¼ cups hot chicken stock
4 tbsp butter
¼ tsp nigella seeds

4 large onions, diced
1 red chile, chopped
1 tsp dark brown (muscovado) sugar
2 tbsp balsamic vinegar
½ cup half-and-half
salt and freshly ground black pepper

1 For a fried onion garnish, put the onion slices in a shallow dish, sprinkle with the sea salt, then set to one side for at least 2 hours. Using your hands, squeeze out the liquid, then pat dry with paper towels. Deep-fry in hot oil for 1–2 minutes or until golden, then drain on paper towels.

2 Bring a small pan of water to a boil, add the almonds, turn off the heat, and cover with a lid. Let soak for 15 minutes, then drain and slip off the skins once the nuts are cool enough to handle. Transfer to a food processor with ½ cup of the stock, then process to a paste and set aside.

3 Meanwhile, melt the butter in a large pan, add the nigella seeds, and cook over low heat for 1 minute. Stir in the diced onions and chile, cover, and cook over very low heat for 20–30 minutes or until soft but not brown, then turn up the heat and remove the lid. When the onions begin to turn golden in color, stir in the sugar and cook until it starts sticking to the bottom of the pan. Add the vinegar and continue cooking until sticky.

4 Add the rest of the stock and the almond paste and simmer for 20 minutes. Process the soup until smooth in a blender, then return to the pan, stir in the cream, and season with salt and freshly ground black pepper. Reheat gently and serve garnished with the fried onions.

Combined with just a few simple ingredients, roasted potatoes can quickly be transformed into a luxuriously smooth, rich, and comforting winter soup.

roasted potato soup

SERVES 4 · **PREP** 15 MINS **COOK** 1 HR 15 MINS · **FREEZE** UP TO 3 MONTHS
BEFORE ONION AND BACON ARE ADDED

1lb (450g) floury potatoes, such as Russet, cut into 2in (5cm) chunks
2 tbsp olive oil
salt and freshly ground black pepper
3 large shallots, coarsely chopped
2 garlic cloves, halved

1 large parsnip, cut into small chunks
3¾ cups hot vegetable stock
4 slices bacon, cut into thin strips
1 onion, halved lengthwise and thinly sliced
¼ cup heavy cream
2 tbsp butter

1 Preheat the oven to 400°F (200°C). Put the potatoes and 1 tbsp of the oil into a small roasting pan and toss to coat well. Season with freshly ground black pepper, then roast for 45 minutes or until golden. Turn occasionally to ensure even roasting. Transfer to a large pot and add the shallots, garlic, and parsnip. Add the stock, bring to a boil, then cover with a lid and simmer for 20 minutes or until the parsnip is tender.

2 Meanwhile, heat the remaining oil in a frying pan, add the bacon, and fry for 5 minutes or until crisp. Remove with a slotted spoon and drain on paper towels. Add the onion along with a pinch of salt, and cook over medium heat for 8–10 minutes or until dark golden brown and well caramelized. Set to one side and keep warm.

3 Remove the soup from the heat, add the cream and butter, and stir until the butter has melted. Process in a blender or food processor until smooth. You may need to do this in batches. Add a little more stock if the soup is too thick. For an extra smooth soup, press the mixture through a fine sieve. Season to taste with salt and freshly ground black pepper, then reheat gently and serve topped with the crispy onion and bacon.

Broccoli and shallots add color and freshness to this rich combination of potato and cheese. You can use Caerphilly or Wensleydale in place of the mascarpone.

potato soup with broccoli, shallots, and mascarpone

SERVES 4   **PREP** 20 MINS **COOK** 40 MINS   **FREEZE** UP TO 3 MONTHS

1 tbsp olive oil
¾ tbsp butter
2 large shallots, finely chopped
12oz (350g) floury potatoes, chopped
    into 1in (2.5cm) chunks
sea salt and freshly ground black pepper

1 large head of broccoli, cut into florets
4 tbsp mascarpone
4 croûtes (see p39)
1oz (30g) creamy, strong-flavored blue
    cheese, such as Roquefort, fourme
    d'Ambert, or Gorgonzola piquante

1 Heat the oil and butter in a sauté pan over medium heat, add the shallots and potatoes, and cook for 5 minutes, stirring often. Meanwhile, boil 1½ quarts (1½ liters) water in a teapot or on the stove.

2 Pour 1¼ quarts (1¼ liters) boiling water into the pan and stir well. Season lightly with sea salt and freshly ground black pepper and bring to a simmer. Lower the heat, cover with a lid, and simmer for 10 minutes. Add the broccoli, stir, cover again, and continue cooking for 10–15 minutes or until the vegetables are tender. Let cool for several minutes, then transfer the contents of the pan to a blender and process until smooth. Strain the soup back into the pan through a sieve, using a wooden spoon to push as much of the mixture through as possible.

3 Pour in the rest of the hot water. Place the pan over medium heat, stir in the mascarpone, and keep stirring until it has blended in. Season with salt and freshly ground black pepper. Spread the croûtes with the blue cheese, ladle the soup into bowls, and float a piece in the center of each one.

If you can't find fresh chanterelle mushrooms for this, you can use jarred or canned. Drain, rinse, and then drain them again before you cook them.

german potato soup

◉ SERVES 6   **🕐 PREP** 25 MINS **COOK** 45 MINS   **❄ FREEZE** UP TO 3 MONTHS
WITHOUT ONIONS AND MUSHROOMS

5 tbsp butter
¼ celeriac, diced
9oz (250g) carrots, diced
1½lb (675g) floury potatoes, diced
1 onion, studded with a bay leaf and a clove
1½ quarts (1½ liters) hot vegetable stock
7oz (200g) leeks, sliced
1 onion, diced

7oz (200g) chanterelles, large ones halved
½ cup heavy whipping cream or
⅔ cup crème fraîche
salt and freshly ground black pepper
pinch of dried marjoram
pinch of freshly grated nutmeg
2 tbsp chopped flat-leaf parsley, chervil,
or chives

1 Melt 3 tbsp of the butter in a large pan, add the celeriac and carrots, and cook, stirring frequently, for 6–8 minutes or until light brown. Add the potatoes, onion, and stock and bring to a boil. Lower the heat, cover with a lid, and simmer for 20 minutes or until tender. Add the leeks, cover again, and cook for 10 minutes more.

2 Meanwhile, melt the rest of the butter in a frying pan, add the diced onion, and cook, stirring continuously, for 4–5 minutes or until soft but not brown. Add the chanterelles and cook, stirring frequently, for 5 minutes.

3 Remove the whole onion from the soup and discard. Transfer about one-third of the contents of the pan to a blender and process until smooth. Stir in the cream and return to the pan. Season with salt and freshly ground black pepper, then add the marjoram, nutmeg, and the cooked onion and chanterelles, and reheat gently. Serve sprinkled with the herbs over the top.

The scallops are a counterpoint to the distinctive taste of the Jerusalem artichoke purée in this traditional soup menu pairing.

scallop and artichoke soup

◉ SERVES 4 **🕐 PREP** 20 MINS **COOK** 25 MINS **❄ FREEZE** UP TO 3 MONTHS
AT THE END OF STEP 1

7 tbsp unsalted butter
1 onion, chopped
1 garlic clove, chopped
2¼lb (1kg) Jerusalem artichokes, peeled
   or scrubbed and cut into small dice
1½ quarts (1½ liters) hot chicken stock
   or water
½ cup heavy cream

salt and freshly ground black pepper
a pinch of freshly grated nutmeg
4 thick slices bacon, cut into
   small dice
4 scallops
2 tbsp sunflower oil
few drops of lemon juice
snipped chives, to garnish

1 Melt 3½ tbsp butter in a large pan and cook the onion gently. Add the garlic and artichokes and sweat over low heat for 3 minutes. Add the stock or water, cover with a lid, and simmer until the artichokes are completely cooked and soft. Purée in a blender with the cream and the remaining butter. You may need to do this in batches. Return to the pan and season with salt and freshly ground black pepper, then sprinkle in the nutmeg and keep warm.

2 Cook the bacon in a frying pan until crisp, then spoon on to paper towels to drain. Season the scallops with salt and freshly ground black pepper, then cook quickly in the sunflower oil—they will be ready almost as soon as they are sealed by the heat. Squeeze a few drops of lemon juice over the top.

3 Divide the artichoke purée among four bowls, spoon the bacon and scallops on top, then garnish with the chives and serve.

Use whatever proportion of carrots and Jerusalem artichokes you have, adding up to 1lb 9oz (700g) in total. The carrots enhance the color and sweetness of the soup.

jerusalem artichoke soup with saffron and thyme

SERVES 4–6   **PREP** 15 MINS **COOK** 35–45 MINS   **FREEZE** UP TO 3 MONTHS

2 tbsp extra-virgin olive oil, plus extra
  to garnish
2 medium onions, chopped
3 garlic cloves, chopped
12oz (350g) Jerusalem artichokes, scrubbed
  and coarsely chopped
12oz (350g) carrots, scrubbed and
  coarsely chopped

sea salt and freshly ground black pepper
1.2 quarts (1.2 liters) hot vegetable stock
1 tbsp fresh thyme leaves or
  1½ tsp dried thyme
large pinch (about 30 strands) of saffron
juice of ½ lemon

1 Heat the oil in a large pan over medium heat, add the onions, and cook for 5–10 minutes or until soft and translucent. Add the garlic and cook for another 30 seconds or until fragrant. Stir in the artichokes, carrots, and a little salt, then cover with a lid and sweat, stirring frequently, for 10–15 minutes or until the vegetables are softened.

2 Add the stock, thyme, and saffron, bring to a boil, then lower the heat to a simmer and cook for 20 minutes or until the vegetables are thoroughly soft. Cool briefly, then process until smooth in a blender. Stir in the lemon juice and season to taste with salt and freshly ground black pepper. Serve in warm bowls, with a drizzle of olive oil on top.

Make the effort to cook up your own stock, as the flavor of the celeriac and hazelnuts in this pale, creamy soup is not strong enough to disguise any shortcomings.

celeriac and hazelnut soup

⊘ **SERVES** 6　　🕐 **PREP** 15 MINS **COOK** 40 MINS　　❄ **FREEZE** UP TO 3 MONTHS
WITHOUT LEMON JUICE AND CREAM

3½oz (100g) shelled hazelnuts
3 tbsp butter
1 medium–large celeriac, coarsely diced
1 onion, chopped
2 tbsp long- or short-grain rice

1 quart (1 liter) hot chicken stock
salt and freshly ground black pepper
juice of ½ lemon
½ cup heavy cream

1 Preheat the oven to 375°F (190°C). Spread the hazelnuts out on a baking sheet and roast for 5–10 minutes or until they turn a shade darker and the skins flake off easily. Check regularly to prevent burning. Let them cool slightly, then rub off the skins.

2 Melt the butter in a large pan over low heat. Add the celeriac, onion, rice, and hazelnuts, turn to coat well, then cover and let sweat gently for 10–15 minutes, stirring once or twice. Pour in half the stock, season well with salt and freshly ground black pepper, and bring to a boil. Simmer gently for 15 minutes or until the celeriac and rice are tender.

3 Let the soup cool for a few minutes, then process until completely smooth in a blender, adding the remaining stock to thin the soup down. Return to the pan, stir in the lemon juice and then the cream, and reheat, being sure to taste and balance the seasoning. Serve hot and steaming.

A light, colorful soup with quite a kick from the jalapeño. Large turnips have a stronger flavor, which is perfect for this dish. Don't use delicate baby ones.

spicy turnip soup with pimento and noodles

⊚ **SERVES** 4–6   ⏱ **PREP** 10 MINS **COOK** 30 MINS   ❄ **FREEZE** UP TO 3 MONTHS
AT THE END OF STEP 1

4 scallions, chopped
2 good-sized turnips, diced
½ tsp crushed hot red pepper flakes
1 green jalapeño pepper, seeded
  and cut into thin rings
2 star anise
2 tsp tomato purée

1 quart (1 liter) hot vegetable stock or
  light chicken stock
1 package dried thin Chinese egg noodles
1 preserved pimento, drained and diced
1–2 tsp soy sauce, to taste
freshly ground black pepper
small handful of cilantro, torn

1 Put the scallions, turnips, pepper flakes, jalapeño, star anise, tomato purée, and stock in a saucepan and bring to a boil. Lower the heat, partially cover with a lid, and simmer gently for 30 minutes or until the turnips are very tender. Discard the star anise.

2 Meanwhile, put the noodles in a bowl, cover with boiling water, and let stand for 5 minutes, stirring to loosen, then drain. Stir the noodles into the soup, along with the pimento. Season to taste with soy sauce and freshly ground black pepper, then stir in half the cilantro. Ladle into warm soup bowls, top with the remaining cilantro, and serve.

TURNIPS
Choose organic turnips for the sweetest, most mustardy flavor. To prepare, trim. Small turnips then need only the thinnest layer of skin peeled off. Larger turnips, however, usually have a thicker layer of hard woody skin to peel.

Alice Waters of Chez Panisse restaurant in California writes, "young turnips with their greens are in the markets in spring and fall. Together they make a delicious soup."

turnip soup

◉ **SERVES** 4–6   ◷ **PREP** 20 MINS **COOK** 40 MINS   ❄ **FREEZE** UP TO 3 MONTHS

2 bunches of young turnips with greens, about 1½lb (675g) total in weight
3 tbsp butter or olive oil
1 onion, thinly sliced
1 bay leaf

2 sprigs of thyme
sea salt
1¼ quarts (1¼ liters) well-flavored chicken stock

1 Remove the greens from the turnips, then trim and discard the stems. Rinse and drain the leaves and cut into ½in (1cm) strips. Trim the roots from the bases and, if the skins are tough (taste one to see), peel before slicing thinly. Heat the butter or oil in a heavy pot over low heat, add the onion, and cook very gently for 12 minutes or until soft.

2 Stir in the turnip bases, along with the bay leaf and thyme, and season with salt. Cook for 5 minutes, stirring occasionally, then pour in the stock and bring to a boil. Lower the heat to a simmer, cover, and cook for 10 minutes. Add the turnip greens and cook for another 5–10 minutes or until tender. Remove the bay leaf, check the seasoning, and serve. This is excellent with a little grated Parmesan on top.

Aromatic spicing balances the natural sweetness of the parsnips in this warming soup. Beef stock will give the best flavor, but chicken or vegetable stock can also be used.

curried parsnip soup

🍽 **SERVES** 4   🕐 **PREP** 25 MINS **COOK** 30 MINS   ❄ **FREEZE** UP TO 3 MONTHS
BEFORE CREAM IS ADDED

1 heaped tbsp coriander seeds
1 tsp cumin seeds
1 dried red chile or ½ tsp crushed
   hot red pepper flakes
1 rounded tsp ground turmeric
¼ tsp ground fenugreek
1 medium onion, chopped
1 large garlic clove, split in half

1½lb (675g) parsnips, cored and diced
2 tbsp butter
1 tbsp flour
1 quart (1 liter) vegetable stock, beef stock,
   or chicken stock
salt and freshly ground black pepper
⅔ cup heavy cream
chopped chives or parsley, to garnish

1 Process the first five ingredients in a coffee grinder, or pound the whole spices in a mortar, then mix with the ground. Transfer the mixture to a small jar—you will not need all of it for this recipe.

2 Cook the onion, garlic, and parsnips gently in the butter, lid on the pan, for 10 minutes. Stir in the flour and 1–2 tbsp of the spice mixture. Cook for 2 minutes, stirring from time to time. Pour in the stock gradually, stirring constantly. Bring to a boil and let simmer gently for 10–15 minutes or until the parsnips are really tender.

3 Purée until smooth in a blender, then dilute to taste with water. Season to taste with salt and freshly ground black pepper, then reheat. Add the cream and serve with the chives or parsley scattered over the top.

PARSNIPS
Widely produced organically, parsnips should be heavy for their size, with firm, unblemished skin. To prepare, trim the ends, then peel thinly. Baby parsnips can be cooked whole, while larger ones should be sliced and diced.

The sweetness of the parsnip is balanced by mild curry powder and sharp green apple in this easy-to-prepare and warming, smooth winter soup.

parsnip and apple soup

⊘ SERVES 4   **◷ PREP** 20 MINS **COOK** 30 MINS   **❄ FREEZE** UP TO 3 MONTHS
WITHOUT CREAM AND LEMON JUICE

1 tbsp olive oil
½ tbsp butter
½ Spanish onion, finely chopped
1 garlic clove, crushed
2 tsp mild curry powder
2¼lb (1kg) parsnips, chopped
sea salt and freshly ground black pepper

1 large Granny Smith apple, peeled, cored, and chopped
1 quart (1 liter) hot vegetable stock or light chicken stock
6 tbsp half-and-half
2 tbsp lemon juice

1 Heat the oil and butter in a large sauté pan over low heat. Add the onion, garlic, and curry powder and cook gently, stirring frequently, for 2–3 minutes or until the onion has softened. Add the parsnips and season lightly with salt and freshly ground black pepper. Turn the heat up a little and cook, stirring frequently, for 5 minutes or until the parsnips are golden.

2 Add the apple, stir for 1 minute, then pour in the stock and bring to a boil. Lower the heat and simmer for 10–12 minutes or until the parsnips are tender. Take off the heat and let cool for several minutes, then transfer to a blender or food processor and process until smooth and creamy.

3 Pass the soup through a sieve placed over the pan, then rinse out the blender or food processor with ½ cup hot water and stir this into the soup. Reheat gently, then stir in the half-and half and lemon juice. Adjust the seasoning and serve piping hot.

The vegetables for this soup are cooked in the oven, which brings out their naturally sweet flavor. This is delicious served with warm pita bread.

moroccan roasted sweet potato soup

SERVES 4   **PREP** 20 MINS **COOK** 50 MINS   **FREEZE** UP TO 3 MONTHS
BEFORE THE YOGURT IS ADDED

1½lb (675g) sweet potatoes, cut into
    big chunks
6 large shallots, quartered
3 plump garlic cloves, unpeeled
1 carrot, cut into large chunks
1 tbsp harissa, plus extra to serve
2 tbsp olive oil

salt and freshly ground black pepper
1 quart (1 liter) hot vegetable stock
1 tsp honey
generous squeeze of lemon juice
natural yogurt, to serve
warm pita bread, to serve

1 Preheat the oven to 400°F (200°C). Place the sweet potatoes, shallots, garlic, and carrot in a roasting pan. Mix the harissa with the oil, then pour over the vegetables and toss together so they are all well coated. Season with freshly ground black pepper, then roast, turning occasionally, for 40 minutes or until tender and turning golden. Remove from the oven.

2 Squeeze the garlic out of their skins into the roasting pan. Stir in the stock and honey, then scrape up all the bits from the bottom of the pan. Carefully transfer to a blender and process until smooth. You may need to do this in batches. Pour into a saucepan and reheat gently.

3 Add a good squeeze of lemon juice and season to taste with salt and freshly ground black pepper. Swirl the yogurt with a little harissa and top each bowl with a spoonful. Serve with warm pita bread.

This recipe is based on a classic African soup that is hot and spicy and full of flavor. The peanut butter lends a rich, satisfying earthiness.

african sweet potato soup

🍲 **SERVES** 4   🕐 **PREP** 20 MINS **COOK** 20–25 MINS   ❋ **FREEZE** UP TO 3 MONTHS

2 tbsp olive oil
1 onion, chopped
2 garlic cloves, finely chopped
2 tsp finely grated ginger
¼ tsp crushed hot red pepper flakes
1lb (450g) sweet potatoes, cut into
  small chunks
1 red bell pepper, seeded and chopped
1 x 8oz (230g) can tomatoes

1 tsp cumin seeds, dry-roasted
  and crushed (see p25)
1 tsp coriander seeds, dry-roasted
  and crushed
1 quart (1 liter) hot vegetable stock
2–3 tbsp smooth or crunchy peanut butter
few drops of Tabasco (optional)
chili oil, to serve

1 Heat the oil in a large pan, add the onion, and cook for 3 minutes. Stir in the garlic, ginger, and hot red pepper flakes and cook for 1 minute, then stir in the sweet potatoes, pepper, tomatoes, and crushed spices and cook for 2 minutes. Pour in the stock, bring to a boil, then simmer for 12–15 minutes or until the sweet potatoes are tender.

2 Remove from the heat and process in a blender until smooth. You may need to do this in batches. Pass the soup through a sieve to remove the pepper skin and then stir in the peanut butter, tasting to decide the desired amount. If you want to add more heat, add in some Tabasco. Reheat gently, then drizzle a little chili oil over each bowlful to serve.

As a strictly cold-season vegetable, the rutabaga stores up lots of starch in the edible root base. It is this that gives this rich, wintry soup its velvety texture.

creamy rutabaga soup

⊘ **SERVES** 4–6　　🕐 **PREP** 10 MINS **COOK** 40–50 MINS　　❄ **FREEZE** UP TO 3 MONTHS
BEFORE CREAM IS ADDED

2 tbsp butter
2 medium onions, chopped
1lb 10oz (750g) rutabaga (trimmed weight),
　cut into cubes
sea salt and freshly ground black pepper

1 quart (1 liter) hot vegetable stock
1 tbsp honey
½ nutmeg (to grate)
⅔ cup half-and-half, plus extra to garnish

1 Melt the butter in a large pan over medium heat. Add the onions and cook for 6–8 minutes or until lightly golden. Stir in the rutabaga and a pinch of salt, cover with a lid, and cook for 10 minutes, stirring frequently. Pour in the stock, add the honey, and bring to a boil, grating in a bit of the nutmeg as you do so. Simmer for 20–30 minutes or until the rutabaga is completely soft.

2 Cool briefly, then process in a blender until smooth and velvety. You may need to do this in batches. Season with salt and freshly ground black pepper, then stir in the half-and-half. Serve each bowlful with a swirl of the half-and-half and a good grinding of black pepper.

RUTABAGA
Pick out rutabaga that are heavy for their size, but not too large—small generally equals sweet. They should be firm with an unblemished skin. Avoid any with shriveled roots. Store in a cool dark place for up to a week.

If you are a fan of smooth soups, you can process this in a blender at the end of step 1 and then swirl the pesto through the resulting delicate light green purée.

kohlrabi soup with pesto

SERVES 6   **PREP** 5 MINS **COOK** 15 MINS   **FREEZE** UP TO 3 MONTHS

1 tbsp butter
3–4 kohlrabi, cut into bite-sized dice
1 quart (1 liter) hot vegetable stock

2 tbsp crème fraîche
salt and freshly ground black pepper
6 tsp pesto, to garnish

1 Melt the butter in a heavy saucepan, add the kohlrabi, and cook for 5 minutes or until light golden brown. Pour in the stock and bring to a boil. Add the crème fraîche and season with salt and freshly ground black pepper. Cook for 8–10 minutes or until the kohlrabi is tender but not mushy.

2 Taste and adjust the seasoning, then ladle the soup into warm bowls and garnish each with a teaspoon of pesto.

KOHLRABI
Go for kohlrabi that are somewhere between a golf ball and a tennis ball in size. If they are any larger than this, they will be very tough. Store them in a plastic bag in the crisper drawer of the refrigerator for up to 3 weeks.

The addition of nutmeg to this recipe gives the soup a wonderfully distinctive flavor. Be generous with the nutmeg for the best, and tastiest, results.

butternut squash soup

SERVES 4   **PREP** 10 MINS **COOK** 25 MINS   **FREEZE** UP TO 3 MONTHS
WITHOUT THE CREAM

1½ tbsp butter
1lb 2oz (500g) butternut squash, seeded and
   chopped into 1in (2.5cm) pieces
1 medium onion, chopped
1 garlic clove, crushed

a generous grating of nutmeg
2 cups hot chicken stock
½ cup heavy cream or half-and-half
salt and freshly ground black pepper

1 Melt the butter in a heavy-bottomed saucepan. Add the squash, onion, and garlic, cover with a lid, and cook for 15 minutes, stirring occasionally. Grate in the nutmeg and cook with the lid on for another 5 minutes.

2 Stir in the stock and bring to a boil. When the squash is tender, add the cream and simmer for 1 minute. Transfer the soup to a blender and process until smooth. You may need to do this in batches. Season with salt and freshly ground black pepper and serve.

Roasting the squash concentrates and develops its flavor beautifully, and leaves you free to get on with making a hot rouille sauce, which gives this soup its vigor.

roasted squash soup

SERVES 6　　**PREP** 30 MINS **COOK** 50 MINS　　**FREEZE** UP TO 3 MONTHS

1½–2lb (675–900g) winter squash, such as pumpkin, butternut, or acorn, cut into chunks
1lb (450g) ripe tomatoes, coarsely chopped
6 garlic cloves, unpeeled
1 sprig of rosemary
2 sprigs of thyme
1 red onion, cut into 8 wedges
4 tbsp extra virgin olive oil
1.2 quarts (1.2 liters) hot vegetable stock or chicken stock

salt and freshly ground black pepper
small pinch of saffron
1 garlic clove, chopped
1 red chile, seeded and coarsely chopped
1 egg yolk
1 tbsp red wine vinegar
½ cup sunflower oil
4 tbsp extra virgin olive oil
12 croûtes (see p39)
freshly grated Comté or Gruyère, to serve

1 Preheat the oven to 425°F (220°C). Put the first seven ingredients into a roasting pan and turn to coat in oil. Roast, turning occasionally, for 45 minutes or until everything is very tender. Discard the herb stems, and scrape the rest into a blender. Add the stock and process until smooth. You may need to do this in batches. Pour into a large pot and season with salt and freshly ground black pepper.

2 Meanwhile, make a rouille. Soak the saffron in 1 tbsp warm water. Pound the garlic, chile, and a pinch of salt to a paste in a mortar, then work in the egg yolk and vinegar. Mix the two oils, then drip them in, whisking constantly. When one-third of the oil has been incorporated, increase the flow to a slow trickle. Stir in the drained saffron, then adjust the seasonings.

3 To serve, reheat the soup, then ladle into bowls. Pass the croûtes, the rouille, and the grated cheese around separately, so everyone can smear the croûtes liberally with rouille, float them in the steaming soup, and then finish with a sprinkling of grated cheese.

The sharp basil and lime cream melting into this soup is a perfect finish for special occasions. For a more everyday dinner, however, you can leave it out.

winter squash soup with basil and lime cream

◉ SERVES 6–8   **🕑 PREP** 25 MINS **COOK** 35 MINS   **❄ FREEZE** UP TO 3 MONTHS
AT THE END OF STEP 2

5 garlic cloves
1 large onion, chopped
1in (2.5cm) piece ginger, peeled and
    coarsely chopped
3 tbsp oil
3lb 3oz (1.5 kg) winter squash, such
    as pumpkin, butternut, or acorn, seeds
    and rind removed, coarsely cubed
2 sprigs of parsley
1 sprig of thyme
1 bay leaf

3 star anise
12oz (350g) tomatoes, peeled, seeded,
    and coarsely chopped
2 quarts (2 liters) hot vegetable stock
    or chicken stock
salt and freshly ground black pepper
1¼ cups heavy whipping cream
juice of 1–2 limes
small handful of basil leaves,
    chopped, to serve

1 Chop two of the garlic cloves, but leave the rest whole. Put the chopped garlic and the whole garlic into a large pan with the onion, ginger, oil, and squash. Tie the herbs together in a bundle and toss those in too. Cover with a lid and cook over low heat for 10 minutes, stirring once or twice.

2 Add the star anise, tomatoes, and stock, then season with salt and freshly ground black pepper and bring to a boil. Simmer for 20 minutes or until the squash is tender. Pick out and discard the bundle of herbs and the star anise. Process the soup in a blender until smooth and then pass it through a sieve. Taste and adjust the seasoning, then reheat gently.

3 Meanwhile, pour the cream into a bowl, add the lime juice, and whisk. Once the cream holds its shape loosely, stir in the basil. As you ladle the soup into bowls, top with a floating crown of basil and lime cream.

A thick, creamy soup with an amazing vivid orange color. If you are using a stock cube, be sure to taste the soup before adding any extra salt.

pumpkin soup

SERVES 6   **PREP** 10 MINS **COOK** 20 MINS   ❄ **FREEZE** UP TO 3 MONTHS
WITHOUT THE SAGE GARNISH

1 small pumpkin (or part of a large one), about 1lb 10oz (750g) in total, peeled and cubed
2 medium potatoes, peeled and cubed
1 tbsp olive oil
2½ cups vegetable stock
2 tomatoes, chopped

4 fresh sage leaves
sea salt and freshly ground black pepper

for the garnish
olive oil, for frying
18 large fresh sage leaves

1 Heat the oil in a saucepan and cook the pumpkin and potatoes for 5 minutes. Add the stock, chopped tomatoes, and the 4 sage leaves. Cover and simmer for about 10 minutes, until the vegetables are soft.

2 Using a blender, process the soup until smooth, then gently reheat. Season with salt and pepper, to taste.

3 For the garnish, heat a little oil in a frying pan and, once hot, fry the large sage leaves until crisp. Scatter the crispy leaves over the soup and serve immediately.

This recipe first appeared in *Fork to Fork* by Monty and Sarah Don, published by Conran Octopus and reproduced by kind permission

You can cook the apples—skin, core, and all—as you will be sieving the end result. For special occasions, use dry sherry or white wine instead of water.

pumpkin and apple soup

SERVES 6   **PREP** 20 MINS **COOK** 40 MINS   **FREEZE** UP TO 3 MONTHS

4 tbsp unsalted butter
1 medium onion, finely chopped
7oz (200g) pumpkin flesh, diced
2 sharp-tasting apples such as
 Granny Smith, diced

½ cup hot water
4 cups cold vegetable stock or
 chicken stock
salt and freshly ground black pepper
2 tsp toasted pumpkin seeds, to garnish

1 Melt the butter in a large saucepan, add the onion, and cook very gently, stirring often, for 10 minutes or until soft. Do not let it brown. Add the pumpkin and apples and stir to coat well. Pour in the hot water, cover with a lid, and leave on a very, very low heat for 30 minutes, stirring from time to time. If the liquid evaporates, pour in a little more hot water. The vegetables and fruit should be very soft at the end of cooking.

2 Stir in the stock, then blend the soup in batches. As each batch is done, pour it into a sieve set over a clean saucepan. Press the contents through with the back of a ladle, a wooden spoon, or a pestle.

3 When all the soup has been sieved, reheat it very gently, then season to taste with salt and freshly ground black pepper. Serve garnished with the toasted pumpkin seeds.

This chunky country soup takes minutes to prepare and makes a good light supper or lunch dish. For a vegetarian option, leave out the bacon.

french cabbage soup

SERVES 4   **PREP** 15 MINS **COOK** 30 MINS   **FREEZE** UP TO 3 MONTHS
WITHOUT THE BACON GARNISH

1 tbsp olive oil
3½oz (100g) diced bacon
1 Spanish onion, finely chopped
1 garlic clove, crushed
1 large Savoy cabbage, halved, core
   discarded, and leaves cut into shreds

sea salt and freshly ground black pepper
3 sprigs of parsley
croûtons (see p39), to garnish

1 Heat the oil in a large heavy saucepan over medium heat. Add the bacon (setting aside 2 tbsp to garnish), onion, and garlic. Cook, stirring frequently, for 3–4 minutes or until the onion and garlic start to color. Add the cabbage shreds, reserving a handful to finish. Stir well and season lightly with sea salt and generously with pepper. Continue cooking for 2–3 minutes, stirring occasionally.

2 Bring about 3½ cups water to a boil in a teapot. Pour the boiling water over the vegetables and bacon pieces, stir well, and add the parsley. Cover, lower the heat a little, and simmer gently for about 20 minutes, stirring occasionally.

3 Meanwhile, place a nonstick cooking pan over medium heat. Add the reserved bacon and cook until crisp and golden. Then add the reserved cabbage shreds and cook them until they have wilted, stirring frequently. Season with a little pepper.

4 Taste the soup and adjust the seasoning as needed. Remove the parsley. Ladle into individual bowls and scatter the fried bacon and cabbage mixture over the top. Garnish with croûtons, if using, to finish off the soup.

You can prepare the meatballs ahead for this recipe. Allow approximately 30 minutes to reheat the broth, add the meatballs, and finish off the cooking.

cabbage and tomato soup with meatballs

SERVES 4   **PREP** 40 MINS **COOK** 1 HOUR   ✱ **FREEZE** UP TO 3 MONTHS
SOUP AND MEATBALLS SEPARATELY

for the meatballs
1 garlic clove, crushed
½ Spanish onion, finely chopped
½ tsp hot smoked paprika
½ tsp ground cumin
1 tsp dried thyme (or fresh leaves)
2 tbsp freshly grated Parmesan cheese
breadcrumbs made from 2 slices bread
14oz (400g) ground steak
1 large egg
sea salt and freshly ground black pepper
3 tbsp flour
3 tbsp vegetable oil
1 tbsp butter

for the soup
2 tbsp vegetable oil
½ Spanish onion, coarsely chopped
1 garlic clove, crushed
9oz (250g) tomatoes, seeded and chopped
1 large Savoy cabbage, halved, core and ribs
    discarded, and leaves sliced into
    bite-sized pieces
sea salt and freshly ground black pepper
1 quart (1 liter) beef stock
2 tbsp finely chopped parsley, to finish
3 tbsp grated or shaved Parmesan cheese

1 For the meatballs, put the first nine ingredients in a bowl, season, and mix well. Shape into walnut-sized balls and refrigerate for 30 minutes.

2 Heat the oil in a large deep pan over medium heat. Add in the onion, garlic, and tomatoes. Cook for 3–5 minutes, stirring. Add the cabbage and stir for 3 minutes. Stir in the stock and simmer for 15–20 minutes.

3 Meanwhile, sift the flour onto a plate and coat the meatballs. Heat the oil and butter in a pan over medium-high heat. Add the meatballs and cook for 3 minutes until they are a rich brown all over. Add to the soup and simmer for 15–20 minutes. Serve scattered with parsley and Parmesan.

Many variations of this Polish dish exist. Bacon, sauerkraut, and smoked Polish sausage are essential, but you could try lamb or beef instead of the duck or venison.

bigos

◎ SERVES 4 **🕐 PREP** 40 MINS **COOK** 2 HRS **❄ FREEZE** UP TO 3 MONTHS

1 small Savoy cabbage, cored, ribs removed, leaves shredded
salt and freshly ground pepper
1lb 2oz (500g) sauerkraut, drained
3½oz (100g) smoked bacon, cubed
7oz (200g) smoked Polish sausage, sliced
7oz (200g) duck breast or lean venison, cubed
1 large red onion, diced
1 clove garlic, crushed

5½oz (150g) mushrooms, sliced
½ tsp smoked paprika
1 bay leaf
½ tsp juniper berries
1 tsp dried marjoram
½ tsp caraway seeds, crushed using a pestle and mortar
¾ cup red wine
1 cup beef stock

1 Heat a heavy saucepan over medium heat. Add the cabbage and cover with boiling water. Season with salt and pepper. Return to a simmer and cook for 10 minutes. Drain and reserve. Repeat with the sauerkraut, but simmer for 5 minutes. Drain, reserving the sauerkraut and the cooking liquid.

2 Heat a nonstick frying pan over medium heat. Cook the bacon until crisp. Place them on a platter lined with paper towels. Cook the sausage and duck or venison for 5 minutes, stirring, then add to the platter with the bacon. Set aside. Now cook the onion, garlic, and mushrooms in the same pan until softened. Then add to the saucepan, along with the cooked meats.

3 Place the saucepan over medium heat. Stir in the paprika, bay leaf, juniper berries, marjoram, and caraway seeds. Pour in the wine and stock. Bring to a simmer, stirring. Cover, reduce the heat a little, and simmer for 1 hour, stirring from time to time.

4 Add the boiled cabbage, stir, cover, and cook for 10 minutes, and then stir in the sauerkraut. Add some or all of the reserved cooking liquid (the mixture should be a thick soup rather than a stew). Simmer for another 15 minutes. Taste, adjust the seasoning, and serve very hot.

Sauerkraut is an excellent source of vitamin C. This hearty soup is redolent of Eastern Europe, although Chinese cooks were pickling cabbage in wine as early as 200 BCE.

sauerkraut soup

◎ SERVES 4   **🕐 PREP** 10 MINS **COOK** 30 MINS   **❄ FREEZE** NOT SUITABLE

2 tbsp vegetable oil
1 onion, finely chopped
3½oz (100g) bacon, diced
1 x 14oz (400g) jar or can sauerkraut,
  coarsely chopped

1 x 14oz (400g) can chopped tomatoes, peeled
2 tsp sugar
2½ cups hot vegetable or chicken stock
¾ cup heavy cream
freshly ground black pepper

1 Heat the vegetable oil in a large saucepan over low heat. Add the chopped onion and cook gently until softened but not browned. Then add the diced bacon and cook for another 3 minutes. Finally add the chopped sauerkraut, cover, and continue to cook for another 5 minutes, stirring from time to time.

2 Increase the heat under the saucepan slightly and add the chopped tomatoes, sugar, hot stock, heavy cream, and freshly ground black pepper and stir well. Bring to a simmer over medium heat for 15 minutes until the sauerkraut is tender. Ladle the soup into bowls to serve and eat with toasted rye bread.

Start off with a good-quality, home-made stock for this fragrant, light, refreshing soup, then serve it piled high with fresh herbs and chiles.

vietnamese noodle soup

⊘ **SERVES** 4   🕐 **PREP** 25–30 MINS PLUS SOAKING TIME   ❄ **FREEZE** NOT SUITABLE
COOK 25 MINS PLUS SITTING TIME

1¼ quarts (1¼ liters) chicken stock, preferably homemade
6 slices ginger (no need to peel)
½ tsp coriander seeds
4 star anise
2 stalks lemongrass, sliced
2 skinless, boneless chicken breasts
3½oz (100g) rice noodles
2 bok choy, very thinly sliced

Asian fish sauce, to taste
3½oz (100g) bean sprouts
small bunch cilantro, about ¾oz (20g), coarsely chopped
small handful mint leaves, finely shredded
2 scallions, thinly sliced
1 large fresh red chile, seeded (unless you like it hot) and thinly sliced
lime wedges

1 Pour the stock into a large saucepan, and add the ginger, coriander seeds, star anise, and lemongrass. Simmer gently for 10 minutes. Lower the chicken breasts into the stock and continue simmering for 15 minutes. Remove from the heat and let sit for 5 minutes. Meanwhile, break the noodles (so they are easier to eat) into a large heatproof bowl and cover with boiling water. Let soak for the time suggested on the package.

2 Remove the chicken from the stock with a slotted spoon and transfer it to a cutting board. Slice the chicken into very thin bite-sized strips. Strain and discard the flavorings from the stock and return the stock to the pan. Drop in the bok choy (off the heat) and let it wilt in the warmth of the stock. Return the chicken to the stock along with a dash of fish sauce.

3 Drain the noodles and divide between 4 big bowls. Lay the bean sprouts on top. To serve, ladle the chicken and hot stock over the noodles and top each bowl with a generous scattering of the cilantro, mint, scallions, and chile; add another splash of fish sauce. Offer lime wedges for squeezing over the top.

Potato and kale soup (*caldo verde*) is ubiquitous in Portugal, where cooks use incredibly finely shredded cabbage. Here we have to substitute our own winter greens.

portuguese potato and kale soup

⊘ SERVES 4   **⏱ PREP** 15–20 MINS **COOK** 20–25 MINS   ❄ **FREEZE** UP TO 3 MONTHS

1lb (450g) potatoes, peeled and sliced
4 garlic cloves, sliced
1 small onion, finely chopped
salt and freshly ground black pepper

8oz (225g) curly kale, or cavolo nero or
  Savoy cabbage
4oz (110g) chorizo, skin removed and sliced
extra virgin olive oil, to serve

1 Place the potato slices in a large saucepan with the garlic and onion. Season with salt and pepper and add enough water to cover generously. Simmer until tender. Pass through the fine blade of a mouli-legume, or mash to a smooth purée using a potato masher. Add a little more water if necessary to thin to a soupy consistency. Return to the pan and adjust the seasoning, adding plenty of pepper.

2 While the potatoes are cooking, cut the stems from the kale, then roll up the leaves and shred very thinly—the resulting threads of cabbage should be around ⅛in (3mm) wide. Bring the soup back to a boil. Stir in the kale and sausage. Simmer for 5 minutes. Ladle into soup bowls, pour a little olive oil into each, and serve.

KALE
Intense in flavor and vibrant in color, use locally grown kale with firm stems and fresh, curly leaves. Or you could grow this hardy vegetable yourself. The tough central stems should be removed before cooking.

Cauliflower is transformed when treated to gentle heat and aromatic spicing. For a vegetarian option, garnish this with croûtons and Parmesan cheese instead of bacon.

cauliflower soup with toasted coriander

⊘ SERVES 4–6   **⏱ PREP** 15–20 MINS **COOK** 40 MINS   **❄ FREEZE** UP TO 1 MONTH
WITHOUT HALF-AND-HALF OR BACON

2 tsp coriander seeds
3 tbsp unsalted butter
1 onion, diced
1 potato, diced
1 head cauliflower, finely chopped
2 cups vegetable stock

1 bay leaf
8 slices bacon
¾ cup milk
½ cup half-and-half
salt and freshly ground black pepper

1 Heat a sturdy frying pan and lightly roast the coriander seeds, stirring all the time, for about a minute. Grind the seeds to a coarse powder using a mortar and pestle and set aside.

2 Melt the butter in a large saucepan over low heat. Add the onion and potato, cover, and leave to soften for 10 minutes. Add the cauliflower and ground coriander, season well, cover, and continue cooking for another 10 minutes.

3 Pour in the stock, add the bay leaf, cover, and simmer for about 15 minutes, until the cauliflower has softened. Meanwhile, cook the bacon under the broiler until crisp. Drain on paper towels, coarsely chop, and set aside.

4 Remove the bay leaf and blend the soup to a purée with an immersion blender. Stir in the milk and add the half-and-half. Reheat and season with salt and pepper. Ladle the soup into bowls and scatter with the chopped bacon before serving.

Make sure your cauliflower is impeccably fresh, and check that the cheese really is smoked, and not just laced with fake smoke flavoring, as some are.

smoked cauliflower cheese soup

SERVES 6   **PREP** 15–20 MINS **COOK** 25–30 MINS   **FREEZE** UP TO 3 MONTHS
BEFORE CHEESE IS ADDED

1 cauliflower, broken into florets
1 large onion, chopped
1 medium floury potato, cut into cubes
2 garlic cloves, sliced
1 bouquet garni (see p24)
2 tbsp butter
1 quart (1 liter) hot vegetable
  or chicken stock

salt and freshly ground black pepper
3½oz (100g) coarsely grated smoked cheddar
a shake of cayenne pepper, freshly chopped
  parsley or chives, croûtons, or a dollop of
  sour cream, to garnish

1 Cook the vegetables, garlic, and bouquet garni with the butter in a covered pan over low heat for 10 minutes, stirring once or twice. Add the stock, a little salt, and lots of freshly ground black pepper and bring to a boil. Simmer until the cauliflower and potato are just tender (don't overcook). Remove the bouquet garni and process the soup in a blender until smooth, adding more stock or a little milk to thin it down as necessary.

2 Reheat the soup gently, but do not allow it to boil. Stir in two-thirds of the cheese, taste, and see if you think it needs more. Add it if it does. Taste one more time, then serve with the garnish of your choice.

CAULIFLOWER
You can find various types of organic cauliflower, including purple, orange, white, and miniature. Look for those with tight, firm heads and bright green leaves. The stalks can be used for flavoring soup or stock.

This is an unexpectedly good soup, with all the fresh, nutty flavor of Brussels sprouts tempered by the natural sweetness of the onion.

brussels sprout soup

SERVES 4–6   **PREP** 20 MINS **COOK** 1 HR 10 MINS   **FREEZE** UP TO 3 MONTHS
WITHOUT THE SOUR CREAM

1lb (450g) onions, sliced
2 tbsp butter
1 tbsp sugar
1lb (450g) Brussels sprouts, trimmed
　and halved
1 generous sprig thyme

1¼ quarts (1¼ liters) chicken or
　vegetable stock
salt and freshly ground black pepper
sour cream, crème fraîche, or
　Greek-style yogurt, to serve
paprika or cayenne pepper, to serve

1 Place the onions in a pan with the butter. Cover and cook over low heat for about 30–40 minutes until the onions are incredibly tender and soft. Sprinkle in the sugar and cook, uncovered, for another 10–15 minutes or so until the onions are lightly colored and concentrated, stirring occasionally.

2 Add the sprouts and the thyme and stir. Pour in the stock and season with salt and pepper. Bring to a boil and simmer for 10–15 minutes until the sprouts are just tender. Cool slightly, remove the thyme, and process in two batches. Reheat gently if needed, then taste and adjust the seasoning. Serve piping hot, with a spoonful of sour cream, crème fraîche, or yogurt in each bowlful, and a light dusting of paprika or cayenne.

BRUSSELS SPROUTS
Look for locally grown sprouts. They can range from the size of a thumbnail to a golf ball, but smaller equals sweeter. Before using home-grown sprouts, soak them in cold water, as they may contain a few worms.

This earthy soup combines mildly nutty celeriac and more assertive celery to create a fragrant, satisfying winter warmer.

celery and celeriac soup

⊚ **SERVES** 4   🕐 **PREP** 15 MINS **COOK** 20 MINS   ❄ **FREEZE** UP TO 3 MONTHS
WITHOUT THE CHILLED BUTTER

1 tbsp sunflower, peanut, or mild-flavored
  olive oil
2 tbsp butter
1lb 2oz (500g) celeriac, peeled and chopped
1 large head celery, cored and chopped
1 medium floury potato, peeled and chopped

sea salt and freshly ground black pepper
1 quart (1 liter) vegetable stock or
  chicken stock
2 tbsp chilled butter, diced
4 slices walnut bread, lightly toasted,
  to serve

1 Put the oil and 2 tbsp butter in a large sauté pan over medium heat. Add the celeriac, celery, and potato. Stir well for 2–3 minutes then reduce the heat a little. Add 3–4 tbsp water, and season lightly. Partially cover and let stew gently until very soft. Stir the vegetables from time to time and keep the heat low.

2 Transfer the cooked vegetables to a food processor and purée. Return to the pan and add the stock. Season, stir briskly to blend, and bring to a simmer over medium heat, stirring frequently. Reduce the heat a little and let simmer gently for 10–15 minutes, still stirring occasionally. Taste and adjust the seasoning.

3 Just before serving, whisk in the chilled diced butter. Serve hot with toasted walnut bread.

CELERY
Most celery found in markets is naturally vibrantly green, but look out for the less bitter blanched white variety, too. Celery's thick outer stalks are best in soups, stews, and casseroles, rather than eaten raw.

Here's a refreshing soup for a warm summer's day. You could use romaine lettuce or even a bunch of watercress instead of chicory, if you prefer.

chicory gazpacho

⊘ SERVES 4   **🕐 PREP** 15 MINS PLUS CHILLING   **❄ FREEZE** UP TO 3 MONTHS

1 large orange
2 heads white chicory
2 slices bread, crusts removed
1 garlic clove, coarsely chopped
4 scallions, trimmed and
    coarsely chopped
1 large beefsteak tomato, peeled, quartered,
    and seeded

2 cups cold vegetable stock
2 tbsp olive oil, plus extra for garnish
2 tbsp white balsamic condiment
4 large basil leaves
salt and freshly ground black pepper

1 Thinly pare the zest of half the orange. Cut in thin strips and boil in water for 1 minute. Drain, rinse with cold water, and drain again. Set aside for garnish. Finely grate the zest from the remaining orange, squeeze the juice into a bowl, and set aside.

2 Cut a cone shape out of the base of each head of chicory and discard. Separate the heads into spears. Reserve four of the smallest spears for the garnish. Coarsely chop the remainder.

3 Soak the bread in water for 2 minutes. Squeeze out some of the moisture then put the bread in a blender with the chopped chicory, garlic, scallions, tomato, stock, olive oil, white balsamic condiment, and the basil leaves, the orange juice and finely grated zest. Purée the soup in a blender or food processor then season to taste. Chill until ready to serve.

4 Ladle into four bowls, and drizzle with a little olive oil. Garnish each with a tiny chicory spear and a few strands of blanched orange zest. Serve cold.

This simple soup recipe with onion, garlic, and parsley brings out the flavor of mixed wild mushrooms beautifully. Delicious served with sour cream.

mixed mushroom soup

SERVES 4   **PREP** 15 MINS **COOK** 1 HR   **FREEZE** UP TO 3 MONTHS

4½ tbsp unsalted butter
1 cup onions, finely chopped
1 garlic clove, finely chopped
1 tbsp (15g) flat-leaf parsley, chopped
8oz (225g) mixed wild mushrooms, diced
4 tbsp milk

salt and freshly ground black pepper
grated nutmeg
4 tbsp flour
1¼ quarts (1¼ liters) vegetable or
   chicken stock
4 tbsp sour cream

1 Heat half the butter with the onion, garlic, and parsley in a sauté pan and cook for 3 minutes. Add the mushrooms and sauté for another 3 minutes. Pour in the milk and season with salt and nutmeg. Cook for a few more minutes and set aside.

2 In another saucepan, melt the remaining butter. Remove the pan from the heat and beat in the flour. Return the pan to low heat and cook until the mixture deepens in color. Remove the pan from the heat once more, and add the stock gradually by the ladleful. Stir constantly to keep lumps from forming, and return the pan to low heat.

3 When all the stock has been combined with the flour, add the mushroom mixture and the juices. Bring to a boil and simmer for 15–20 minutes. Season with salt and pepper to taste. Spoon a tablespoon of sour cream into each bowl and serve.

MUSHROOMS
Many different varieties of wild mushrooms can be found in farmers' markets or by foraging in the wild. If you're unsure about which mushrooms are safe to eat, take a good identification book, or stick to the market.

This hearty Italian country soup has deep, earthy flavors. Check the mushrooms after soaking, because there may be bits of dirt or straw that need to be removed.

porcini mushroom soup

⊘ SERVES 4   **🕐 PREP** 20 MINS, PLUS 30 MINS STANDING   **❄ FREEZE** UP TO 3 MONTHS
                          COOK 1 HR   WITHOUT THE BREAD

1oz (30g) dried porcini mushrooms
3 tbsp extra virgin olive oil, plus extra
　to serve
2 onions, finely chopped
2 tsp chopped fresh rosemary leaves
1 tsp fresh thyme leaves
2 garlic cloves, finely sliced

4oz (115g) chestnut mushrooms, sliced
2 celery ribs with leaves, finely chopped
1 x 14oz (400g) can chopped tomatoes
3¼ cups vegetable stock
salt and freshly ground black pepper
½ stale ciabatta or small crusty white loaf,
　torn into chunks

1 Put the dried porcini in a heatproof bowl, pour over 1¼ cups boiling water, and let stand for 30 minutes. Drain, reserving the soaking liquid, then chop any large pieces of porcini.

2 Heat the oil in a saucepan, add the onions, cover, and let cook for 10 minutes, or until soft. Add the rosemary, thyme, garlic, chestnut mushrooms, and celery, and continue cooking, uncovered, until the celery has softened.

3 Add the tomatoes, porcini, and the stock. Strain the soaking liquid through a piece of muslin or a fine sieve into the pan. Bring the soup to a boil, then lower the heat and simmer gently for 45 minutes.

4 Season to taste with salt and pepper, and add the chunks of bread. Remove the pan from the heat. Cover and let stand for 10 minutes before serving. Spoon into deep bowls and drizzle each serving with a little olive oil.

in praise of...
mushrooms

Nothing is more satisfying to a cook than a mushroom soup: first the foraging in the woods or choosing the best specimens from the market; then the making of the dish, and finally the eating.

Using a selection of both wild and cultivated mushrooms produces a soup bursting with flavor. The horseradish cream provides a welcome kick.

mushroom soup

SERVES 4   **PREP** 10 MINS **COOK** 45 MINS   **FREEZE** UP TO 3 MONTHS

2 tbsp butter
1 onion, finely chopped
2 celery ribs, finely chopped
1 garlic clove, crushed
1lb (450g) mixed mushrooms, coarsely chopped

7oz (200g) potatoes, peeled and cubed
1 quart (1 liter) vegetable stock
2 tbsp finely chopped fresh parsley
salt and freshly ground black pepper
horseradish cream, to serve (optional)

1 Melt the butter in a large saucepan, add the onion, celery, and garlic, and cook for 3–4 minutes, or until softened.

2 Stir in the mushrooms and continue to cook for another 5–6 minutes. Add the potatoes and the stock, and bring to a boil. Reduce the heat and let simmer gently for 30 minutes.

3 Using a blender, process the soup until smooth, working in batches if necessary. Sprinkle the parsley over the top and season to taste with salt and pepper. Serve immediately, stirring a little horseradish cream into each soup bowl, if desired, for an extra kick.

legumes and nuts

This soup contains annatto. If you've never used the spice before, it has a sweet peppery flavor and an orangey red color. It is widely used in Latin America.

cuban black bean soup

SERVES 4   **PREP** 20 MINS, PLUS OVERNIGHT SOAKING   **FREEZE** UP TO 3 MONTHS
COOK 1¾ HRS

8oz (225g) dried black beans, soaked in cold
  water overnight
1 bay leaf
2 cups chicken stock or ham stock
1 tbsp sunflower oil
1 large onion, finely chopped
1 garlic clove, crushed
½ tsp ground cumin
½ tsp ground annatto

pinch of ground cloves
1 beefsteak tomato, peeled and chopped
1 tsp white wine vinegar
4oz (115g) cooked ham, diced
1½ tsp brown sugar
salt and freshly ground black pepper
a few torn cilantro leaves, to garnish
corn tortilla chips, crushed, to serve
grated Cheddar, to serve

1 Drain the soaked beans and put in a large saucepan with enough water to cover by 2in (5cm). Add the bay leaf, bring to a boil, then boil rapidly for 10 minutes. Reduce the heat, cover loosely with a lid, and simmer gently for 1 hour or until really tender. Drain, reserving the liquid. Add enough stock to the cooking liquid to make 1 quart (1 liter) in all.

2 Discard the bay leaf and coarsely purée the beans and some of the stock in a blender—the mixture should not be completely smooth. Alternatively, crush with a potato masher, then set aside.

3 Heat the oil in the rinsed-out pan, add the onion, and cook gently, stirring, for 3–4 minutes or until softened but not browned. Add the garlic and cook for 1 minute, then add the spices and cook for 30 seconds. Add the tomato and vinegar and cook, stirring, for 3–5 minutes or until pulpy.

4 Add the beans, the remaining stock, and the ham. Bring to a boil, reduce the heat, and simmer gently for 20 minutes or until thickened. Season with salt and freshly ground black pepper, then ladle into bowls, garnish with the cilantro, and sprinkle with tortilla chips and cheese.

If you can, make this soup in advance and let it stand for a while before reheating—it will be even better. It's also good made with shelled overgrown runner beans.

black-eyed pea soup

◉ SERVES 4–6   **🕐 PREP** 15 MINS **COOK** 40 MINS   **❄ FREEZE** UP TO 3 MONTHS

1 tbsp canola oil or sunflower oil
3 leeks, cleaned and sliced
1 small red bell pepper, chopped
1 small yellow bell pepper, chopped
3 garlic cloves
2in (5cm) piece fresh ginger, peeled and
   grated or coarsely chopped
1 small red chile
1 tsp cumin seeds

sea salt and freshly ground black pepper
2 x 14oz (400g) cans black-eyed peas,
   drained, rinsed, and drained again
1¾ cups coconut milk
2 cups hot vegetable stock
1 tsp brown sugar
fresh cilantro, to garnish
lime wedges, to serve

1 Heat the oil in a deep saucepan over medium heat, add the leeks and peppers, cover, and cook, stirring frequently, for 5–7 minutes or until soft. Meanwhile, put the garlic, ginger, chile, cumin, and 1 tsp salt in a blender with 4 tbsp water and process until completely smooth. Add to the pan, using a little more water to rinse out every last bit. Cook, stirring, for 2–3 minutes or until most of the liquid has evaporated.

2 Add the peas, coconut milk, stock, sugar, and a good grinding of black pepper and bring to a boil. Reduce the heat to a simmer and cook gently for 30 minutes, stirring frequently. Taste for seasoning, then serve each bowlful garnished with fresh cilantro and a lime wedge.

BLACK-EYED PEAS
So called because of the "black eye" where the bean was originally joined to the pod, black-eyed peas have a creamy, pealike flavor. When shopping for them, choose organic peas that have been canned without sugar and salt.

This hearty, substantial soup improves with reheating, so it benefits from being made a day in advance. Reheat gently over low heat.

tuscan bean soup

SERVES 4   **PREP** 15 MINS **COOK** 1 HR 20 MINS   **FREEZE** UP TO 3 MONTHS

4 tbsp extra virgin olive oil, plus extra
   for drizzling
1 onion, chopped
2 carrots, sliced
1 leek, sliced
2 garlic cloves, chopped
1 x 14oz (400g) can chopped tomatoes
1 tbsp tomato purée
1 quart (1 liter) chicken stock

salt and freshly ground black pepper
1 x 14oz (400g) can borlotti beans, navy
   beans, or cannellini beans, drained
   and rinsed
9oz (250g) baby spinach leaves or spring
   greens, shredded
8 slices ciabatta bread
grated Parmesan cheese, for sprinkling

1 Heat the oil in a large saucepan and cook the onion, carrot, and leek over low heat for 10 minutes, or until softened but not colored. Add the garlic and cook for 1 minute. Add the tomatoes, tomato purée, and stock. Season to taste with salt and pepper.

2 Mash half the beans with a fork and add to the pan. Bring to a boil, then lower the heat and simmer for 30 minutes. Add the remaining beans and spinach to the pan. Simmer for another 30 minutes.

3 Toast the bread until golden, place 2 pieces in each soup bowl, and drizzle with olive oil. To serve, spoon the soup into the bowls, top with a sprinkling of Parmesan, and drizzle with a little more olive oil.

Robust, garlicky, and fragrant with rosemary and sage, this is a hearty, satisfying soup. Serve it with some fresh crusty bread and a drizzle of good-quality olive oil.

bean and rosemary soup

⊘ SERVES 8   **🕒 PREP** 15 MINS **COOK** 40 MINS   **❄ FREEZE** UP TO 3 MONTHS

2 tbsp olive oil
2 onions, finely chopped
salt and freshly ground black pepper
1 tbsp finely chopped fresh rosemary leaves
a few fresh sage leaves, finely chopped
4 celery ribs, finely chopped

3 garlic cloves, grated or finely chopped
2 tbsp tomato purée
2 x 14oz (400g) cans borlotti beans, drained, rinsed, and drained again
1¼ quarts (1¼ liters) hot chicken stock
5½lb (2.5kg) potatoes, cut into chunky pieces

1 Heat the oil in a large pan, add the onions, and cook over low heat for 6–8 minutes or until soft and translucent. Season well with salt and freshly ground black pepper, then stir in the rosemary, sage, celery, and garlic and cook over very low heat, stirring occasionally, for 10 minutes.

2 Stir in the tomato purée and beans and cook gently for 5 minutes. Pour in the stock, bring to a boil, then add the potatoes and simmer gently for 15 minutes or until cooked. Taste, season with salt and freshly ground black pepper, if needed, and serve.

This is so thick and hearty it is a meal in itself—a real family soup. For children, try topping it with some broken-up tortilla chips.

mexican chili bean soup

SERVES 4   **PREP** 10 MINS **COOK** 40 MINS   **FREEZE** UP TO 3 MONTHS
AT THE END OF STEP 2

2 tbsp sunflower oil
1 onion, chopped
1 small red bell pepper, seeded and
   finely chopped
2 garlic cloves, finely chopped
14oz (400g) lean ground beef
1 tsp ground cumin
2 tsp medium or hot chili powder
½ tsp dried oregano
1 x 14oz (400g) can chopped plum tomatoes

2 tbsp tomato purée
3¼ cups hot vegetable stock
   or chicken stock
1 x 14oz (400g) can red kidney beans,
   drained, rinsed, and drained again
handful of chopped flat-leaf parsley
salt and freshly ground black pepper
sour cream or natural yogurt, to serve
grated Cheddar, to serve
4 warm tortillas (optional), to serve

1 Heat the oil in a large saucepan, add the onion, and cook for 5 minutes. Add the pepper and garlic and stir-fry for 2 minutes. Add the beef and stir-fry for 5 minutes or until it has broken up and browned. Stir in the cumin, chili powder, and oregano and cook for another minute or so.

2 Stir in the tomatoes, tomato purée, and stock, then simmer for about 20–25 minutes or until reduced slightly and a good soupy consistency. Add the beans and simmer for another 5 minutes. Stir in half the parsley and season with salt and freshly ground black pepper.

3 Ladle into bowls and serve topped with a spoonful of sour cream or yogurt, a scattering of Cheddar, and the rest of the parsley.

RED KIDNEY BEANS
Valued for their color and the robust, sweet flavor they acquire during cooking, red kidney beans are sometimes known as chili beans. When buying them canned, go for organic beans preserved without salt or sugar.

This hearty, wholesome soup takes the edge off chilly winter weather. It's worth using dried beans, which have a much fuller flavor than the canned variety.

creamy kidney bean soup

SERVES 6　　**PREP** 20 MINS **COOK** 3¼ HRS
OR 30 MINS IN A PRESSURE COOKER

FREEZE UP TO 3 MONTHS
AT THE END OF STEP 3

8oz (225g) dried kidney beans, soaked
　overnight in cold water
2 red onions, diced
1 x 14oz (400g) can chopped tomatoes
1 tbsp tomato purée
5 garlic cloves, halved
2in (5cm) fresh ginger, coarsely chopped
3 large green chiles, left whole
salt and freshly ground black pepper

⅔ cup half-and-half
squeeze of fresh lime juice, to taste

for the garnish
4–6 red radishes, sliced
1 large green chile, finely chopped
2 tbsp chopped fresh cilantro leaves
squeeze of fresh lime juice, to taste

1 Drain the kidney beans, discarding the soaking liquid. Put the beans in a very large heavy-bottomed pan and cover with 1¾ quarts (1¾ liters) of water. Add the onions, tomatoes, tomato purée, garlic, ginger, and chiles and bring to a boil.

2 Cover the pan, lower the heat, and simmer for about 3 hours, until the beans are just breaking up. Add more liquid if needed during cooking. You could also use a pressure cooker—the beans will be tender in about 30 minutes.

3 Once the beans have cooled slightly, scoop out the chiles. Using a blender, process the soup in batches until smooth, then sieve to remove the skins. Season well with salt and pepper.

4 Stir in the half-and-half, and reheat. Add lime juice to taste. For the garnish, combine the sliced radish with the green chile and cilantro. Sharpen with a squeeze of lime, then top each bowl of soup with a small heap of the thin radishes.

A quick homemade version of pesto is spooned on top of this fava bean soup, giving it extra flavor, color, and texture—perfect for serving at a dinner party.

fava bean soup with arugula pesto

SERVES 4   **PREP** 20 MINS **COOK** 20 MINS   **FREEZE** UP TO 3 MONTHS
SOUP AND PESTO SEPARATELY

2 tbsp olive oil
1 onion, chopped
2 celery ribs, halved lengthwise, sliced
2 garlic cloves, chopped
4 slices prosciutto, chopped
pinch crushed hot red pepper flakes
handful basil leaves, shredded
1 quart (1 liter) vegetable or chicken stock
1¾oz (50g) spaghetti, broken into pieces
1 x 14oz (400g) can fava beans, drained

for the pesto
scant 1oz (25g) arugula, very finely chopped
2 tbsp very finely chopped basil
scant 1oz (25g) Parmesan cheese, grated
scant 1oz (25g) pine nuts, toasted, very
  finely chopped
1 small garlic clove, finely chopped
3 tbsp olive oil
salt and freshly ground back pepper

1 Heat the oil for the soup in a large saucepan. Add the onion and celery and cook for 4–5 minutes until the onion is soft but not brown. Add the garlic and cook for 1 minute. Stir in the prosciutto and pepper flakes and cook another 1–2 minutes until the prosciutto is starting to crisp. Stir in the basil, stock, and spaghetti. Bring to a boil. Simmer for about 10 minutes or until the spaghetti is *al dente*. Add the fava beans and warm through.

2 Spoon 3 ladlefuls of the soup into a food processor or blender and process until smooth. Stir it back into the rest of the soup and season with salt and pepper to taste.

3 Mix all the ingredients for the pesto together in a bowl or coarsely chop in a small blender. Season it with pepper and a pinch of salt. Reheat the soup and serve with a spoonful of pesto on top.

Leeks, rather than onions, are used as the basis of this soup, which gives the soup a certain sweetness from the outset.

cannellini bean and carrot soup

⊘ **SERVES** 4-6   🕐 **PREP** 10 MINS **COOK** 1 HR   ❄ **FREEZE** UP TO 3 MONTHS

3–4 leeks, finely sliced
1 tbsp olive oil
1½ tbsp butter
1 x 14oz (400g) can cannellini beans, drained
   and rinsed, then drained again

3 medium carrots, finely chopped
salt and freshly ground black pepper
1 tsp medium curry powder (optional)
3¼ cups cold water
extra virgin olive oil, to serve

1 Heat the oil and melt the butter in a large, deep pan over very low heat. Add the leeks and cook for at least 10 minutes, adding a tiny bit of water when the leeks start to stick to the bottom of the pan.

2 Add the cannellini beans and carrots, then turn up the heat and stir well with a wooden spoon to mix the vegetables and flavors together. Let it simmer for 5–6 minutes. Season the soup with salt and pepper, and stir in the curry powder, if using. Add the water and bring to a boil. Cover with a lid, and simmer for 45 minutes.

3 Transfer the mixture to a blender and process until smooth, then ladle into serving bowls. Encourage your guests to add a bit of olive oil and some freshly ground black pepper to their soup—it makes a wonderful finishing touch.

This thick soup from northern Italy is guaranteed to keep out the winter chills. Soak the beans overnight to rehydrate them and cut down on the cooking time.

white bean soup

⊘ SERVES 4　　**⏱ PREP** 30 MINS **COOK** 2 HRS　　❄ **FREEZE** UP TO 3 MONTHS
AT THE END OF STEP 3

3 tbsp olive oil
2 onions, finely chopped
2 garlic cloves, crushed
8oz (225g) dried cannellini beans,
　soaked overnight
1 celery rib, chopped
1 bay leaf
3–4 parsley stems, without leaves

1 tbsp lemon juice
1¼ quarts (1¼ liters) vegetable stock
salt and freshly ground black pepper
3 shallots, thinly sliced
2oz (60g) pancetta, chopped (optional)
3oz (85g) Fontina or Taleggio cheese,
　chopped into small pieces

1 Heat 2 tbsp olive oil in a saucepan, add the onions, and cook over low heat for 10 minutes, or until softened, stirring occasionally. Add the garlic and cook, stirring, for 1 minute.

2 Drain the soaked beans and add to the pan with the celery, bay leaf, parsley stems, lemon juice, and stock. Bring to a boil, cover, and simmer for 1½ hours, or until the beans are soft, stirring occasionally.

3 Remove the bay leaf and process the soup in batches in a blender, or through a hand mill. Rinse out the pan. Return the soup to the pan and season to taste with salt and pepper.

4 Heat the remaining olive oil in a small frying pan, and cook the shallots and pancetta (if using) until golden and crisp, stirring frequently to keep them from sticking to the pan. Reheat the soup, adding a little stock or water if it is too thick. Stir the Fontina into the soup. Ladle into individual bowls, and sprinkle each serving with the shallots and pancetta.

Navy beans give texture while rosemary and dried mushrooms provide loads of flavor for this rustic Italian-style soup.

rosemary's bean soup with italian cheese crisps

🥄 **SERVES** 4   🕐 **PREP** 10 MINS PLUS 20 MINS SOAKING **COOK** 15–20 MINS   ❄ **FREEZE** UP TO 3 MONTHS WITHOUT CHEESE CRISPS

½oz (12g) dried porcini mushrooms, covered in water to soak
1¾oz (50g) pecorino or Parmesan cheese, coarsely grated
1½ tsp very finely chopped rosemary
2 tbsp olive oil
1 onion, chopped

2 garlic cloves, chopped
3 rosemary sprigs
2 x 14oz (400g) cans navy (or flageolet) beans, drained and rinsed
2½ cups vegetable stock
extra virgin olive oil, for drizzling
ciabatta loaf cut into chunks, to serve

1 Preheat the oven to 400°F (200°C). Let the mushrooms soak for 20 minutes. Meanwhile, make the cheese crisps. Line a baking sheet with parchment paper. Scatter the cheese and half the rosemary in a thin, even layer on the sheet in an 7in (18cm) circle. Bake for 8 minutes or until it starts to turn golden around the edges. Remove and let cool and firm on the sheet. Strain the mushrooms (reserving the liquid) and coarsely chop.

2 Heat the oil in a large saucepan, add the onion, and soften for 4–5 minutes. Stir in the garlic, chopped mushrooms, and rosemary. Cook for 2–3 minutes. Add the beans, stock, and 6 tbsp of the reserved mushroom liquid. Simmer for 10 minutes. Remove the rosemary. Coarsely purée about three-quarters of the soup. Pour this back into the pan with the rest of the soup. Season to taste with salt and pepper, then warm through.

3 Break the cheese crisps into large pieces. For each serving, sprinkle with the rest of the chopped rosemary, drizzle with the oil, and accompany with the cheese crisps and ciabatta.

Lime gives a distinctive, vibrant twist to this clean-tasting, healthy soup from New Mexico. It has the added advantage of being very quick and easy to prepare.

green lentil soup with lime

SERVES 4 **PREP** 5 MINS **COOKING** 30 MINS **FREEZE** UP TO 3 MONTHS
AT THE END OF STEP 3

1 quart (1 liter) chicken stock
2–3 sprigs fresh thyme
10oz (300g) green lentils

sea salt and freshly ground black pepper
grated zest and juice of 1 organic lime

1 Pour the stock into a saucepan over medium heat. Add the thyme and bring to a simmer.

2 Add the lentils, and season lightly with salt and pepper. Return to a simmer, cover, reduce the heat a little. Cook for 20–25 minutes until the lentils are very soft.

3 Turn off the heat and let cool for several minutes. Transfer to a blender or food processor, and process until just smooth.

4 Pour the soup back into the saucepan and stir in the lime zest and juice. Reheat gently, taste, and adjust the seasoning. Serve very hot.

This hearty vegetarian soup has just a touch of spice and is quick and easy to prepare. Serve with plain, low-fat yogurt and good crusty bread.

lentil soup

SERVES 4 **PREP** 20 MINS **COOK** 35 MINS **FREEZE** UP TO 3 MONTHS

1 tbsp olive oil
2 onions, finely chopped
2 celery ribs, finely chopped
2 carrots, finely chopped
2 garlic cloves, crushed

1–2 tsp curry powder
5½oz (150g) red lentils
1½ quarts (1½ liters) vegetable stock
½ cup tomato or vegetable juice
salt and freshly ground black pepper

1 Heat the oil in a large pan over medium heat, then add the onions, celery, and carrots. Cook, stirring, for 5 minutes, or until the onions are soft and translucent.

2 Add the garlic and curry powder and cook, stirring, for another minute, then add the lentils, stock, and tomato juice.

3 Bring to a boil, then lower the heat, cover, and simmer for 25 minutes, or until the vegetables are tender. Season to taste with salt and pepper, and serve hot.

This Moroccan bean and lentil soup is a meal in a bowl often eaten for breakfast during Ramadan, to keep people going right through a day of fasting.

harira

⊘ **SERVES** 6–8   ◷ **PREP** 15 MINS **COOK** 1 HR 5 MINS   ✳ **FREEZE** UP TO 3 MONTHS

1 large onion, chopped
2 tbsp olive oil
10oz–1lb 2oz (300–500g) shoulder
   of lamb on the bone
1 tsp ground ginger
1 tsp ground cinnamon
leaves of 1 small bunch parsley,
   finely chopped
leaves of 1 small bunch cilantro,
   finely chopped

5½oz (150g) brown lentils, rinsed
1 x 14oz (400g) can chopped tomatoes
2 tbsp tomato purée
salt and freshly ground black pepper
3½oz (100g) vermicelli noodles
1 x 14oz (400g) can chickpeas, drained, or
   14oz (400g) cooked chickpeas
3 tbsp flour
lemon wedges, to serve

1 Cook the onion gently in the oil until translucent. While it cooks, cut the meat from the lamb bones in 1¼in (3cm) cubes. Reserve the bones.

2 Once the onions are tender, stir in the ginger, cinnamon, half the parsley, and half the cilantro, then add the lamb chunks and bone and turn to coat evenly. Now add the lentils, tomatoes, and tomato purée and season with salt and freshly ground black pepper. Mix well and simmer for a few minutes, then add 1¾ quarts (1¾ liters) of water. Let simmer for 45 minutes, then remove the lamb bones and add the vermicelli and chickpeas.

3 Put the flour in a small bowl with a ladleful of the cooking liquid and stir to make a smooth paste the consistency of thick cream, adding more liquid if needed. Stir this back into the soup and simmer for another 3–4 minutes until it has thickened and the vermicelli is cooked.

4 Just before serving, stir in the remaining herbs, and adjust the seasoning. Serve with wedges of lemon.

This vegetable and lentil dish is best served piping hot, in cavernous bowls. You can find pink lentils (*masoor dal*) in most Asian food stores.

kichidi

◉ **SERVES** 6–8   🕐 **PREP** 15 MINS **COOK** 50 MINS   ❄ **FREEZE** UP TO 3 MONTHS
AT THE END OF STEP 3

1 butternut squash, about 1lb 9oz (700g)
½ tsp garam masala
salt and pepper
2 tbsp olive oil
3½oz (100g) basmati rice
3½oz (100g) pink or red lentils
2in (5cm) ginger, peeled and finely grated

2 tbsp ghee or clarified butter
2 tsp cumin seeds
½ tsp crushed hot red pepper flakes
juice of 1 lime
3 tbsp chopped cilantro
2 tbsp unsalted butter

1 Preheat the oven to 400°F (200°C). Halve the squash lengthwise and scoop out the seeds and fibers. Put it in a roasting pan, cut side up, sprinkle with the garam masala, season with salt and pepper, and drizzle with the oil. Cover with foil and roast for 45 minutes, or until meltingly tender. Let cool slightly, then scoop out the flesh, lightly crush it with a fork, and set aside.

2 Meanwhile, combine the rice and lentils in a large saucepan and cover with 2 quarts (2 liters) of water. Add the ginger, bring to a boil, then reduce the heat and simmer for about 30 minutes until the rice grains have lost their texture and broken down. Add more hot water to loosen the texture, if desired. Stir in the lightly crushed squash.

3 Heat the ghee in a separate pan and cook the cumin and red pepper flakes for about 30 seconds, until aromatic and darker in color. Tip the spices and ghee into the rice and lentils and stir well, seasoning with plenty more salt and pepper.

4 Stir in the lime juice and cilantro. Divide between deep bowls and finish with a generous dollop of butter in the center of each helping.

Small, dark green, and with a distinctive earthy flavor, puy lentils are less floury than paler or red lentils, and they cook quickly without disintegrating.

puy lentil soup

🍲 **SERVES** 4   🕐 **PREP** 20 MINS **COOK** 45 MINS   ❄️ **FREEZE** UP TO 3 MONTHS
AT THE END OF STEP 2

3 tbsp fruity olive oil, plus extra for serving
1 Spanish onion, finely chopped
1 garlic clove, crushed
14oz (400g) puy lentils, rinsed and drained
salt and freshly ground black pepper
2 thick ham steaks, about 3½oz (100g) each

2 sprigs of fresh thyme
2 sprigs of flat leaf parsley
1 tbsp finely chopped parsley, to serve
1 tsp grated zest of an unwaxed lemon,
   to serve

1 Put 1½ tbsp oil in a large, heavy saucepan over medium heat. Cook the onion and garlic for 2–3 minutes until golden and softened, stirring frequently. Stir in the lentils and season with salt and pepper. Put one of the ham steaks on top of the lentils and add the thyme and parsley. Pour in enough cold water to cover the lentils and ham with an extra 1¼in (3cm) water on top. Bring gently to a simmer, partially cover, and cook for 25–30 minutes until the lentils are cooked through.

2 Lift out the cooked ham steak and chop into small pieces. Discard the parsley and thyme. Reserving 3 ladlefuls of soup, put the contents of the pan with the chopped ham in a blender or food processor and process until smooth. Return to the pan and stir in the reserved mixture.

3 Gently reheat until piping hot. Meanwhile, using the rest of the oil, cook the second ham steak in a nonstick frying pan over medium-high heat for 4–5 minutes, turning after 3 minutes, until cooked through and crisp and golden on both sides. Cut into small chunky pieces.

4 Taste and adjust the seasoning. Stir the soup and ladle into warmed bowls. Scatter the crispy ham over the top and add a drizzle of extra virgin olive oil. Finish with a little chopped parsley and lemon zest, mixed together, and serve.

This chunky vegetable soup owes much of its appeal to the robust nature of homemade harissa, which can be made in advance and stored in the refrigerator.

harissa and chickpea soup

🍲 **SERVES** 4   🕐 **PREP** 25 MINS **COOK** 45 MINS   ❄️ **FREEZE** UP TO 3 MONTHS

for the harissa paste
1 red bell pepper
2 tbsp olive oil
½ tsp coriander seeds
2 tsp cumin seeds
1 tsp caraway seeds
2 tsp tomato purée
3 garlic cloves, coarsely chopped
4 red chiles, seeds removed, coarsely
  chopped
1 tsp smoked paprika
juice of 1 lemon

for the soup
1 tbsp olive oil
3½oz (100g) smoked pancetta, cubed
2 red onions, diced
1 potato, peeled and diced
3 celery ribs, diced
1 small fennel, thinly sliced
3 tbsp oregano leaves, chopped
1 x 14oz (400g) can chopped tomatoes
3¼ cups vegetable stock
1 x 14oz (400g) can chickpeas, drained
1 bay leaf

1 To make the harissa, rub the red bell pepper with olive oil and cook under the broiler for 10–15 minutes, turning frequently, until the skin is blackened and charred. Remove to a bowl, cover with plastic wrap, and let cool. Peel away the skin, discard the seeds, and coarsely chop the flesh.

2 Heat a small frying pan over low heat and roast the coriander, cumin, and caraway seeds for about a minute, stirring. Using a mortar and pestle, pound the spices to a powder. Transfer to a food processor and add the red bell pepper along with the tomato purée, garlic, red chiles, paprika, and lemon juice. Process until smooth, gradually adding the remaining olive oil.

3 To make the soup, heat the olive oil in a large saucepan and cook the pancetta until golden, then remove. Add the onion, potato, celery, fennel, and oregano to the pan. Cover and soften over low heat for 10 minutes. Stir in 1–2 tbsp of the harissa paste and the tomatoes and continue cooking for 5 minutes. Add the stock, pancetta, chickpeas, and bay leaf. Season well, and simmer in a half-covered pan for 20 minutes. Remove the bay leaf and serve.

The chicken drumstick makes this a questionable dish for your vegetarian friends—unless you don't mind stretching the truth. It can, of course, be left out.

chickpea soup

⊘ SERVES 6　　**🕐 PREP** 15 MINS, PLUS OVERNIGHT SOAKING　　**❄ FREEZE** UP TO 3 MONTHS
COOK 1 HR 40 MINS

7oz (200g) chickpeas, soaked in water
　overnight, then drained
2.5 quarts (2.5 liters) cold water
1 chicken drumstick
4 tbsp olive oil
2 celery ribs, chopped
1 medium onion, chopped

1 medium leek, chopped
3 garlic cloves, finely sliced
salt and freshly ground black pepper
½ cup dry white wine
1 tbsp lemon juice
6 tbsp extra virgin olive oil, to serve
2 tbsp chopped chives and parsley, to garnish

1 Place the chickpeas in a saucepan with plenty of cold water and bring to a boil. Skim away any foam with a slotted spoon, then drain and return to the pan. Add the cold water and chicken, bring to a boil, and skim again. Cover with a lid and simmer for 1½ hours or until the peas are done. Lift out the chicken after 45 minutes, remove the meat, and set to one side.

2 Heat 1 tbsp of the oil in a frying pan, add the celery, onion, and leek, and cook for 5–10 minutes or until soft. Add the garlic, season with salt and freshly ground black pepper, then cook for another minute. Add the contents of the frying pan to the chickpeas, then stir in the cooked chicken. Pour in a little water if the mixture seems too thick to blend.

3 Transfer the soup to a blender and process in batches until smooth, adding the wine, lemon juice, and the remaining 3 tbsp olive oil in three or four stages. Season with salt and freshly ground black pepper, then return to the pan and heat through. Divide the soup among six bowls, float 1 tbsp of extra virgin olive oil on the top of each one, then serve garnished with the chopped chives and parsley.

If chervil isn't available, you can replace it with a few leaves of fresh mint to finish. You can also use frozen peas if fresh peas are out of season.

potage saint germain

SERVES 4   **PREP** 15 MINS **COOK** 1 HR   **FREEZE** UP TO 3 MONTHS
BEFORE MADEIRA IS ADDED

1 tbsp sunflower, peanut, or
   mild-flavored olive oil
1 tbsp butter plus 2 tbsp chilled
   butter, diced
4 large scallions (white parts only), chopped
1½ quarts (1½ liters) hot chicken or
   vegetable stock
5½oz (150g) split green peas, rinsed
   and drained

sea salt and freshly ground black pepper
1lb 2oz (500g) fresh green peas
   (about 1¾lb/800g unshelled)
1 small head soft lettuce, leaves snipped
1 large egg yolk
3 tbsp crème fraîche
1–2 tbsp Madeira or port
few sprigs of chervil

1 Put a large sauté pan over medium heat. Add the oil and 1 tbsp butter, then stir in the scallions. Reduce the heat a little and cook for 5 minutes, stirring frequently. Pour the hot stock into the pan, and then add the split peas. Season lightly with salt and pepper, and bring back to a simmer. Reduce the heat, cover, and cook for another 20 minutes, stirring occasionally.

2 Add the garden peas and the lettuce, stir, and cook for 5 minutes. Let cool a little, then pour the contents of the pan into a blender or food processor and process until smooth. Push the soup back into the pan through a fine sieve, mashing the vegetables with the back of a spoon to extract as much as possible. Pour ½ cup water through the sieve to thin down the soup. Reheat gently over low heat.

3 In a cup or small bowl combine the egg yolk and the crème fraîche with 2–3 tablespoons of the hot soup. Whisk this into the pan a little at a time. Continue cooking until the soup is piping hot. Adjust the seasoning. Just before serving, stir in the Madeira or port. Whisk in the diced butter and sprinkle a little snipped chervil over the top.

Be careful when seasoning this hearty soup, as the bacon means that little, if any, extra salt will be needed. Try this soup with olive oil croûtons.

split pea and bacon soup

SERVES 6   **PREP** 30 MINS **COOK** 1 HR 10 MINS   **FREEZE** UP TO 3 MONTHS

9oz (250g) dried split green peas, rinsed and drained
1½ quarts (1½ liters) water
4–5 slices thick-cut bacon
¼ celeriac, peeled and diced
1 large carrot, diced
1 small leek, diced

1 medium floury potato, peeled and diced
1 tsp dried marjoram
1 tbsp butter
1 onion, diced
freshly ground black pepper
3–4 tsp chopped chives, to garnish

1 Put the peas in a large saucepan with the water and bring to a boil. Add the bacon, cover, and cook for about 40 minutes over medium heat. Add the celeriac, carrot, leek, and potato, and stir in the marjoram. Bring to a boil again, cover, and cook for another 20 minutes.

2 Melt the butter in a separate pan, and add the onion. Brown slightly, stirring continuously, then set aside.

3 Remove the bacon from the soup, chop, and return it to the soup together with the cooked onion. Season with pepper. Sprinkle with chopped chives to serve.

You can use pre-cooked chestnuts for this soup from Piedmont, Italy, but fresh ones have a more velvety texture (although you should allow time for peeling.)

piedmont chestnut soup

SERVES 6   **PREP** 5 MINS USING COOKED CHESTNUTS   **FREEZE** UP TO 3 MONTHS
COOK 1 HR 55 MINS   BEFORE RICE IS ADDED

8oz (225g) fresh chestnuts or
  6oz (180g) cooked peeled chestnuts
2 sprigs thyme
1 bay leaf
1¼ quarts (1¼ liters) chicken stock

salt and freshly ground black pepper
2oz (60g) risotto rice
2 tbsp butter
1¼ cups milk
a little truffle oil, to serve

1 If using fresh chestnuts, score each one with a small sharp knife (see below), then put half a dozen at a time into a microwaveproof bowl. Cover tightly with plastic wrap and cook on High for 20–30 seconds or until the skins have split, then peel. Put the peeled chestnuts in a pan with the herbs, stock, and a little salt and freshly ground black pepper, bring to a boil, then simmer for 1½ hours.

2 Add the rice and simmer for 10 minutes. Stir in the butter and the milk and simmer for a final 10 minutes. Remove the bay leaf and thyme, taste, and adjust the seasonings, if necessary. Serve with a few drops of truffle oil in each bowlful to turn this peasant soup into a major treat.

PEELING FRESH CHESTNUTS

Score a deep cross in the skin of each chestnut with a knife, to keep it from exploding as it cooks.

After cooking, the shells will have split. Peel off the outer and inner skin with your fingers.

If fresh chestnuts aren't in season, use canned whole unsweetened chestnuts or dried peeled ones. You could also use pancetta or bacon instead of ham.

chestnut soup with ham

⊙ SERVES 4   **🕐 PREP** 30 MINS **COOK** 45 MINS   **❄ FREEZE** UP TO 3 MONTHS
WITHOUT THE HAM GARNISH

1lb 5oz (600g) fresh chestnuts
1½–2 tbsp sunflower, peanut, or
   mild-flavored olive oil
¾ oz (20g) butter
½ Spanish onion, finely chopped
1 garlic clove, crushed
3 bay leaves

2 tsp dried fennel seeds, plus 1 heaping tsp,
   to garnish
sea salt and freshly ground black pepper
1¼ quarts (1¼ liters) light vegetable stock
3½ oz (100g) slice of cooked ham, diced
1½ tbsp mascarpone, to finish (optional)

1 Score each chestnut with a small sharp knife (see below left), then place in a saucepan, cover with cold water, and bring to a boil. Drain, set aside until cool enough to handle, then peel and set aside. (You could also peel them using the microwave method on the opposite page.)

2 Place a large, heavy-based saucepan over medium heat. Add the oil and half the butter. Cook the onion and garlic until golden and softened, about 2–3 minutes, stirring frequently. Add the peeled chestnuts, the bay leaves, and the 2 tsp fennel seeds. Stir and season with salt and pepper. Pour in the stock. Bring to a gentle simmer, partly cover, and cook for 20–30 minutes, stirring occasionally, until the chestnuts are soft.

3 Leave to cool. Discard the bay leaves. Transfer the soup to a blender or food processor and process until smooth. Strain the soup through a sieve back into the pan, pressing with the back of a spoon. Gently reheat the soup.

4 Meanwhile, place a nonstick frying pan over fairly low heat. Add the reserved butter, and then add the diced ham and the extra fennel seeds. Cook gently, stirring a few times. Taste and adjust the seasoning. Stir the soup and ladle it into bowls. Scatter over a little of the diced ham and fennel seeds. If you like, add a small dollop of mascarpone to each serving.

As delicate as it is delicious, this pretty, pastel-green soup is scented with citrusy cardamom notes, which make a marvelous marriage with the pounded pistachios.

creamy pistachio soup

◉ SERVES 2–3   **◕ PREP** 40 MINS **COOK** 20 MINS   **❄ FREEZE** UP TO 3 MONTHS
WITHOUT HALF-AND-HALF
AND CILANTRO

4½oz (125g) (shelled weight) unsalted
   pistachio nuts
1 green chile, cut in half and seeded
½ cup hot water
6 green cardamom pods, crushed and
   seeds extracted
1 small blade of mace
½ tsp coriander seeds, dry-roasted (see p25)
2 tbsp butter
2 large garlic cloves, finely chopped

small bunch of scallions (white parts only),
   finely chopped
1in (2.5cm) piece of ginger, peeled
   and finely chopped
½ tsp garam masala
2 cups hot vegetable stock
3½fl oz (100ml) half-and-half
1 tbsp chopped cilantro
salt and freshly ground black pepper

1 Bring a pan of water to a boil, add the pistachios, and cook for about 2–3 minutes. Drain in a colander and refresh under cold running water. Pat the nuts dry with paper towels, then turn out on to a kitchen towel. Give them a vigorous rub with the towel—the skins should slip off easily. Reserve a generous tablespoon for garnishing and put the rest in a food processor. Add the chile and hot water and process to a rough paste, then set aside.

2 Grind the cardamom seeds, mace, and coriander to a powder with a pestle and mortar. Melt the butter in a saucepan over medium heat, add the garlic, scallions, and ginger, and soften for 2–3 minutes. Stir in the ground spices and garam masala and cook for a few seconds, then add the pistachio paste and stock. Simmer without a lid for 10–15 minutes, stirring occasionally.

3 Blend in batches until smooth. Stir in the cream and cilantro, then season with salt and freshly ground black pepper. Serve the soup garnished with the reserved pistachio nuts coarsely chopped.

This Spanish soup is seriously garlicky, but heavenly in summer. You could reduce the number of garlic cloves to as few as two—if you wish.

white gazpacho

🍲 **SERVES** 4   🕐 **PREP** 20 MINS   ❄ **FREEZE** NOT SUITABLE

3oz (85g) white bread (crusts removed), cut into cubes
2 cups ice water
9oz (250g) whole blanched almonds
6 garlic cloves, coarsely chopped

3 tbsp olive oil
3 tbsp sherry vinegar or white balsamic vinegar
salt and freshly ground black pepper
5½oz (150g) seedless white grapes

1 Soak the bread in all but 3 tbsp of the ice water for 10 minutes. Meanwhile, place the almonds in a food processor and process until ground as finely as possible. Add the remaining 3 tbsp ice water and blend to a paste. Remove the bread from the water (reserving the water) and add to the processor, along with the garlic, and blend again.

2 With the motor running, gradually add the water the bread soaked in, followed by the oil. Keep pulsing until the mixture is absolutely smooth. Add the vinegar and season to taste with salt and freshly ground black pepper. To serve, place a handful of grapes in the bottom of each bowl, ladle the soup on top, then drizzle with a little olive oil, if desired.

fish and shellfish

Originally nothing more than a humble fisherman's soup using the remains of the day's catch, bouillabaisse has evolved into one of the great Provençal dishes.

bouillabaisse

🍲 **SERVES** 4   🕐 **PREP** 20 MINS **COOK** 45 MINS   ❄ **FREEZE** NOT SUITABLE

4 tbsp olive oil
1 onion, thinly sliced
2 leeks, thinly sliced
1 small fennel bulb, thinly sliced
2–3 garlic cloves, finely chopped
4 tomatoes, peeled, seeded, and chopped
1 tbsp tomato purée
1 cup dry white wine
1½ quarts (1½ liters) fish or chicken stock
pinch of saffron threads
strip of orange zest
1 bouquet garni
salt and freshly ground black pepper
2 tbsp Pernod

3lb (1.35kg) mixed white and oily fish and shellfish, such as monkfish, red mullet, shrimp, and mussels, heads and bones removed
8 croûtes, to serve

for the rouille
4¼oz (125g) mayonnaise
1 bird's-eye chile, seeded and coarsely chopped
4 garlic cloves, coarsely chopped
1 tbsp tomato purée
½ tsp salt

1 Heat the oil in a large pan over medium heat. Add the onion, leeks, fennel, and garlic and cook, stirring, for 5–8 minutes, or until the vegetables are soft but not colored. Stir in the tomatoes, purée, and wine.

2 Add the stock, saffron, zest, and bouquet garni. Season with salt and pepper, and bring to a boil. Reduce the heat, partially cover, and simmer for 30 minutes, stirring occasionally. Process the rouille ingredients in a blender until smooth. Transfer to a bowl, cover, and chill until required.

3 Just before the liquid finishes simmering, cut the fish into chunks. Remove the zest and bouquet garni and add the firm fish. Reduce the heat to low and simmer for 5 minutes. Add the delicate fish and simmer for 2–3 minutes, or until it is cooked through and flakes easily. Stir in the Pernod and season to taste. To serve, spread the croûtes with rouille and place 2 in the bottom of each bowl. Ladle the soup on top.

The seafood must be just-cooked, so cut dense fish in small pieces or add it earlier. Try red mullet, bass, haddock, cod, salmon, turbot, raw shrimp, or scallops.

north sea fish soup

⊘ **SERVES** 4   🕐 **PREP TIME** 20 MINS **COOK** 20 MINS   ❄ **FREEZE** NOT SUITABLE

1lb 2oz (500g) mixed fish fillets and shellfish
salt and frehly ground black pepper
1 tbsp lemon juice
2½ cups fish or chicken stock
¼ cup white wine
2 shallots, chopped

1 egg yolk
1 tbsp heavy cream
1 tomato, peeled, seeded, and chopped
1 tbsp chopped parsley
croûtons, to serve

1 Skin the fish, if necessary, and cut into 1in (2.5cm) pieces. Season and add the lemon juice. Bring the stock, white wine, and shallots to a boil in a large saucepan.

2 Add the fish in the order it takes to cook depending on which you are using: red mullet or bass first, 2 minutes later the turbot, if using, followed by any haddock, cod, or salmon and, finally, shrimp or scallops. Simmer uncovered until all the fish is just cooked.

3 Stir the egg yolk and cream together in a bowl. Remove the soup from the heat, stir in the egg mixture, then add the tomato and parsley. Serve with croûtons.

This soup was originally a way to use the leftover catch of the day in Brittany. Try it with haddock, smoked haddock, pollock, or cod.

cotriade (fish stew)

⊘ **SERVES** 4   🕐 **PREP** 20 MINS **COOK** 30 MINS   ❄ **FREEZE** NOT SUITABLE

2 large floury potatoes, peeled
2 tbsp peanut, sunflower, or mild olive oil
2 tbsp butter
2 Spanish onions, coarsely chopped
1 quart (1 liter) light fish stock
3 sprigs of thyme
3 bay leaves
3 sprigs of flat-leaf parsley
sea salt and freshly ground black pepper
1¾lb (800g) mixed fish, skinned and cut into
   large chunks
4 thick slices country bread, to serve

for the dressing
5–6 tbsp peanut, sunflower, or mild olive oil
½ tsp Dijon mustard
sea salt and freshly ground black pepper
1 tbsp white wine or cider vinegar
2 tbsp finely chopped parsley

1 Cut the potatoes into quarters and set aside. Heat the oil and butter in a large, heavy sauté pan over medium heat. Add the onions and soften until just golden, stirring frequently. Add the stock, then add in the potatoes and herbs. Season lightly with salt and pepper, stir, cover, and cook for 12–15 minutes or until the potatoes are almost cooked.

2 Place the fish in the pan and season lightly. Gently stir, then cook for 7–10 minutes, or until the fish just starts to flake when pierced with a fork. If you are freezing the soup, cool and do so now. Meanwhile, make the dressing. In a small bowl, mix together the oil and mustard. Season with salt and pepper, then whisk in the vinegar until emulsified. Stir in the parsley.

3 Remove the soup from the heat and adjust the seasoning. Remove the herbs. Put the bread in 4 warm bowls and moisten with a little dressing. Ladle the soup over the top and drizzle on the remaining dressing. Serve hot.

This flavorful soup needs no accompaniment, but croûtes rubbed with garlic, spread with rouille (see p234), or topped with Gruyère cheese are a welcome addition.

soupe de poissons

🌀 **SERVES** 6   🕐 **PREP** 20 MINS **COOK** 1 HOUR   ❄ **FREEZE** UP TO 2 MONTHS

5 tbsp olive oil
4 medium onions, chopped
2 leeks, chopped
3lb 3oz–4½lb (1½–2kg) mixed fish
  and seafood
4 pieces dried fennel stalks, 2in (5cm) long
4 medium, ripe tomatoes, quartered
9 garlic cloves, crushed

5 sprigs of fresh flat-leaf parsley
3 bay leaves
6in (15cm) strip dried orange peel
1 tbsp tomato purée
salt and freshly ground black pepper
pinch of saffron threads
6 croûtes, to serve

1 Put the oil in a large, heavy saucepan. Add the onions and leeks and soften over medium heat until just golden.

2 Gut the larger fish, and rinse all the fish and seafood. Add to the pan and stir, then add the fennel, tomatoes, garlic, parsley, bay leaves, orange peel, and tomato purée. Stir and cook for 8–10 minutes until the fish is just beginning to flake when pierced with a fork. Pour in 2½ quarts (2½ liters) hot water and season lightly with salt and pepper. Reduce the heat and simmer gently for 20 minutes.

3 Remove from the heat. Let cool a little, stirring and mashing down the soft fish pieces with the back of a large wooden spoon. Remove the fennel, orange peel, and bay leaves. If you like, process the soup to a coarse purée in a blender. Push the soup through a chinois or a very fine sieve into a clean saucepan. Return the soup to a simmer over medium heat.

4 Soften the saffron in a ladleful of the soup, then stir into the rest of the soup in the pan. Adjust the seasoning. Ladle the soup into bowls. Serve hot, with croûtes.

This rustic, Mediterranean-style fish soup—robustly flavored with brandy, orange, and fennel—is simple to prepare and sure to please.

fish soup with fennel

⊘ **SERVES** 4–6 🕐 **PREP** 10 MINS **COOK** 1 HR ❄ **FREEZE** NOT SUITABLE

2 tbsp butter
3 tbsp olive oil
1 large fennel bulb, finely chopped
2 garlic cloves, crushed
1 small leek, sliced
4 ripe plum tomatoes, chopped
3 tbsp brandy
¼ tsp saffron threads, infused in a little hot water
zest of ½ orange
1 bay leaf

1¾ quarts (1¾ liters) fish stock
10oz (300g) potatoes, diced and parboiled for 5 minutes
4 tbsp dry white wine
1lb 2oz (500g) fresh black mussels, scrubbed and debearded
salt and freshly ground black pepper
1lb 2oz (500g) monkfish or other firm white fish, cut into bite-sized pieces
6 raw whole tiger prawns
parsley, chopped, to garnish

1 Heat the butter with 2 tbsp of the oil in a large, deep pan. Stir in the fennel, garlic, and leek, and cook over medium heat, stirring occasionally, for 5 minutes, or until softened and lightly browned.

2 Stir in the tomatoes, add the brandy, and boil rapidly for 2 minutes, or until the juices are reduced slightly. Stir in the saffron, orange zest, bay leaf, fish stock, and potatoes. Bring to a boil, then reduce the heat and skim off any foam from the surface. Cover and simmer for 20 minutes, or until the potatoes are tender. Remove the bay leaf.

3 Meanwhile, heat the remaining oil with the wine in a large, deep pan until boiling. Add the mussels, cover, and continue on high heat for 2–3 minutes, shaking the pan often. Discard any mussels that do not open. Strain, reserving the liquid, and set the mussels aside. Add the liquid to the soup and season to taste. Bring to a boil, add the monkfish and prawns, then reduce the heat, cover, and simmer gently for 5 minutes, or until the fish is just cooked and the prawns are pink. Add the mussels to the pan and bring almost to a boil. Serve the soup sprinkled with chopped parsley.

A German soup, from the region of Schleswig-Holstein on the North Sea coast. You can use any white fish, so choose whatever is freshest.

büsumer fish soup

⊘ **SERVES** 6–8   🕐 **PREP** 15 MINS **COOK** 20 MINS   ❄ **FREEZE** NOT SUITABLE

2 large carrots, chopped
1 large potato peeled and diced
1 large onion, diced
1 quart (1 liter) hot vegetable stock
1 bay leaf
salt and freshly ground black pepper
1lb 2oz (500g) white fish fillets, such as
  haddock, cleaned and cubed

juice of 1 lemon
7oz (200g) button or cremini
  mushrooms, sliced
3½oz (100g) raw peeled jumbo shrimp
½ cup heavy cream
½ bunch of dill, chopped

1 Put the carrots, potato, and onion into a saucepan, add the hot stock and bay leaf, and bring to a boil. Reduce the heat and simmer for 10 minutes.

2 Sprinkle a little salt and pepper and half the lemon juice over the fish pieces, then add these to the stock along with the mushrooms and simmer for another 5 minutes over low heat.

3 Add the shrimp to the pan along with the remaining lemon juice, and cook for 3 minutes, or until they turn pink. Remove the bay leaf and season with salt and pepper, to taste. Stir in the cream and half the dill and serve immediately, using the remaining dill to garnish.

If you enjoy the intense salty-sweetness of eel, you'll love this German-style soup. Contact your fishmonger in advance to order a fresh eel, asking for it to be prepared.

hamburg eel soup

SERVES 6   **PREP** 15 MINS **COOK** 1 HR 20 MINS   **FREEZE** UP TO 2 MONTHS

3¼ cups Riesling wine
2 tbsp white wine vinegar
2 tbsp chopped fresh parsley
1 onion, sliced
2 carrots, diced
1 bay leaf
salt and freshly ground black pepper

1 prepared eel (cleaned, skinned, and cut
   into 2in/5cm pieces)
2 tbsp butter
1½ tbsp flour
2 quarts (2 liters) hot vegetable stock
bouquet garni (see p24)

1 Pour the wine and 2 cups of water into a large saucepan with the vinegar, then add the chopped parsley, onion, carrots, and bay leaf, and season with salt and pepper. Bring to a boil and cook for 4–6 minutes. Add the eel pieces and simmer over low heat for 10 minutes, or until the flesh is tender, then let cool.

2 Melt the butter in a saucepan, add the flour, and cook until blended. Stir in the stock a little at a time. Add the bouquet garni to the pan, and cook slowly for 1 hour.

3 To serve, remove the eel pieces from the cooking liquid. Stir half the cooking liquid into the vegetable stock, divide the eel pieces between six bowls, and ladle the soup over.

Henningsvaer is a picturesque little port town in Norway's Lofoten Islands, and this soup is the speciality of a small restaurant there.

henningsvaer fish soup

SERVES 6-8 **PREP** 15 MINS **COOK** 45 MINS   **FREEZE** NOT SUITABLE

1½ quarts (1½ liters) fish stock
12oz (350g) cod fillet
4 tbsp butter
1 onion, finely chopped
1 large carrot, finely chopped
1 large leek, finely chopped

2 tsp sugar
2 tbsp white wine vinegar
salt and freshly ground black pepper
1¼ cups crème fraîche
chopped parsley, to serve

1 Bring the stock to a boil. Add the cod, bring gently back to a boil, then remove from the heat. When cool enough to handle, lift out the cod and flake, discarding skin and stray bones. Set aside the fish and stock.

2 Melt the butter in a large pan and add the vegetables. Stir to coat, then cover the pan, reduce the heat to very low, and let cook for 20 minutes, stirring once or twice. Add the stock, sugar, and vinegar, season with salt and pepper, and bring to a boil. Simmer for 10 minutes. Stir in the crème fraîche and flaked fish. Taste and adjust the seasoning, then reheat gently without boiling. Serve immediately, sprinkled with the parsley.

Replace the mussels with shell-on shrimp in this Flemish soup if you prefer; peel, and add the empty shells to the reduced stock for 3 minutes before straining.

waterzooi (flemish stew)

🍲 **SERVES** 4　　⏱ **PREP** 20 MINS **COOK** 30 MINS　　❄ **FREEZE** NOT SUITABLE

1 large waxy potato, peeled
1 large carrot, peeled
1 medium-large zucchini
1 bunch asparagus
10oz (300g) monkfish
1 sole, filleted and skinned
2½ cups chicken or fish stock

½ cup dry white wine
3 large scallions, finely chopped
1lb 2oz (500g) mussels, rinsed and scrubbed
½ cup heavy (whipping) cream
salt and freshly ground black pepper
1 tbsp finely chopped tarragon, to serve

1 Cut the potato and carrot in ½ x 2in (1 x 5cm) batons. Slice the zucchini into diagonal pieces. Cut off the asparagus tips, then chop the spears into 2in (5cm) lengths. Cut the monkfish into 1½in (4cm) chunks and cut each sole fillet crosswise in half. Set the vegetables and fish aside separately.

2 Place the stock, wine, and scallions (reserving a few to serve) in a heavy saucepan. Bring to a boil over medium heat. Add the potato, reduce the heat to a simmer, and cook for 5 minutes, then add the carrot and cook for 5 minutes. Add the zucchini and asparagus and cook for 1–2 minutes, or until all is *al dente*. Remove the vegetables and set aside.

3 Bring the stock to a boil over high heat and reduce by a third. Reduce the heat to a simmer, add in the mussels, cover and cook for 3–4 minutes. Strain through a muslin-lined sieve into a bowl, let cool briefly, then discard any mussels that haven't opened. Shell the rest and set aside. Return the stock to the pan and simmer over medium heat, then stir in the cream and season to taste with salt and pepper. Add the monkfish, cook for 2–3 minutes, then the sole for 1 minute, then the vegetables and mussels for a final 2 minutes.

4 Using a slotted spoon, distribute the vegetables between the bowls. Place the fish on top, ladle over the broth, and scatter with mussels. Sprinkle with chopped tarragon and the reserved scallion. Serve hot.

This combination of South Indian and South East Asian flavors is a marvelous match for any firm-fleshed fish or seafood. Shrimp is a good alternative to cod.

pineapple broth with cod

🍲 **SERVES** 4   🕐 **PREP** 30 MINS **COOK** 40 MINS   ❄️ **FREEZE** UP TO 2 MONTHS

1 onion, diced
1¾oz (50g) raw peanuts, skinned
2 tbsp shredded coconut
1¼in (3cm) piece of ginger, chopped
1 tsp coriander seeds
2 tsp sesame seeds
1 tsp cumin seeds
1 tsp poppy seeds
3 tbsp tamarind pulp
½ tsp turmeric
¾ tsp chili powder

salt and freshly ground black pepper
2 tbsp vegetable oil
1 tsp palm sugar
1¾ cups fish stock
1 cup pineapple juice
1¾ cups coconut milk
1 cup cod, chopped
juice of 1 lime
4½oz (125g) fresh pineapple pieces, chopped
2 tbsp mint leaves, coarsely torn
2 tbsp raw peanuts, toasted and chopped

1 Heat a cast-iron pan. Add the onion, peanuts, coconut, ginger, and all the seeds. Stir over low heat until the coconut darkens and spices turn aromatic, about 5 minutes. Transfer to a bowl to cool, then place in a food processor and process to a coarse paste. Add the tamarind pulp, turmeric, chili powder, and salt and pepper, and process to a smooth paste.

2 Heat the vegetable oil in a large saucepan and cook the paste for about 10 minutes over low heat. Stir in the sugar and continue cooking until the paste begins to stick to the bottom of the pan. Pour in the stock and pineapple juice and simmer for 20 minutes, partially covered.

3 Remove the soup from the heat and process in a blender until smooth. You might need to do this in batches. Stir in the coconut milk and return the pan to the heat. Once it begins to bubble, add the fish and simmer for 3 minutes. Add the lime juice and stir in the pineapple pieces and mint leaves. Ladle into bowls and scatter the peanuts over the top.

Chowder makes a hearty lunchtime soup for any time of year. When possible, try to purchase your wild salmon from a sustainable source.

wild salmon chowder

SERVES 4   **PREP** 15 MINS   **FREEZE** NOT SUITABLE
                      COOK 25 MINS PLUS 5–10 MINS RESTING

2 tbsp olive oil
4 slices bacon, chopped
6 scallions, cut into 1in (2.5cm) slices
3 sprigs of thyme
2 bay leaves
1lb 5oz (600g) small waxy potatoes, thickly sliced
2 tbsp butter

1 tbsp flour
3 cups fish or chicken stock
14oz (400g) salmon fillets, skinned and cut into chunks
⅔ cup half-and-half
2–3 tbsp snipped dill
zest of ½ lemon, finely grated
salt and freshly ground black pepper

1 Heat 1 tbsp of the oil in a wide, deep sauté pan. Add the bacon and cook until crisp. Drain on paper towels and set aside. Pour the remaining oil into the pan, add the scallions, thyme, and bay leaves, and stir-fry for 1 minute. Add the potatoes and cook 2–3 minutes.

2 In another saucepan, melt the butter and beat in the flour. Cook for 1–2 minutes and then gradually add the stock. Bring to a boil and then simmer gently for 3–4 minutes or until thickened slightly. Add the thickened stock to the potatoes and bring to a boil. Cook for 10 minutes without stirring, until the potatoes are just tender.

3 Reduce the heat and submerge the salmon chunks into the stock. Simmer very gently for 3–5 minutes, until the fish is just cooked. Do not stir or the fish will break up.

4 Remove from the heat. Without stirring, pour in the half-and-half and scatter with the dill and lemon zest. Let the soup sit for 5–10 minutes for all the flavors to blend. When ready to serve, gently warm through, discard the thyme and bay leaves, and add seasoning if needed. Ladle into bowls and serve with black pepper and the crispy bacon scattered over the top.

This is a complete meal in a bowl. Raw mangoes add bite to a citrusy broth flecked with fiery red chiles. Raw mangoes are available in many Asian markets.

mango and snapper broth

SERVES 4   **PREP** 15 MINS, PLUS 20 MINS MARINATING   **FREEZE** NOT SUITABLE   **COOK** 15 MINS

1 tbsp soy sauce
2 tsp Asian fish sauce
1 tbsp toasted sesame oil
1 tbsp mirin
1 tsp sugar
juice of 1 lime
1lb (500g) skinless red snapper fillets, cut into 1in (2.5cm) cubes
2 stalks lemongrass, finely chopped
2 tbsp vegetable oil
4 bird's eye red chiles, finely sliced
4 scallions, finely sliced
2in (5cm) fresh ginger, finely shredded
4 garlic cloves, coarsely chopped

4 small raw green mangoes, or under-ripe mangoes, peeled and finely chopped
2 tsp palm sugar or brown sugar
2 tbsp rice wine vinegar
1 quart (1 liter) fish stock
8 kaffir lime leaves, torn in half
1 tbsp Asian fish sauce
4oz (100g) medium egg noodles
4oz (100g) thin green beans, halved
salt to season
juice of 1 lime, to taste
2 tbsp chopped fresh cilantro leaves
1 tbsp shredded fresh mint leaves

1 Combine the soy and fish sauce, sesame oil, mirin, sugar, and lime juice, and spoon over the fish. Refrigerate for 20 minutes. Pound the lemongrass to a paste with a dash of water, using a mortar and pestle. Set aside.

2 Heat the oil in a wok or large pan and cook the chiles, scallions, ginger, and garlic for 30 seconds over high heat. Add the mangoes and cook for 1 minute. Stir in the sugar until it begins to caramelize. Add the vinegar, lemongrass, stock, lime leaves, and fish sauce. Bring to a boil.

3 Stir in the noodles, beans, and fish pieces (not the marinating liquid). Simmer for 3–5 minutes, until the noodles are cooked and the fish flakes easily. Season with salt, sharpen with lime juice, and add the herbs.

The strong flavors of cavolo nero and smoked haddock develop in minutes, making this soup very satisfying. If you want to freeze it, do so before adding the fish.

portuguese haddock soup

SERVES 4   **PREP** 20 MINS **COOK** 20 MINS   **FREEZE** NOT SUITABLE

10oz (300g) leaves of cavolo nero, kale, or savoy cabbage
2 tbsp olive oil
1 Spanish onion, finely chopped
3 garlic cloves, peeled and crushed

1 large waxy potato, peeled and diced
1 cup milk
salt and freshly ground black pepper
10oz (300g) smoked haddock fillet, skinned and flaked

1 Rinse the greens, cut out and discard the large ribs, and shred the leaves finely. Set aside. Place a heavy saucepan over medium heat and add the oil. Once it is hot, add the onion and garlic and cook for 4–5 minutes, or until softened.

2 Add the potato and milk, then pour in enough water to cover everything by ¾–1¼in (2–3cm). Season, bring to a simmer, and cook for 5 minutes, then add the greens and continue cooking for 10–15 minutes until the vegetables are tender.

3 Stir in the haddock and simmer for 1 minute, then take off the heat and cover. Let stand for 5 minutes before serving.

This comforting soup is based on a simple roux-based sauce, so it is vital to use very good stock to make it really sing. It makes an excellent light lunch.

creamy smoked trout soup

SERVES 6 **PREP** 15 MINS **COOK** 10 MINS **FREEZE** UP TO 2 MONTHS

3½ tbsp butter
¼ cup flour
3¼ cups hot vegetable or fish stock
1 cup heavy (whipping) cream
4 tbsp white wine
2–3 tsp Worcestershire sauce

salt and freshly ground black pepper
squeeze of lemon juice
13oz (375g) smoked trout fillets,
   skinned and flaked
2 tbsp chopped parsley

1 Over low heat, melt the butter in a large saucepan, stir in the flour, and mix until smooth. Cook for 2–3 minutes, stirring constantly. Gradually pour in the hot stock, making sure there are no lumps by whisking vigorously. Bring to a boil and then cook, uncovered, over low heat for about 3 minutes, stirring occasionally.

2 Add the cream, white wine, Worcestershire sauce, salt, pepper, and a little lemon juice, then bring to a boil again. Add the fish pieces and briefly heat them through. Sprinkle the soup with parsley and serve.

TROUT
Be sure to buy smoked trout for this dish, as it is already cooked. Go for whole moist fillets, because some pre-flaked fish can be dry. Always keep yourself informed of fish sustainability guidelines.

Make sure you don't boil the soup after adding the miso paste, as it spoils the flavor. You'll find wakame (dried seaweed) and miso in large supermarkets.

miso soup with tuna

SERVES 4   **PREP** 25 MINS **COOK** 15 MINS   **FREEZE** NOT SUITABLE

4in (10cm) piece wakame
2 tbsp dried shiitake mushrooms
2 scallions, chopped
1 tsp grated fresh ginger
1 long thin carrot, thinly sliced

2 cups chicken stock
7oz (200g) fresh tuna steak, diced
2 tbsp miso paste
soy sauce, to season
1 tbsp snipped chives

1 Put the wakame and mushrooms in a bowl and cover with cold water. Soak for 15 minutes. Drain, reserving the liquid. Lift out the wakame, remove any hard central ribs, and cut into strips.

2 Put the wakame, mushrooms, scallions, ginger, and carrot into a saucepan. Combine 1¼ cups of the soaking water with the stock and add to the saucepan. Bring to a boil, reduce the heat, cover, and simmer for 10 minutes until the carrot is just tender.

3 Add the tuna and cook for another 5 minutes. In a small bowl, blend the miso paste with 2 tbsp water and stir in to the soup. Season to taste with soy sauce. Heat through but do not boil. Ladle into warm soup cups and sprinkle with snipped chives.

A rich main meal soup naturally thickened with okra—
a classic gumbo ingredient. In its native Louisiana, sweet
ground sassafras leaves would be used.

mixed seafood gumbo

⊘ **SERVES** 6   🕐 **PREP** 20 MINS **COOK** 50 MINS   ❄ **FREEZE** UP TO 2 MONTHS
AT THE END OF STEP 2

1 tbsp sunflower oil
1 onion, chopped
2 celery ribs, chopped
1 large garlic clove, chopped
4oz (115g) chorizo, sliced
2 tbsp plain flour
2½ cups fish or chicken stock
1 x 14oz (400g) can chopped tomatoes
1 green bell pepper, diced

9oz (250g) okra, trimmed and cut
   into short lengths
¼ tsp cayenne pepper
½ tsp dried oregano
½ tsp sugar
salt and freshly ground black pepper
7oz (200g) mixed raw seafood
8oz (225g) long-grain rice
chopped parsley, to serve

1 Heat the oil in a large saucepan. Add the onion and celery and cook gently, stirring, for about 5 minutes, or until lightly golden. Stir in the garlic and chorizo and cook for 2 minutes. Stir in the flour and cook for another minute. Remove from the heat and gradually blend in the stock, then the tomatoes. Return to the heat and bring to a boil, stirring. Add the remaining ingredients, except the seafood and rice, bring back to a boil, reduce the heat, partially cover, and simmer gently for 30 minutes.

2 Add the seafood and simmer for another 5 minutes, stirring from time to time. Taste and season again to taste.

3 Meanwhile, cook the rice in plenty of boiling, lightly salted water for 10 minutes or until just tender (or as the package directs). Drain in a colander, rinse with boiling water, and drain again.

4 Spoon some rice into each of 6 large soup bowls. Ladle the gumbo over the top, sprinkle with a little chopped parsley, and serve hot.

in praise of...
shellfish
There are few greater
pleasures than
gathering mussels
at low tide, and then
feasting on these
delicious fruits of
the sea.

A delicious fall soup for the whole family. Purée it for the younger members, so they get to eat their required vegetables without noticing.

potato and clam soup

⊘ **SERVES** 4–6   ◷ **PREP** 25 MINS **COOK** 1 HR 30 MINS   ❋ **FREEZE** NOT SUITABLE

2¼lb (1kg) clams
¼ cup dry white wine
2–3 tbsp olive oil
2 celery ribs, finely diced
1 red onion, finely chopped
1 carrot, finely chopped
4 tomatoes, peeled, seeded, and chopped

2 medium potatoes, finely diced
1 quart (1 liter) cold water
1 sprig of rosemary
1 tbsp finely chopped flat-leaf parsley
   or chervil
salt and freshly ground black pepper
4–6 slices thick country bread

1 Wash the clams thoroughly in cold running water, throwing away any with broken shells and any that are open and won't close when gently tapped. Put them in a large frying pan with the wine, cover with a lid, and place over high heat for 5 minutes or until the shells open. Discard any that remain closed, as they will not be edible. Drain, reserving the liquid. Remove the clams from their shells, place in a bowl, cover, and refrigerate until needed. Strain the cooking liquid through a fine sieve.

2 Heat the oil in a large heavy-bottomed pan, add the celery, onion, and carrot, and cook on low heat for 10 minutes or until light brown. Add the tomatoes, potatoes, the reserved cooking liquid, and the water, and bring to a boil. Add the rosemary, then lower the heat, cover with a lid, and simmer for 1 hour.

3 Stir in the clams and the parsley or chervil, then season with salt and freshly ground black pepper. Remove the rosemary, put a slice of bread in the bottom of each bowl, and ladle over the soup.

This traditional, creamy soup is often served with oyster crackers, although crusty bread is also good. The clams must be cooked on the day of purchase.

new england clam chowder

⊘ SERVES 4 **⏱ PREP** 15 MINS **COOK** 35 MINS **❄ FREEZE** NOT SUITABLE

36 live clams
1 tbsp oil
4oz (115g) thick-cut bacon, diced
2 floury potatoes, such as russet, peeled and
   cut into ½in (1cm) cubes
1 onion, finely chopped

2 tbsp flour
2½ cups whole milk
salt and freshly ground black pepper
½ cup half-and-half
2 tbsp finely chopped flat-leaf parsley

1 Discard any open clams, then shuck the rest, reserving the juices. Add enough water to the juices to make 2½ cups. Chop the clams. Heat the oil in a large, heavy saucepan and cook the bacon over medium heat for 5 minutes or until crisp. Remove and drain on paper towels.

2 Add the potatoes and onion to the pan and cook for 5 minutes or until the onion has softened. Add the flour and stir for 2 minutes. Stir in the clam juice and milk and season to taste. Cover with a lid, lower the heat, and simmer for 20 minutes or until the potatoes are tender. Add the clams and simmer gently, uncovered, for 5 minutes. Stir in the half-and-half and reheat without boiling. Serve sprinkled with the bacon and parsley.

SHUCKING CLAMS

Work the tip of a knife between the top and bottom shell, then twist upward to open the clam.

Sever the muscle at the top, then do the same at the bottom to release the clam meat.

There are several variations on Manhattan clam chowder, using vegetables such as celery and green bell peppers. Its defining feature, however, is its tomato base.

manhattan clam chowder

⊚ SERVES 4　　**◑ PREP** 15 MINS **COOK** 35 MINS　　**❄ FREEZE** NOT SUITABLE

36 live clams, freshly bought
1 tbsp oil
3–4 slices thick-cut bacon, diced
1 onion, finely chopped
2 floury potatoes, such as russet, peeled
　and cut into ½ in (1cm) cubes

2 tbsp flour
2 x 14oz (400g) cans chopped tomatoes
　with their juice
salt and freshly ground black pepper
fresh thyme, to garnish

1 Discard any clams that are open. Shuck the clams and reserve the juice, adding enough water to make 2½ cups. Chop the clams.

2 Heat the oil in a large, heavy saucepan and cook the bacon over medium heat, stirring frequently, for 5 minutes, or until it is crisp. Remove from the pan with a slotted spoon, drain on paper towels, and set aside.

3 Add the onion and potatoes to the pan and cook for 5 minutes, or until the onion has softened. Add the flour and stir for 2 minutes.

4 Stir in the tomatoes and their juice and season to taste with salt and pepper. Cover the pan, reduce the heat, and let simmer for 20 minutes or until the potatoes are tender. Add the clams and simmer gently, uncovered, for 5 minutes. Serve the chowder hot, sprinkled with bacon and thyme.

This is a wonderful, unusual, inspired soup. The combination of saffron and curry powder gives it an interesting aromatic quality.

mussel and saffron soup

SERVES 4   **PREP TIME** 15 MINS **COOK** 35 MINS   **FREEZE** NOT SUITABLE

½ cup dry white wine
2 cups fish or chicken stock
4½lb (2kg) mussels, scrubbed
   and debearded
2 tbsp butter
4½oz (125g) onions, finely chopped
2 carrots, diced
3oz (85g) celeriac, diced

1 thin leek, finely sliced
1 garlic clove, chopped
1½ tsp curry powder
good pinch of saffron threads,
   soaked in 2 tbsp hot water
1 cup heavy cream
salt and pepper
2 tbsp parsley, finely chopped

1 Bring the wine and stock to a boil in a large deep pan over high heat. Add the mussels, discarding any that will not shut when tapped, and cover. As the mussels open, remove them to a bowl. When all are open, filter the liquid through muslin into another bowl. Discard two-thirds of the shells.

2 Clean the pan. Melt the butter over low heat and add the vegetables and garlic, stirring well. Cook gently for 10 minutes, then stir in the curry powder and add the mussel liquid and the saffron in its water. Add the cream and cook without boiling for 5 minutes. Return the mussels to the pan, heat through gently, and season well. Sprinkle over the parsley, and serve.

SCRUBBING AND DE-BEARDING MUSSELS

Scrub the mussels under cold running water, then scrape off any barnacles with a knife.

Pinch the dark stringy "beard" between forefinger and thumb and pull it firmly away.

A typical Provence concoction, this mussel and fennel soup harmoniously combines seafood and vegetables in a fragrant broth.

mussel and fennel soup

 SERVES 4   **PREP TIME** 15 MINS **COOK** 45 MINS   **FREEZE** UP TO 1 MONTH

2¼lb (1kg) fresh mussels
2 cups dry white wine
4 medium, ripe tomatoes
3 tbsp olive oil
1 leek, chopped
2 sprigs of fresh flat-leaf parsley
2 sprigs of thyme

1 bay leaf
¼ small fennel bulb, chopped
2in (5cm) piece dried orange peel
fine sea salt and freshly ground black pepper
1 large floury potato, peeled and chopped
pinch of saffron strands

1 Rinse and debeard the mussels. Place them in a large saucepan and add the wine. Cover the pan, put over high heat, and cook for 5–6 minutes, shaking occasionally, until the mussels open (discard any that remain closed). Remove from the heat. Line a sieve with muslin or cheesecloth and place over a bowl. Transfer the mussels into the sieve and leave until cool enough to handle, then remove and discard the shells. Reserve both the mussels and the cooking liquid.

2 Pierce the tomatoes with a knife, put them in a bowl, and pour over boiling water to cover. Leave for 1 minute, then drain and peel away the skins. Quarter, remove and discard the seeds, and chop the flesh. Heat the oil in a large sauté pan over medium heat. Add the tomatoes, leek, herbs, fennel, and orange peel and season. Cook until softened, stirring frequently.

3 Add the mussel cooking liquid to the pan, then 2 cups of just-boiled water. Bring to a simmer. Add the potato and cook until soft. Remove from the heat, let cool a little, then remove the herbs and orange peel. Mash the potato pieces into the soup to thicken.

4 Soften the saffron in a small bowl with a spoonful of soup, then stir it back in. Taste and adjust the seasoning, add the mussels, reheat gently, and serve immediately.

This aromatic, mussel soup comes from France's Atlantic coast. You can prepare it ahead, but be sure to reheat the mussels gently, or they will overcook.

mouclade

⊚ **SERVES** 4   🕐 **PREP** 20 MINS **COOK** 30 MINS   ❄ **FREEZE** NOT SUITABLE

3lb 3oz (1.5kg) small fresh mussels, well scrubbed and washed
2¼ tbsp butter
1 large shallot, finely chopped
1½ cups dry white wine
several sprigs of flat-leaf parsley
¼ small fennel bulb, chopped
1 bay leaf
sea salt and freshly ground black pepper

pinch of cayenne
1 large egg yolk
5 tbsp sour cream or crème fraîche
1 large garlic clove, crushed
½ tsp mild paprika or 1 tsp mild curry powder
a few strands of saffron or ¼ tsp ground saffron
fresh warm bread, to serve

1 Place a large sauté pan over medium heat. Add in the mussels with 1 tbsp of the butter, the shallot, wine, and 1½ cups water. Add the parsley, fennel, and bay leaf, season lightly with salt and pepper, and add the cayenne. Increase the heat and bring to a boil. Cover and cook the mussels for 4–5 minutes, or until they open, shaking the pan a few times.

2 Using a slotted spoon, lift out the mussels and put in a bowl. Discard any that haven't opened and set aside the rest. Strain the liquor through a muslin-lined sieve into a bowl and set aside. In a small bowl, mix the egg yolk with the sour cream until smooth. In a separate bowl, using a fork, mash the remaining butter with the garlic, paprika, and saffron.

3 Shell the mussels, keeping 12 in their shells, and moisten them all with a little of the cooking liquid. Keep warm.

4 Place a large pan over a low heat. Add the butter and, when it bubbles, pour in the mussel liquor, stir, and bring to a simmer. Remove 3 tbsp and whisk it into the egg mixture, then whisk this back into the pan and stir until hot and blended. Adjust the seasoning and divide the mussels between 4 warm bowls. Pour the broth over and serve with the bread.

These succulent mussels in their moat of gingery juices are terrific with a mound of fluffy rice on the side, but crusty bread mops up the broth just as nicely.

mussels in a ginger and chile broth

⊘ **SERVES** 2–4 🕔 **PREP** 20 MINS **COOK** 30–35 MINS ❄ **FREEZE** NOT SUITABLE

3lb (1.5 kg) mussels, in their shells, cleaned
1 stick (8 tbsp) butter
2 onions, finely chopped
2 bird's-eye red chiles, finely chopped
2in (5cm) fresh ginger, finely shredded
5 large garlic cloves, finely chopped
2 stalks lemongrass, split lengthwise
   and lightly bruised

½ cup ginger liqueur
1¾ cups fish stock
⅔ cup coconut milk
3 tbsp coconut cream
salt and freshly ground black pepper
juice of 1–2 limes, to taste
3 tbsp chopped fresh cilantro

1 Wash the mussels under cold running water. Give any open ones a firm tap against the counter top and discard any that don't close.

2 Melt the butter in a large pan over low heat and soften the onions, chiles, ginger, garlic, and lemongrass for 10 minutes without coloring.

3 Turn the heat up to high and add the ginger liqueur followed by the stock. Bring to a boil before adding the mussels. Cover the pan and cook for 5–7 minutes, until the mussel shells have opened. Discard the lemongrass along with any mussels that remain closed.

4 Pour in the coconut milk and cream, and bring to a boil. Season with salt and pepper, sharpen with lime juice, stir in the cilantro, and serve.

A wonderfully elegant soup that marks the crossover between foods that are coming into season and those that are going out of season.

soup of the first and last

⊘ **SERVES** 4–6   🕐 **PREP** 30 MINS **COOK** 45 MINS   ❄ **FREEZE** NOT SUITABLE

10 oysters, opened, and with juice
1 tbsp butter
1 white onion, finely diced
2 garlic cloves, finely chopped
1 celery rib, finely diced
salt and freshly ground black pepper
¾ cup heavy cream
1¾ cups cold water
½ celeriac, peeled and finely diced

7oz (200g) russet potatoes, cut into thin slices
2 small–medium turnips, cut in two, then sliced into half-moons
7oz (200g) garlic leaves, cut into roughly 1¾in (4cm) pieces (or substitute baby spinach and extra garlic)
a handful of wild garlic flowers, to garnish (optional)

1 Wash 4–6 oyster shells (one per serving) to remove any grit. Cover with boiling water, to clean and keep warm. Heat the butter in a pan, add the onion, garlic, celery, and a pinch of salt, cover with a lid, and cook over low heat for 5 minutes or until soft. Add the cream, water, and celeriac and simmer, covered, for 10 minutes. Add the potatoes and cook for 10 minutes, then add the turnips and cook for 10 more minutes.

2 Take off the heat and ladle half the soup into a blender. Add 4–6 oysters (depending on how many you need to serve) and half the garlic leaves and blend until smooth. Tip the mixture back in the pan, rinse the blender out with 1¾ cups cold water, and add that to the pan as well. Season with salt and freshly ground black pepper, add the rest of the garlic leaves, then bring to a gentle simmer and cook for 5 minutes.

3 Meanwhile, put the remaining oysters and their juices in a pan with 2 tbsp water, and poach for 4 minutes or until firm. Turn halfway through. Stir the juice (but not the oysters) into the soup, then check the seasoning and the consistency—add a little hot water if the soup is too thick. Divide among 4–6 bowls. Drop a warm oyster shell in each, fill with a poached oyster, and garnish with wild garlic flowers if desired.

A rich broth sets off the sweetness of the scallops while the chorizo adds a spicy contrast. Try serving as the first course of a dinner party menu.

creamy scallop bisque

SERVES 4   **PREP** 20 MINS **COOK** 40 MINS   **FREEZE** NOT SUITABLE

3 cups water
1¼ cups dry white wine
1 tbsp butter
1 small onion, finely chopped
1 small shallot, very finely chopped
1 medium-sized ripe tomato, chopped
7oz (200g) shrimp, shelled
3½oz (100g) cod or pollock, skinned and cut into chunks

2 tbsp chopped parsley
2 tsp dill seeds
3 tbsp brandy
sea salt and freshly ground black pepper
½ cup half-and-half
2½oz (75g) chorizo, diced
12 small scallops (or 6 large)
1 tbsp finely chopped chives, to finish

1 Boil the 3 cups water with the wine. Place the butter in a sauté pan over medium heat. Add the onion and shallot and soften until golden. Add the tomato, shrimp, fish, parsley, and dill seeds. Stir, and cook for 5 minutes. Stir in the brandy, and cook for a minute. Pour in the wine mixture and season lightly with salt and pepper. Reduce the heat, and simmer gently for 10 minutes. Take off the heat and let cool. Stir and mash down the soup with the back of a spoon, then heat the half-and-half in another pan until hot.

2 Transfer the soup to a blender and purée. Strain through a sieve back into the pan and stir in the hot half-and-half. Return to a simmer. Remove from the heat and adjust the seasoning. Cover and keep warm.

3 Place a nonstick frying pan over medium heat. Add the chorizo and cook for 3–5 minutes until cooked through and crispy. Set aside on a plate lined with paper towels and keep warm.

4 Add the scallops to the pan. Cook for 2 minutes, turn over, and cook for a minute. Remove from the heat. Ladle the soup into 4 bowls and add the scallops. Scatter the chorizo over the top and serve immediately.

Serve this delightful soup with some nutty rye bread and chilled unsalted butter. If you like, you can use crab for a less expensive alternative to the lobster.

brandied lobster chowder

SERVES 4   **PREP** 20 MINS **COOK** 1 HR   **FREEZE** UP TO 2 MONTHS
WITHOUT HALF-AND-HALF
AND SNOW PEAS

1 small cooked lobster
3½ cups water
⅔ cup dry white wine
1 bay leaf
1–2 tbsp unsalted butter
2 shallots, finely chopped
4 tbsp brandy
1 large tomato, peeled and diced

2 tsp anchovy essence
4 large new potatoes, peeled and diced
8 baby corn, cut in short lengths
salt and freshly ground pepper
2oz (60g) snow peas, cut in short lengths
5 tbsp half-and-half
4 thick slices lemon
4 sprigs of parsley

1 Twist the legs and claws off the lobster. Split the body lengthwise and remove the vein that runs along it. Remove the tail meat, cut in small pieces, and reserve. Crack the large claws, remove the meat, dice, and reserve. Keep all other meat in the shell. Coarsely chop it and put it in a saucepan with the claws and legs. Add the water, wine, and bay leaf. Bring to a boil, reduce the heat, cover, and simmer for 30 minutes. Strain and reserve the stock.

2 Melt the butter in another large saucepan over low heat. Add the shallots and cook gently, stirring for 1 minute. Add the brandy, ignite, and shake the pan until the flames subside. Add the tomato, anchovy essence, potatoes, and corn. Return the stock to the pan. Season and bring to a boil. Reduce the heat, cover, and simmer gently for 20 minutes until the potatoes are really tender.

3 Meanwhile, blanch the snow peas in a little boiling water for 2 minutes until just tender. Drain, rinse with cold water, and drain again. Then add to the soup along with the half-and-half and lobster meat. Taste and season again. Reheat the soup but do not boil it. Ladle into deep soup cups. Serve with a slice of lemon and a small sprig of parsley in each bowl.

The name 'bisque' refers to a rich and luxurious shellfish soup with cream and brandy and is thought to have come from the Spanish Biscay region.

lobster bisque

⊘ SERVES 4   **🕑 PREP** 45 MINS **COOK** 1 HR 10 MINS   **❄ FREEZE** UP TO 3 MONTHS

1 lobster, cooked, about 2¼lb (1kg) in weight
3½ tbsp butter
1 onion, finely chopped
1 carrot, finely chopped
2 celery ribs, finely chopped
1 leek, finely chopped
½ fennel bulb, finely chopped
1 bay leaf
1 sprig of tarragon
2 garlic cloves, crushed

2½oz (75g) tomato purée
4 tomatoes, coarsely chopped
½ cup Cognac or brandy
½ cup dry white wine or vermouth
1¾ quarts (1¾ liters) fish stock
½ cup heavy cream
salt and freshly ground black pepper
pinch of cayenne
juice of ½ lemon
chives, to garnish

1 Split the lobster in half, remove the meat from the body, and chop the meat into small pieces. Twist off the claws and legs, break at the joints, and remove the meat, then crack all the shells with the back of a knife. Chop the shells into coarse pieces and put the meat into the refrigerator.

2 Melt the butter in a large pan over medium heat, add the vegetables, herbs, and garlic, and cook for 10 minutes, or until softened, stirring occasionally. Add the lobster shells. Stir in the tomato purée, tomatoes, Cognac, white wine, and fish stock. Bring to a boil and simmer for 1 hour.

3 Let cool slightly, then ladle into a food processor. Process in short bursts, until the shell breaks into very small pieces. Strain through a coarse sieve, pushing through as much as you can, then pass it again through a fine sieve before returning to the heat.

4 Bring to a boil, add the reserved lobster meat and the cream, then season to taste, adding the cayenne and lemon. Serve in warm bowls, garnished with chives.

Buy your crab precooked, or, for optimum freshness, buy it live and cook it yourself. Boiling is the most common way to cook a live crab, although it can also be steamed.

crab bisque

⊘ **SERVES** 4　　🕐 **PREP** 45 MINS **COOK** 1 HR 10 MINS　　❄ **FREEZE** UP TO 2 MONTHS
BEFORE CREAM IS ADDED

1–2 cooked crabs, about 2¼lb
　(1kg) total weight
3½ tbsp butter
olive oil
1 onion, finely chopped
1 carrot, finely chopped
2 celery ribs, finely chopped
1 leek, finely chopped
½ fennel bulb, finely chopped
1 bay leaf
1 sprig of tarragon
2 garlic cloves, crushed

1in (2.5cm) piece fresh ginger, peeled
　and finely chopped
2½oz (75g) tomato purée
4 tomatoes, coarsely chopped
½ cup Cognac or brandy
½ cup dry white wine or vermouth
1¾ quarts (1¾ liters) fish stock
½ cup heavy cream
salt and freshly ground black pepper
pinch of cayenne pepper
juice of ½ lemon

1 Remove the crab meat from the shell and chop into small pieces. Chop the shell up coarsely and set both shell and meat to one side. Heat the butter and oil in a large saucepan over medium heat. Add the vegetables, herbs, garlic, and ginger. Cook, stirring occasionally, for 10 minutes or until softened.

2 Add the chopped shell, then stir in the tomato purée, tomatoes, Cognac, wine, and stock. Bring to a boil and simmer for 1 hour. Let cool slightly, then blend until smooth. Strain through a coarse sieve, pushing as much liquid through as you can with the back of a spatula, and then press through a fine sieve, making sure to remove the chopped shell.

3 Return the soup to the pan and bring to a boil. Add the crab meat and cream, then season to taste with salt and pepper and add cayenne and lemon juice to taste. Garnish with chives and serve in warm bowls.

Seafood and tomatoes make a flavorful pair in this delicate summer chilled soup. You can use the cooked clams or mussels in another dish, such as potato salad.

crab gazpacho

⊘ SERVES 4   **⏱ PREP** 30 MINS   **❄ FREEZE** NOT SUITABLE
COOK 10 MINS CHILLING 2 HOURS

1lb 2oz (500g) clams or mussels, cleaned
4 tbsp fruity olive oil
1 shallot, finely chopped
2 large scallions, finely chopped
2 garlic cloves, crushed
½ cup dry sherry
3 sprigs flat leaf parsley, plus 1 tbsp finely
  chopped parsley to finish
1 tsp fennel seeds, crushed

sea salt and freshly ground black pepper
½ tsp hot paprika
2¼lb (1kg) ripe tomatoes, rinsed and halved
3 tbsp olive oil
2 eggs, hard-boiled and peeled
1 tbsp sherry vinegar
freshly cooked brown and white meat
  of 1 medium prepared crab
8 croûtes (see p39), rubbed with garlic

1 Place a sauté pan over medium heat. Add the clams or mussels along with 1 tbsp oil, the shallot, half the scallions and garlic, the sherry, and 1 cup water. Add the parsley sprigs, fennel seeds, salt, pepper, and paprika. Bring to a boil. Cover and cook for 4–5 minutes, shaking a few times, until the shells open. Strain through a muslin-lined sieve into a bowl and let cool completely. Discard any unopened clams or mussels.

2 Put the tomatoes, the cold stock from the mussels, 1 tbsp olive oil, 1 hard-boiled egg yolk and the remaining scallions and garlic in a blender and process until very smooth. Press through a sieve into a bowl. Rinse out the blender or food processor with 1 cup water mixed with the sherry vinegar. Pour through the sieve into the bowl.

3 Chill the soup for at least 2 hours. Press the remaining egg yolk through a sieve and finely chop the whites. Mix the brown crab meat with 2 tbsp oil and the egg yolk and whites. Add a little pepper and spread on the croûtes.

4 Ladle the soup into bowls and lightly stir in the white crab meat. Float a croûte on each helping and scatter the chopped parsley over the top.

This clear seafood soup uses dashi—a Japanese tuna- and seaweed-based fish stock—as its base. For those avoiding gluten in their diet, tamari may be used.

prawn and sea bass soup

⊘ **SERVES** 4   🕐 **PREP** 10 MINS **COOK** 5 MINS   ❄ **FREEZE** NOT SUITABLE

3½oz (100g) spinach, blanched
1 quart (1 liter) dashi
3½oz (100g) sea bass fillet, cut into 4 cubes
4 large raw prawns or jumbo shrimp, peeled
    and deveined

1 tsp soy sauce
½ small red chile
1 scallion, chopped
1 tbsp arrowroot
few drops lemon juice

1 Squeeze as much water as possible out of the blanched spinach, then cut into strips and set aside.

2 Bring the dashi to a boil in a saucepan and add the cubed fish and the prawns or jumbo shrimp. Cook for 2–3 minutes, then add the soy sauce, chile, and scallion.

3 Whisk the arrowroot with 1 tbsp cold water in a bowl and stir into the soup. Bring to a boil and then remove the chile. Add the lemon juice and spinach and serve.

This lively aromatic soup can be made in a jiffy, if you use canned coconut milk and have a handy supply of chicken stock. It is filling enough to be a lunch in itself.

prawn, chicken, coconut, and lemongrass soup

SERVES 4–6   **PREP** 10 MINS **COOK** 15 MINS   ✱ **FREEZE** NOT SUITABLE

3½ cups coconut milk
1¼ cups chicken stock
12oz (350g) chicken, cut into slivers
3 stalks lemongrass, heavily bruised (see p25)
½in (1.5cm) piece galangal or ginger, cut into thin matchsticks

8oz (225g) uncooked prawns, shelled
1 red chile, seeded and diced
5 scallions, sliced
juice of 1–2 limes
3 tbsp coarsely chopped cilantro
3 tbsp Asian fish sauce

1 Put the coconut milk and stock into a pan. Bring to a boil. Add the chicken, lemongrass, and galangal or ginger and lower the heat to a gentle simmer. Cook for 10 minutes, uncovered.

2 Add the prawns and cook for another 2–3 minutes, then add all the remaining ingredients. Remove the lemongrass and discard. Taste and add more lime juice or fish sauce, if needed, then serve.

PEELING AND DEVEINING PRAWNS

Pull off the head, leaving the tail meat intact, then peel off the shell and legs with your fingers.

Make a shallow cut along the back of the prawn, then remove the dark vein with the knife tip.

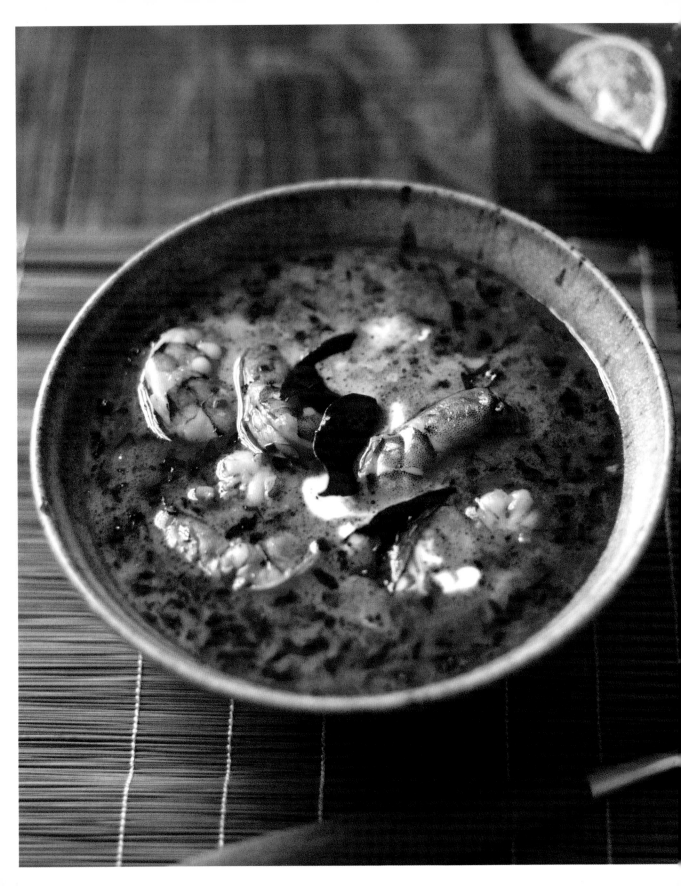

This fragrant soup takes the best ingredients from a cottage garden in the southern Indian state of Kerala. If you are using dried curry leaves, add them with the stock.

keralan shrimp soup

🍲 **SERVES** 4–6   🕐 **PREP** 20 MINS **COOK** 40 MINS   ❄ **FREEZE** NOT SUITABLE

1 tsp black peppercorns
¾ tsp mustard seeds
2 tsp coriander seeds
½ tsp fenugreek seeds
2–3 large red chiles, coarsely chopped
4 garlic cloves, chopped
2in (5cm) piece fresh ginger, chopped
4 tbsp hot water
2–3 tbsp vegetable oil

small handful of fresh curry leaves
2 onions, finely chopped
3¼ cups fish stock
1 cup coconut milk
9oz (250g) raw jumbo shrimp, shelled
1 tbsp coconut cream
2 tbsp fresh cilantro, chopped
juice of 1 lime, to taste

1 Heat a sturdy frying pan over low heat. Roast the peppercorns, mustard, coriander, and fenugreek seeds for about 30 seconds, until they give off a spicy aroma and the mustard seeds start to pop. Grind the spices to a powder using a mortar and pestle, and set aside.

2 Put the chiles in a small food processor with the garlic and ginger. (If you like a milder flavor, use just 2 chiles and remove the seeds.) Pour in the hot water and process to a paste. Set aside.

3 Heat the oil in a wok or saucepan. When hot, toss in the curry leaves and cook for 20 seconds, Be careful; curry leaves spit when added to hot oil. Add the onions, cover, and soften for 10 minutes, stirring occasionally.

4 Stir in the chile, garlic, and ginger paste and cook for 2–3 minutes, until the water evaporates. Add the ground spice mixture and cook for another 30 seconds, stirring all the time. Pour in the stock and simmer for 20 minutes or until reduced by one-third. Stir in the coconut milk and reheat before adding the shrimp and cooking for another 4–5 minutes. Add the coconut cream and finish with the cilantro and enough lime juice to sharpen.

poultry, game, and meat

A universal favorite, this soup has a zingy parsley and lemon finish. It can also be made with leftover meat and the carcass of a roasted chicken.

traditional chicken soup

SERVES 4   **PREP** 2½ HRS **COOK** 30 MINS   **FREEZE** UP TO 3 MONTHS
BEFORE HALF-AND-HALF IS ADDED

for the stock
1 small to medium free-range chicken
1 large carrot, chopped
1 leek, cut into segments
3 garlic cloves, unpeeled
¾oz (20g) dried mushrooms
3 celery ribs, chopped
2–3 sprigs each of parsley and thyme
sea salt and freshly ground black pepper

for the soup
3½oz (100g) short grain rice or pearl barley
1½ tbsp vegetable oil plus 10g (¼oz) butter
½ large red onion, finely chopped
2 garlic cloves, crushed
9oz (250g) button mushrooms, thinly sliced
4 tbsp half-and-half
2 tbsp finely chopped parsley
2 tsp finely grated zest of an unwaxed lemon

1 For the stock, place the chicken in a large saucepan over low heat. Cover with water and bring slowly to a boil, skimming the surface as needed. Add the carrot, leek, garlic, dried mushrooms, celery, and herbs. Season lightly. Bring back to a simmer, partially cover, and cook for 1 hour.

2 Remove from the heat. Once cool, lift out the chicken, strip the meat from the carcass, and reserve. Return the carcass to the pan and boil for 1 hour. Let cool, strain through a sieve into a bowl, and chill the stock.

3 Soak the rice or barley in cold water for 30 minutes. Rinse and drain. Skim the fat from the chilled stock. You'll need 3¼ cups of stock for the soup recipe, but you can add boiling water if needed.

4 Put the oil and butter in a deep saucepan over medium heat. Add the vegetables and cook for 3–5 minutes. Add the rice or barley, and stir for 2 minutes. Add the stock and cook for 15–20 minutes. Shred about 7oz (200g) of the reserved chicken and add to the soup. Taste, season if necessary, and return to a simmer. Stir in the half-and-half, parsley, and lemon zest, and serve very hot.

The traditional method involves slow-simmering a whole chicken, but this version takes less time and effort. To make a more substantial meal, add a few boiled potatoes.

cock-a-leekie soup

SERVES 4 **PREP** 10 MINS **COOK** 1¼ HRS **FREEZE** UP TO 3 MONTHS

1lb (450g) chicken breasts
 and thighs, skinned
2 bay leaves
1 quart (1 liter) chicken or
 vegetable stock
2oz (60g) long-grain rice

2 leeks, thinly sliced
2 carrots, grated
pinch of ground cloves
1 tsp sea salt
1 tbsp chopped fresh parsley

1 Place the chicken in a large pan with the bay leaves and pour in the stock. Bring to a boil, then reduce the heat, cover the pan, and simmer for 30 minutes.

2 Skim the surface of the soup and discard any foam that has formed. Add the rice, leeks, carrots, cloves, and salt. Bring back to a boil, reduce the heat, cover the pan, and simmer for another 30 minutes.

3 Remove the bay leaves and discard. Lift out the chicken, remove the meat from the bones, then return the meat to the soup. Ladle the soup into a warm tureen or divide between individual serving bowls, and serve hot, garnished with parsley.

CHICKEN
Free-range chickens are afforded space to move around in and access to the open air, making them healthier than caged birds, and this is reflected in the taste. Choose a bird with a firm, plump breast and tight skin.

This Mexican soup is made with thin *fideo* noodles, which are similar to angel-hair pasta. The avocado and sour cream offset the spiciness of the broth.

sopa seca de fideos

⊘ SERVES 4　　**⊙ PREP** 20 MINS PLUS 30 MINS SOAKING
　　　　　　　　COOK 15 MINS　　　　　　　　　　**✱ FREEZE** NOT SUITABLE

2 dried chipotle chiles
2 large ripe tomatoes, peeled and seeded
2 garlic cloves
1 small onion, coarsely chopped
1 quart (1 liter) chicken stock
3 tbsp vegetable oil

2 skinless boneless chicken breasts, diced
8oz (225g) Mexican *fideo* noodles or dried
　angel-hair pasta
4 tbsp sour cream, to serve
1 avocado, pit removed, chopped,
　to serve

1 Soak the dried chiles in water for 30 minutes, then drain, discarding the soaking water. Using a blender, process the tomatoes, garlic, onion, chiles, and 2 tbsp of the stock until smooth. Set aside.

2 Heat 2 tbsp of the oil in a large pan over medium heat and stir-fry the chicken for 2–3 minutes, or until just cooked. Remove from the pan, drain on paper towels, and set aside.

3 Pour the remaining oil into the pan, add the noodles, and cook over low heat, stirring constantly, until the noodles are golden.

4 Pour in the tomato mixture, stir until the noodles are coated, then add the remaining stock and return the chicken to the pan. Cook for 2–3 minutes, or until the noodles are just tender. To serve, ladle into bowls, topping each with sour cream and chopped avocado.

Here, a nourishing chicken stock combines with the sweetness of sweet corn and satisfying vermicelli to create a soothing meal in a bowl.

chinese chicken noodle soup

◉ SERVES 4   **◐ PREP** 10 MINS PLUS 30 MINS SOAKING
COOK 15 MINS   **❄ FREEZE** NOT SUITABLE

1½oz (45g) dried Chinese mushrooms
2½ cups chicken stock
2 skinless boneless chicken breasts

6oz (175g) dried rice vermicelli
3½oz (100g) sweet corn kernels

1 Place the dried Chinese mushrooms in a heatproof bowl, pour in 1¼ cups boiling water, and let stand for 30 minutes. Reserving the mushrooms, strain the soaking water into a large saucepan and add the stock. Bring the pan to a boil.

2 Slice the mushrooms and cut the chicken breasts into bite-sized pieces or thin strips. Break the rice vermicelli into short lengths and stir into the pan. Bring to a simmer and cook for 2 minutes.

3 Add the mushrooms, chicken, and sweet corn kernels to the pan, bring back to a boil, and simmer for another 2 minutes, or until the vermicelli is tender. Spoon into bowls and serve at once.

The pasta and the liberal quantities of vegetables ensure that this chicken soup goes a long way. You can use whatever fresh vegetables are available.

chicken soup with pasta

SERVES 4–6 **PREP** 10 MINS **COOK** 1 HR **FREEZE** UP TO 3 MONTHS

4 chicken drumsticks
2¾lb (1.25kg) mixed vegetables, e.g., carrots (diced), kohlrabi (diced), green beans (ends trimmed and strings removed), cauliflower or broccoli (small florets), leeks (sliced), zucchini (sliced), peas

3½oz (100g) vermicelli pasta
sea salt and freshly ground black pepper
2 tablespoons chopped parsley

1 Place the chicken drumsticks in a large saucepan, cover with 1¼ quarts (1¼ liters) cold water, and bring to a boil. Cover and cook over medium heat, skimming occasionally with a slotted spoon, for about 40 minutes. Remove from the heat and strain into a clean pan, then allow the stock to cool slightly before skimming the fat from the surface with a spoon.

2 Remove and discard the skin from the chicken drumsticks, strip the meat from the bones, shred, and reserve.

3 Bring the stock back to a boil, then add the vegetables. Add those with longer cooking times first, cover, and simmer for 5 minutes; then add the remaining vegetables and the vermicelli, cover, and cook for another 5 minutes.

4 Season the soup with salt and pepper to taste. Add the reserved meat and heat it through. Ladle into bowls, garnish each with a little chopped parsley, and serve piping hot.

Based on a Thuringian vegetable soup, this recipe requires a good-quality, well-flavored chicken stock, so make your own for best results.

german chicken broth

SERVES 4-6   **PREP** 10 MINS **COOK** 25 MINS   **FREEZE** UP TO MONTHS
AT THE END OF STEP 1

1¼ quarts (1¼ liters) chicken stock
5oz (150g) green beans, ends trimmed
   and strings removed
2 large carrots, peeled and sliced
7oz (200g) kohlrabi, diced

5½oz (150g) sugar snap peas, ends trimmed
salt and freshly ground black pepper
heavy cream, to serve
1 bunch chervil, finely chopped

1 Bring the stock to a boil in a medium-sized saucepan, add the green beans, and simmer for 5 minutes. Add the carrots and kohlrabi and cook for another 5 minutes, then add the sugar snap peas and cook for 5 minutes more—be careful not to overcook these or they will lose their delightful crunchiness.

2 Season with salt and pepper and remove the pan from the heat. Ladle into serving bowls, add a swirl of cream to each, and sprinkle with chervil before serving.

SUGAR SNAP PEAS
These are most often steamed, lightly boiled, or stir-fried, but they can also be enjoyed raw. The fresher the produce, the better the flavor and texture, so make sure you go for firm, smooth, bright green pods.

This is a traditional soup with a modern twist. Adding baking powder and mashed potato to the balls gives them a really light, fluffy texture.

matzo ball soup

⊘ SERVES 4　　**⏱ PREP** 15 MINS **COOK** 1 HR 10 MINS　　**❄ FREEZE** UP TO 3 MONTHS
BROTH ONLY

1 chicken leg and thigh portion
1 onion, finely chopped
1 leek, thinly sliced
1 large carrot, finely diced
1 quart (1 liter) water
1 sprig of fresh thyme
1 tsp celery salt
salt and freshly ground black pepper

for the matzo balls
1 potato, about 4oz (115g), cooked
　and mashed

1½oz (45g) fine matzo meal
½ tsp baking powder
½ tsp grated fresh ginger
1 tbsp chopped fresh thyme
1 tbsp chopped fresh parsley
1 garlic clove, finely chopped
salt and freshly ground black pepper
1 tbsp sunflower oil
1 egg, beaten
4 small sprigs of fresh thyme, to garnish

1 Put the soup ingredients in a large saucepan. Bring to a boil, reduce the heat, cover, and simmer gently for 1 hour, adding more water if it gets low. Meanwhile, mix the mashed potatoes with the matzo meal, baking powder, ginger, thyme, parsley, garlic, and a little salt and pepper. Add the oil, then mix with the beaten egg to form a soft, slightly sticky dough. Shape into 8 balls.

2 Discard the thyme sprig from the soup. Carefully lift out the chicken and remove all meat from the bones, discarding the skin. Chop the meat and return to the soup. Taste and adjust the seasoning, if necessary.

3 Bring the soup back to a simmer, drop in the balls, cover, and simmer gently for about 10 minutes until fluffy and cooked through. Ladle into warm soup bowls and garnish each with a small sprig of fresh thyme.

Consommé regularly has some garnish or herb to lend interest, but it is the quality and clarity of the soup itself that is at its heart.

chicken consommé

SERVES 4   **PREP TIME** 15 MINS PLUS CHILLING   **FREEZE** NOT SUITABLE
COOK 1 HR 20 MINS

2 large egg whites
1 tbsp passata or 1 tsp tomato purée
1 chicken leg, boned and minced or
   finely chopped
1 onion, chopped
1 carrot, chopped

1 leek, chopped
1 garlic clove, chopped
1 tbsp chopped parsley
2 quarts (2 liters) cold chicken stock
salt and freshly ground pepper
chervil, to garnish

1 To make the clarification mixture, whisk the egg whites just enough to loosen them and form a few bubbles. Add the passata or tomato purée and mix thoroughly.

2 Place the chicken, vegetables, garlic, and parsley in a bowl, add the egg white mixture, and mix thoroughly—use an electric mixer with paddle attachment if need be. Refrigerate until well chilled.

3 Combine the stock with the clarification mixture in a deep, narrow saucepan. Heat slowly, uncovered, until the stock comes to a boil. Gently stir to keep the egg from sticking. Once the stock reaches boiling point, turn the heat down immediately and let simmer gently for at least an hour, or until a white crust forms. When it is hard, poke a hole through it to check on the clarity.

4 When the consommé is clear and the clarification ingredients cooked, widen the hole and strain the consommé through a muslin-lined sieve into a clean container. Season with salt and pepper, garnish with chervil, and serve.

This can be a simple chicken broth with just the drizzled egg, but it's more tasty and filling with the addition of vegetables and Chinese seasonings.

chinese egg drop soup

⊘ SERVES 4   **⏱ PREP** 5 MINS **COOK** 25 MINS   **❄ FREEZE** NOT SUITABLE

1 quart (1 liter) chicken stock
1 garlic clove, crushed
½ tsp grated fresh ginger
2 scallions, chopped
2 tbsp soy sauce
½ tsp Chinese five-spice powder

2 corn on the cob or 1 x 7oz (200g) can
  sweet corn
2 good handfuls of fresh baby leaf spinach
2 tbsp cornstarch
2 eggs, beaten

1 Put the stock in a pan with the garlic, ginger, scallions, soy sauce, and five-spice powder. If using fresh corn, place each corn on the cob on its end and slide a sharp knife down the length to remove all the kernels. Add the kernels to the pan, bring to a boil, reduce the heat, cover, and simmer gently for 20 minutes.

2 Add the canned sweet corn if using, including any liquid, and the spinach. Bring back to a boil, reduce the heat, and simmer for 1 minute or until the spinach has just wilted. Taste and add more soy sauce if necessary.

3 Blend the cornstarch with 4 tbsp water and stir in. Bring back to a boil and simmer, stirring, for 1 minute to thicken slightly. Gradually trickle in the beaten egg, stirring gently, so that it forms thin strands. Serve in warm soup bowls.

This lemon, chicken, and rice soup is claimed by countries across the eastern Mediterranean. The stock must be well flavored, or it will not withstand the lemon juice.

avgolemone

SERVES 4 **PREP** 5 MINS **COOK** 20 MINS **FREEZE** NOT SUITABLE

¼ cup long-grain rice
1¼ quarts (1¼ liters) well-flavored
  chicken stock
3 eggs

juice of 1 large lemon
salt and freshly ground black pepper
lemon wedges, to serve

1 Bring the rice and stock to a boil in a saucepan. Simmer, uncovered, for 15 minutes, or until the rice is completely cooked.

2 Whisk the eggs and lemon juice in a bowl until the mixture becomes frothy. Add a ladleful of hot stock and continue to whisk.

3 Remove the rice and stock from direct heat. Whisk the egg, lemon, and stock mixture into it. Return to the heat and cook gently and briefly at a temperature below boiling point, whisking until the texture is velvety—do not allow to boil. Season with salt and pepper and serve with lemon wedges.

Although this recipe uses coconut milk as its base and key Thai flavorings, it makes no pretense of authenticity. No extra salt should be necessary, as *nam pla* is salty.

thai chicken soup

◎ SERVES 4   **🕐 PREP** 10 MINS **COOK** 45 MINS   **❄ FREEZE** NOT SUITABLE

4 stalks lemongrass, bruised and cut
 into ½in (1cm) lengths
7oz (200g) galangal, peeled and diced
5 kaffir lime leaves, bruised
1 chicken leg
2 cups water

2 small red chiles
1 litre (1¾ pints) coconut milk
1 tbsp *nam pla* or Asian fish sauce
juice of 3 limes
3 scallions, finely chopped
2 tbsp chopped cilantro

1 Put the lemongrass, galangal, lime leaves, chicken, and water in a pan and bring to a boil. Simmer uncovered for 30 minutes, or until the chicken is cooked. Remove with a slotted spoon, dice the flesh, discarding the skin and bones, and set aside.

2 Add the chiles to the pan and bring the soup back to a boil. Pour in the coconut milk and heat slowly—you want the soup to become hot enough for the flavors to infuse the coconut milk without coming to a boil.

3 Strain the soup into a clean pan or tureen. Remove the chiles from the sieve and cut into slivers. Add the *nam pla*, lime juice, scallions, cilantro, and chicken to the soup, then taste to check the seasoning. Serve garnished with the chile slivers.

CHILES
Look for fresh, bright, shiny-looking chiles, and avoid any that have soft patches or look wrinkled. Wrapped in a biodegradable plastic bag, they will keep in the crisper drawer of the refrigerator for up to 2 weeks.

This recipe depends on the quality of its few ingredients, so always try to use homemade stock, organic eggs, and the best Parmesan cheese you can find.

stracciatella with pasta

SERVES 4–6   **PREP** 10 MINS **COOK** 20 MINS   **FREEZE** NOT SUITABLE

1½ quarts (1½ liters) chicken stock
½ cup soup pasta
4 eggs
salt and freshly ground black pepper

½ tsp freshly grated nutmeg
2 tbsp grated Parmesan cheese
1 tbsp chopped parsley
1 tbsp olive oil

1 Place the stock in a large pot and bring to a boil. Add the pasta and cook according to packet directions, or until *al dente*.

2 Break the eggs into a small bowl, add the nutmeg, season to taste with salt and pepper, and whisk lightly with a fork to break up the egg. Add the Parmesan and parsley.

3 Add the olive oil to the simmering stock, reduce the heat to low, then stir the stock lightly to create a gentle "whirlpool." Gradually pour in the eggs and cook for 1 minute, without boiling, so they set into fine strands. Let stand for 1 minute before serving.

This broth is filled with contrasting sweet, sour, hot, and salty flavors, and is made in minutes. Instead of chicken, you could try using fish stock and shelled shrimp.

hot and sour chicken broth

SERVES 4 **PREP** 15 MINS **COOK** 20 MINS **FREEZE** UP TO 1 MONTH
AT THE END OF STEP 2

1 quart (1 liter) chicken stock
2in (5cm) piece ginger, sliced
8 lime leaves, shredded
5 garlic cloves, coarsely chopped
2 tbsp chopped cilantro stems
2 stalks lemongrass, split lengthwise and
   lightly bruised
salt and freshly ground black pepper
2 chicken breasts, about 4½oz (125g) each,
   cleaned and thinly shredded

2–3 bird's eye chiles, finely sliced
2 tsp sugar
3 small shallots, sliced
juice of 2 limes
3 tbsp Asian fish sauce
2 tbsp sweet chili sauce
2 small bok choy, coarsely chopped
handful of bean sprouts

1 Pour the chicken stock into a large pan and add the ginger, lime leaves, garlic, cilantro stems, and lemongrass. Season with salt and pepper, bring the stock to a boil, turn down the heat, and simmer for 10 minutes.

2 Strain the stock into a clean pan and stir in the chicken, chiles, sugar, shallots, lime juice, fish sauce, and chili sauce. Simmer for 4–5 minutes, until the chicken is cooked.

3 Add the bok choy and cook the broth for another minute. Stir in the bean sprouts and serve at once.

Chicken, honey, and herb sausages are used in this hearty soup, but it is also excellent made with any other tasty pure-meat sausages or chorizo.

sausage and bean soup

⊘ SERVES 4   **⏱ PREP** 20 MINS **COOK** 30–35 MINS   **❄ FREEZE** UP TO 3 MONTHS

9oz (250g) cherry tomatoes, halved
4 tbsp olive oil, plus extra to serve
salt and freshly ground black pepper
1 onion, finely chopped
7oz (200g) organic chicken or other good-quality pure-meat sausages or chorizo, peeled and roughly crumbled
4 garlic cloves, finely chopped

½–1 tsp crushed hot red pepper flakes (according to taste)
1 x 14oz (400g) can cannellini beans, drained, rinsed, and drained again
about 3 cups hot chicken stock or vegetable stock
1 tbsp balsamic vinegar
1 handful flat-leaf parsley or basil, chopped

1 Preheat the oven to 350°F (180°C). Place the tomatoes on a baking sheet, drizzle with half the oil, sprinkle with a couple of pinches each of salt and freshly ground black pepper, then turn to coat well. Roast for about 15 minutes or until softened and slightly wilted, then remove from the oven and drizzle with the balsamic vinegar.

2 Meanwhile, heat the remaining oil in a heavy-bottomed pot over medium heat. Add the onion and cook for 5 minutes or until soft. Stir in the sausagemeat, garlic, and hot red pepper flakes, and cook, stirring, for 5–10 minutes or until the onion is pale yellow. Stir in the beans and stock, bring to a boil, adjust the heat to a steady simmer and cook for 10 minutes. Add the tomatoes and their juices and stir in half the parsley or basil.

3 Ladle out a cupful of the beans and tomatoes without too much liquid, and process until smooth in a blender. Stir back into the pot, then simmer the soup steadily for 10 minutes. If it is too thick, thin with a little hot stock or water. Stir in the rest of the herbs and adjust the seasoning, adding salt, freshly ground black pepper, pepper flakes, and balsamic vinegar to taste. Ladle into warmed bowls, drizzle with a little more olive oil, and serve.

You can vary this dish by substituting smoked pork sausage for pancetta or using duck instead of chicken. You may wish to add a little filé powder, if you have it.

chicken and pork gumbo

⊘ SERVES 6 　　　 **🕐 PREP** 20 MINS **COOK** 1½ HRS 　　　 **❄ FREEZE** UP TO 3 MONTHS
WITHOUT THE RICE

2 chicken leg and thigh portions
7oz (200g) diced pancetta
2 boneless belly pork slices, rinded and diced
1 quart (1 liter) chicken stock
1 bay leaf
2 red bell peppers
2 tbsp butter
1 onion, chopped
1 garlic clove, chopped
1 celery rib, sliced
3 tbsp flour
2 beefsteak tomatoes, peeled and chopped

2 tbsp tomato purée
4oz (115g) thin green beans, trimmed
　and cut in short lengths
5½oz (150g) okra, cut in short lengths
2 large sprigs of fresh thyme, chopped,
　plus a little extra to garnish
2 tsp sweet paprika
1 tsp smoked paprika
1 tsp brown sugar
a few drops of Tabasco
salt and freshly ground black pepper
8oz (225g) long-grain rice, cooked

1 Put the chicken, pancetta, and pork slices in a saucepan with the stock and bay leaf. Bring to a boil, reduce the heat, cover, and simmer gently for 1 hour. Meanwhile, roast the peppers under a broiler for 10–15 minutes until blackened. Put in a plastic bag, let cool, then peel off the skin, discard the stalks and seeds, rinse, and dice the flesh.

2 Strain the stock through a sieve and set aside. Lift the chicken out of the sieve and place on a board. Remove all the meat from the bones and cut into small pieces, discarding the skin. Add to the pork and set aside.

3 Melt the butter in the pan. Cook the onion, garlic, and celery for 2 minutes, stirring. Stir in the flour and cook for 3 minutes, stirring, until golden. Remove from the heat and blend in the stock. Return to the heat and bring to a boil. Add the remaining ingredients except the meat and rice. Bring back to a boil, reduce the heat, partially cover, and simmer for 30 minutes. Stir in the meats, taste and season with Tabasco, salt, and pepper. Remove the bay leaf. Spoon the rice into bowls, ladle the gumbo over, and garnish with thyme.

An Anglo-Indian soup from colonial days, mulligatawny has many variations. For extra heat, pop a split red chile in the pan when you add in the stock.

mulligatawny

🍲 **SERVES** 4   🕐 **PREP** 20 MINS **COOK** 45 MINS   ❄ **FREEZE** UP TO 3 MONTHS

2½ tbsp butter
1 large onion, chopped
2in (5cm) fresh ginger, finely chopped
2 garlic cloves, finely chopped
1 apple, diced with peel
1 carrot, sliced
1 celery rib, sliced
1 heaped tbsp mild curry powder
1 tbsp flour

4 tomatoes, coarsely chopped
2 tsp tomato purée
2 cups hot chicken stock
2 bay leaves
salt and freshly ground black pepper
¾ cup coconut milk or half-and-half
7oz (200g) cooked chicken meat, shredded
2 tbsp chopped fresh cilantro
juice of ½ lime

1 Melt the butter in a large pan and soften the onion, ginger, and garlic for 10 minutes, without coloring. Add the apple, carrot, and celery to the pan and continue cooking, covered, for 5 minutes.

2 Stir in the curry powder and cook for 1 minute, stirring all the time. Sprinkle in the flour and continue cooking for another 20 seconds.

3 Add the tomatoes and tomato purée followed by the chicken stock. Add the bay leaves and season with salt and pepper. Bring to a boil, stirring, then reduce the heat and simmer, half-covered, for 20 minutes.

4 Remove the bay leaf and blend until smooth, using a stick blender or liquidizer. Sieve the soup to remove any fibers and skin. Reheat, stir in the coconut milk or half-and-half, and add the diced chicken. Sharpen with a squeeze of lime and add the chopped cilantro.

Make good use of leftover turkey by simmering your own stock with the carcass after a roast dinner. This broth is every bit as appealing when made with chicken.

turkey broth

🌀 **SERVES** 6   🕐 **PREP** 20 MINS **COOK** 25 MINS   ❄ **FREEZE** UP TO 3 MONTHS
BEFORE CREAM IS ADDED

1 quart (1 liter) turkey stock or
    chicken stock
½ cup dry white wine
1 carrot, finely diced
1 parsnip, finely diced
2 celery ribs, finely diced
1 leek (white part only), finely diced

1 small turnip, finely diced
salt and freshly ground black pepper
8oz (225g) cooked turkey meat, finely diced
½ cup half-and-half
2 tbsp chopped parsley
crusty bread, to serve

1 Bring the stock and wine to a boil in a large pan, then stir in the carrot, parsnip, celery, leek, and turnip. Season with salt and freshly ground black pepper, half-cover with a lid, and simmer for 20 minutes.

2 Stir in the cooked turkey, cream, and chopped parsley and reheat gently. Serve the soup with plenty of crusty bread.

This thick and creamy soup is perfect for using up leftover turkey, and tastes even richer if you have some homemade turkey stock on hand.

chunky turkey soup

⊘ SERVES 4   **🕐 PREP** 15 MINS **COOK** 30 MINS   **❄ FREEZE** UP TO 3 MONTHS

1 tbsp olive oil
3¾ tbsp butter, softened
1 onion, chopped
1 large potato, peeled, cut into small chunks
2 carrots, cut into small chunks
1 leek, cut into small chunks
2 bay leaves
1 quart (1 liter) turkey or chicken stock, preferably homemade

3 scant tbsp flour
1¾oz (50g) frozen peas
7oz (200g) cooked turkey, cut in chunks
big handful of coarsely chopped parsley
salt and freshly ground black pepper
hot garlic bread, to serve

1 Heat the oil and half of the butter in a large sauté pan. Add the onion and cook for 4–5 minutes until just starting to turn golden. Add the potato, carrots, leek, and bay leaves and cook for a few more minutes over high heat until the vegetables are going golden and sticky on the base of the pan. With the heat still high, pour in the stock, scraping the bottom of the pan so you have a lovely golden-colored stock. Lower the heat, cover with a lid, and simmer for 15 minutes.

2 Work the rest of the butter into the flour with a spoon. Drop this in small pieces into the pan, whisking all the time after each addition with a wire whisk, until you have a thin sauce consistency. Simmer for about 10 minutes to finish cooking the vegetables, adding the peas for the last 2 minutes. Remove the bay leaves.

3 Stir in the turkey and parsley, grind in lots of black pepper, and add salt if needed. Warm through then serve with slices of hot garlic bread.

This spicy soup is equally delicious made with other game birds, but if they are small, such as pigeon or partridge, use the whole bird including the breasts.

pheasant and apple soup

◉ SERVES 4–6   **◔ PREP** 20 MINS
COOK 1 HR 15 MINS PLUS REHEATING

✷ FREEZE UP TO 3 MONTHS
WITHOUT THE HALF-AND-HALF

1 small pheasant
1 tbsp butter
1 onion, coarsely chopped
1 small sweet potato, coarsely chopped
1 small cooking apple, peeled and diced
2 cups medium-sweet cider or apple juice

2 cups chicken stock
2in (5cm) piece of cinnamon stick
1 bay leaf
salt and freshly ground black pepper
⅔ cup half-and-half
4 small fresh parsley sprigs, to garnish

1 Remove the breast meat from the pheasant and reserve to cook for a separate dish. Cut the rest of the bird in pieces using a large sharp knife or poultry shears.

2 Melt the butter in a saucepan. Add the onion and cook gently, stirring, for 2 minutes until softened but not browned. Add the remaining ingredients except the half-and-half. Season with salt and pepper, bring to a boil, reduce the heat, cover, and simmer gently for 1 hour.

3 Remove the pheasant and let cool slightly. Discard the bay leaf and cinnamon stick and purée the remaining soup in a blender or with a stick blender. Return to the rinsed-out pan and stir in the half-and-half. Taste and adjust the seasoning if necessary.

4 Take the pheasant meat off the bones, discarding the skin, and shred it. Add half to the soup. Reheat the soup, but do not boil. Remove the bay leaf and cinnamon stick. Ladle into shallow soup plates, put a small pile of the remaining diced pheasant in the center, and garnish each with a small sprig of parsley.

This is a substantial soup that is a great way to make one partridge feed four people. You could use any other small game bird in exactly the same way.

partridge soup

⊘ SERVES 4　　**🕐 PREP** 20 MINS **COOK** 1 HR 5 MINS　　**❄ FREEZE** UP TO 3 MONTHS
WITHOUT THE SHERRY

1 tbsp sunflower oil
1 partridge, quartered
1 onion, unpeeled and quartered
1 quart (1 liter) chicken stock
1 bouquet garni
salt and freshly ground black pepper
1 potato, diced
1 carrot, diced

1 small turnip, diced
2 tbsp plain flour
4 tbsp water
7oz (200g) cooked peeled
　chestnuts, quartered
2 tbsp amontillado sherry
a few drops of soy sauce
a little chopped fresh parsley

1 Heat the oil in a saucepan and brown the partridge pieces all over. Add the onion, stock, bouquet garni, and a little salt and pepper. Bring to a boil, reduce the heat, cover, and simmer gently for 1 hour.

2 Strain the stock and return to the saucepan. Add the potato, carrot, and turnip. Bring back to a boil, partially cover, and simmer gently for about 20 minutes until the vegetables are really tender. Meanwhile, take all the meat off the partridge, discarding the skin, and shred the meat.

3 Remove the bouquet garni from the soup and discard. Blend the flour with the water and add to the soup. Bring to a boil, stirring, until lightly thickened, and simmer for 2 minutes.

4 Add the shredded meat, chestnuts, and sherry to the soup and simmer for 2 minutes. Add a few drops of soy sauce to taste. Ladle into warm soup bowls and garnish with a little chopped parsley.

You can buy ready-diced mixed game which includes furred game and pigeon, or use diced venison, rabbit, or hare. Aged beef is another option.

puff-crusted game soup

⊘ SERVES 4   **🕐 PREP** 20 MINS **COOK** 1 HR 20 MINS   **❄ FREEZE** UP TO 3 MONTHS
AT THE END OF STEP 2

1–2 tbsp butter
6oz (175g) diced game meat, thawed
   if frozen, cut into small pieces
1 red onion, chopped
2 tbsp plain flour
1 quart (1 liter) beef stock
1 tbsp redcurrant jelly

3 button mushrooms, halved and sliced
1 tbsp chopped fresh sage
4 tbsp ruby port
salt and freshly ground black pepper
1 sheet ready-rolled puff pastry,
   thawed if frozen
1 egg, beaten

1 Melt the butter in a saucepan and cook the meat and onion for 5 minutes, stirring, until browned.

2 Blend in the flour and cook for 1 minute. Remove from the heat, gradually stir in the stock, add the jelly, and bring to a boil, stirring. Add the mushrooms, sage, port, and some seasoning. Bring back to a boil, reduce the heat, cover, and simmer very gently for 1 hour, stirring from time to time until rich and really tender. Taste and adjust the seasoning if necessary.

3 Meanwhile, preheat the oven to 425°F (220°C). Cut four circles from the pastry slightly larger than deep oven-proof soup cups and brush with beaten egg. Stand the soup cups on a baking sheet. Brush the edges with beaten egg. Ladle in the soup. Top with the circles of pastry, pressing down lightly with a fork around the edge to secure. Make a small slit in the top of each pie lid with a sharp knife to allow the steam to escape. Bake in the oven for about 15 minutes or until puffy, crisp, and golden brown. Allow to cool for 3–5 minutes before serving.

This classic French soup takes time to make, but is well worth waiting for. Try serving this with coarse-grained mustard, gherkins, and creamed horseradish.

pot au feu

⊘ SERVES 4   **⏱ PREP** 40 MINS **COOK** 2 HRS   **❄ FREEZE** NOT SUITABLE

a few beef bones, if possible
2¼lb (1 kg) braising steak cut into 2–2½in (5–6cm) pieces
salt and freshly ground black pepper
1 large carrot, thickly cut on the diagonal
2 turnips, thickly sliced
1 medium-to-large waxy potato, cut into 8 pieces

1 Spanish onion, halved
2 garlic cloves, crushed
3 cloves
1 large leek, thickly sliced
3 celery ribs, chopped
3 bay leaves
several sprigs each of thyme and parsley

1 Put any bones in a large, deep, heavy pan. Place the meat on top of the bones. Cover with plenty of cold water, at least 2½in (6cm) above the meat, and very slowly bring to a simmer over low heat. Season lightly with salt and pepper. Skim off any foam that rises to the surface. Cover and let simmer very gently for 1 hour, while you prepare the vegetables. Cut one half of the onion into slices and press the cloves into the other half.

2 Skim the meat again. Add the prepared vegetables to the pan, with the bay leaves, thyme, and parsley. Bring back to a simmer and skim again. Season lightly. Reduce the heat, partially cover, and cook gently for at least 45 minutes, until the meat and vegetables are tender.

3 Skim again if necessary, then lift out the meat and vegetables and put in a large shallow bowl or in individual bowls. Discard the bones, the onion stuck with cloves, bay leaves, thyme, and parsley.

4 Strain the stock into a saucepan through a muslin-lined sieve. Bring to a simmer and season if required. Ladle sufficient stock over the meat and vegetables. Let the remaining stock cool. There should be plenty left for you to use in other dishes (keep refrigerated for up to 3 days, or freeze).

Warming and hearty, this soup is great served with tortilla chips and some guacamole (avocado mashed with lime juice) on hand to spoon in.

beef chili

SERVES 4 **PREP** 10 MINS **COOK** 35 MINS **FREEZE** UP TO 3 MONTHS

1 tbsp olive oil
1 onion, chopped
8oz (225g) lean ground beef
½ tsp crushed dried chiles
1–2 fresh red chiles, seeded and chopped
1 tsp ground cumin
1 tsp dried oregano
2 cups passata

2 cups beef stock
1 x 14oz (400g) can red kidney beans, drained and rinsed
1 tbsp tomato purée
½ tsp sugar
salt and freshly ground black pepper
1 tbsp chopped fresh cilantro or parsley
grated Manchego or Cheddar cheese, to serve

1 Heat the olive oil in a large saucepan, add the onion, and cook for 4–5 minutes or until softened but not colored. Add the beef and cook, stirring, until the grains of meat are separated and no longer pink.

2 Stir in the dried and fresh chiles and cumin and cook for 30 seconds, stirring. Add the oregano, passata, stock, red kidney beans, tomato purée, sugar, and salt and pepper. Bring to a boil, stirring. Reduce the heat, partially cover, and simmer gently for 30 minutes, stirring occasionally. Taste and adjust the seasoning if necessary.

3 Ladle into warm soup bowls and sprinkle with the cilantro or parsley. Serve topped with grated Manchego or Cheddar cheese.

The warming flavors of steak and onions make this soup a rich and satisfying meal. For an authentic touch, use Hungarian paprika—it is fairly readily available these days.

hungarian goulash soup

SERVES 6–8   **PREP** 15 MINS **COOK** 2 HRS   **FREEZE** UP TO 3 MONTHS

4 tbsp olive oil
1½lb (675g) onions, thinly sliced
2 garlic cloves, crushed
1½lb (675g) chuck steak, cut into
   2in (5cm) cubes
salt and freshly ground black pepper

2 tbsp paprika
1 tsp caraway seeds
1 tsp cayenne pepper, plus extra to garnish
4 tbsp tomato purée
1 quart (1 liter) beef stock
sour cream, to garnish

1 Heat 3 tbsp of the olive oil in a large heavy saucepan over medium heat, add the onions, and cook, stirring occasionally, for 10 minutes or until they are golden brown. Add the garlic for the final 2 minutes, then remove from the heat.

2 Heat the remaining oil in a frying pan, add the steak, and cook, stirring often, for 5 minutes or until brown on all sides. Season with salt and add to the onions, along with the spices and tomato purée. Return the saucepan to the heat and cook for 5 minutes, stirring all the time, then pour in the stock. Cover with a lid and simmer gently for 1¾ hours.

3 Season to taste with salt and freshly ground black pepper, then serve the soup garnished with sour cream, a sprinkling of cayenne, and some more freshly ground black pepper.

Choose firm, waxy potatoes that will keep their shape and texture in this deliciously savory soup. Cooking the beans until just *al dente* retains maximum taste and color.

beef and green bean soup

⊘ **SERVES** 6   ⏱ **PREP** 20 MINS **COOK** 1 HR   ❄ **FREEZE** UP TO 3 MONTHS

2 tbsp sunflower oil
1lb 2oz (500g) braising beef (from the
    shoulder), diced into ¾in (2cm) cubes
salt and freshly ground black pepper
1 onion, chopped
2–3 sprigs of thyme

1 quart (1 liter) vegetable stock
1 large potato, cut into chunks
9oz (250g) fresh green beans, trimmed and
    cut into small pieces
1–2 tbsp chopped fresh parsley (optional)

1 Heat the oil in a pan, season the cubed meat with salt and pepper, and add half the meat to the hot oil. Brown the meat until golden all over. Remove from the pan and repeat with the the next batch. When finished, remove all the meat from the pan, add the onion, and cook until softened.

2 Transfer the browned meat back to the pan, tie the thyme sprigs together with kitchen string, and add them to the pan with the stock. Bring to a boil, cover, and cook over medium heat for about 40 minutes.

3 Add the potato, bring back to a boil, cover, and cook for 10–15 minutes, or until just tender. Add the chopped beans and cook for 4–5 minutes, or until the beans are *al dente*.

4 Remove the thyme. Season to taste with salt and pepper, break up the meat pieces slightly, and sprinkle with parsley, if using, before serving.

Enriched with sherry, this slow-cooked soup is a classic for flavorful comfort eating. If you prefer a chunky texture, the soup also tastes good unblended.

oxtail soup

⊘ **SERVES** 6 🕐 **PREP** 20 MINS, PLUS 1 HR CHILLING **COOK** 4 HRS 45 MINS ❄ **FREEZE** UP TO 3 MONTHS WITHOUT THE SHERRY

2 tbsp vegetable oil
salt and freshly ground black pepper
1lb 5oz (600g) oxtails, disjointed, available
   from your butcher
1 onion, sliced
2 carrots, diced
2 celery ribs, diced

1 x 14oz (400g) can chopped tomatoes
¼ bunch of parsley
1 bay leaf
2 sprigs of fresh thyme
1 tbsp flour
1 tbsp butter
⅔ cup dry sherry

1 Heat the oil in a large saucepan, season the oxtails with salt and pepper, add them to the hot oil, and cook until golden on all sides. Add the onion and cook until softened slightly. Add 2 quarts (2 liters) of water, season with salt and pepper, and simmer, uncovered, for about 2 hours. Cover and continue to simmer for another 2 hours. Check to see if you need more liquid during cooking, and add as needed.

2 Add the carrots, celery, and tomatoes. Tie the parsley, bay leaf, and thyme sprigs together with kitchen string and place in the pan. Bring to a boil and simmer for 30 minutes, or until the vegetables are tender.

3 Remove the herb bundle and discard. Scoop out the meat, remove from the bones, and discard the skin and bones. Strain the stock, reserving the vegetables. Refrigerate the stock for an hour or more. Using a blender, process the meat and vegetables and set aside.

4 Once the stock is chilled, remove the fat from the top and discard. Reheat the stock. In a large, dry frying pan, brown the flour over high heat. Cool slightly. Add the butter and blend. A little at a time, stir in the stock and the meat-vegetable purée. Season with salt and pepper to taste, and add the sherry just before serving.

A favorite from Goa in southern India, the vindaloo is Portuguese in heritage and notable for its garlicky masala, spiked with wine vinegar and softened with sugar.

pork vindaloo broth

SERVES 6   **PREP** 35 MINS PLUS OVERNIGHT CHILLING   **FREEZE** UP TO 3 MONTHS
COOK 3 HRS   AT THE END OF STEP 3

6 dried red chiles
1½lb (650g) boneless pork belly with rind,
   cut into 1 x 2in (2.5 x 5cm) chunks
1 tsp cumin seeds
½ tsp black peppercorns
6 garlic cloves, coarsely chopped
2 in (5cm) fresh ginger, coarsely chopped
1 tsp sweet paprika
3 tbsp tamarind pulp
3 tbsp white wine vinegar
4–6 tbsp vegetable oil

2in (5cm) cinnamon stick
2 star anise
3 onions, finely chopped
¾ cup white wine
1¾ quarts (1¾ liters) chicken stock
2–3 tsp palm sugar or dark brown
   (muscovado) sugar, to taste
salt
1 red chile, seeded and cut into
   strips, to serve
2 tbsp fresh cilantro, to serve

1 Soak the chiles in hot water for 10 minutes (for a milder flavor, remove the seeds first). Put the pork in a pan, cover with boiling water, bring to a boil and simmer for 5 minutes. Drain, discard the liquid, and set aside.

2 Dry-roast the cumin and peppercorns (see p25) and grind using a mortar and pestle. In a small food processor, process the ground spices, drained red chiles, garlic, ginger, paprika, tamarind, and vinegar. Set aside.

3 Heat the oil in a pan. When hot, cook the cinnamon and star anise for 30 seconds. Add the onions and cook for 10–15 minutes. Add the spice paste and cook for 1 minute. Pour in the wine and stock and bring to a boil. Add the pork, turn the heat down, and simmer for 2 hours. Chill overnight. The next day, scoop out the meat, strip away the rind, and dice. Skim the fat from the stock and strain the liquid into a clean pan.

4 Bring to a fast boil over high heat and cook for 5–10 minutes. Sweeten with sugar and season with salt. Before serving, stir in the pork and garnish with the chile strips and cilantro.

The Italian name for this soup is *Minestra Maritata*, which simply means the flavors marry well together. Recipes vary, but it is always a robust, rustic mixture.

italian wedding soup

🍲 **SERVES** 4–5   🕐 **PREP** 10 MINS **COOK** 1 HR 40 MINS   ❄ **FREEZE** 3 MONTHS

5½oz (150g) stewing beef, diced
1 boneless belly pork slice, rinded and diced
4oz (115g) piece of salami, diced
1 chicken portion, with bones
1 large onion, chopped
1 quart (1 liter) beef stock
1 sprig of fresh rosemary
1 bay leaf

salt and freshly ground black pepper
¼ head spring greens or 4–6 cavolo nero leaves, shredded
1 head of green or red chicory
2oz (60g) soup pasta shapes
freshly grated Parmesan cheese
crusty bread, to serve

1 Put all the meats in a large pan with the onion, stock, rosemary, and bay leaf. Season well with salt and pepper. Bring to a boil, skim the surface, reduce the heat, cover, and simmer very gently for 1½ hours until the meat is meltingly tender. Remove and discard the herbs.

2 Lift out the chicken, discard the skin, remove all flesh from the bones, cut into bite-sized pieces, and return to the pot. Add the greens, chicory, and pasta. Bring back to a boil, reduce the heat, and simmer for 10 minutes. Taste and adjust the seasoning, if necessary. Ladle into large open soup plates, sprinkle with grated Parmesan cheese, and serve with crusty bread.

CAVOLO NERO
This dark green cabbage almost looks black. It is popular in Italy, but you can find it in some speciality stores. It has a strong, rich flavor, and the best ones have firm stalks and fresh-looking leaves.

Thick and hearty, this German meat and vegetable soup is as filling as a stew. It is versatile enough to work with pork or beef instead of lamb.

pichelsteiner

⊙ SERVES 6 **🕐 PREP** 20 MINS **COOK** 1 HR 10 MINS **❄ FREEZE** UP TO 3 MONTHS
BEFORE CABBAGE IS ADDED

2 tbsp sunflower oil
1lb 2oz (500g) lamb from shoulder or neck,
   cut into ¾in (2cm) cubes
salt and freshly ground black pepper
2 onions, halved and sliced
pinch of dried marjoram
pinch of dried lovage or thyme

1½ quarts (1½ liters) vegetable stock
2 medium carrots, diced
1 leek, diced
2 medium potatoes, peeled and diced
½ Savoy cabbage, finely shredded
2 tbsp chopped fresh parsley

1 Heat the oil in a large pan, season the cubed meat with salt and pepper, and add half the meat to the hot oil. Brown the meat lightly, stirring continuously. Remove from the pan and repeat with the rest of the meat. Remove the meat from the pan, add the onions, and cook for 2–3 minutes or until softened slightly.

2 Transfer the browned meat back to the pan and add the marjoram, lovage or thyme, and more black pepper. Add the stock, bring to a boil, cover, and cook over medium heat for about 40 minutes.

3 When the meat is tender, add the carrots, leek, and potatoes. Bring to a boil, season with salt and pepper to taste, cover, and cook for another 15 minutes. Add the shredded cabbage and cook for 5 minutes, or until just tender. Sprinkle with parsley before serving.

This light version of Irish stew has a richly aromatic broth. Lamb's neck—good value and meaty, with just enough flavorful fat—is best for this soup.

lamb broth

SERVES 4   **PREP** 20 MINS **COOK** 1 HR 45 MINS   **FREEZE** UP TO 3 MONTHS

6 neck of lamb cutlets
1 celery rib, including leaves, cut into chunks
1 parsnip, cut into chunks
1 large carrot, cut into chunks
1 large floury potato, peeled and chopped
3 large scallions, chopped

3 large sprigs of flat-leaf parsley plus 2 tbsp finely chopped parsley, to finish
sea salt and freshly ground black pepper
1 small green cabbage, cored, leaves shredded
a few allspice berries
a few black peppercorns
Irish soda bread, heated in a low oven, to serve

1 Put the lamb in a large saucepan or stockpot. Cover it with cold water to 2in (5cm) above the meat. Add the celery, parsnip, carrot, potato, scallions, and 3 sprigs of parsley. Season with salt and pepper. Bring to a boil over medium heat, reduce the heat, partially cover, and simmer gently for about 1 hour. Remove any foam that forms at the top with a slotted spoon. Remove from the heat. Lift out the meat and set aside until cool enough to handle. Separate the meat from the bones, reserving the meat.

2 Skim any surface fat from the broth. Lift out and discard the parsley sprigs. Add the meat, cabbage, allspice berries, and peppercorns. Cover and return to a simmer over low heat for about 5 minutes. Taste, season if required and stir in the chopped parsley. Serve very hot with warm Irish soda bread.

SCALLIONS
When shopping for scallions—also called spring onions—look for crisp ones with firm stalks. Avoid if dry and brown on the outer skin, or if the green tops are browning or yellowing.

This broth is best with a puff-pastry lid on each bowl. As you break the lid, the spicy aroma is unleashed. The broth itself is best if you make it the day before.

spiced lamb broth

SERVES 4   **PREP** 30 MINS **COOK** 2 HRS 30 MINS   **FREEZE** UP TO 3 MONTHS
WITHOUT THE PASTRY LID

1½ quarts (1½ liters) chicken stock
12oz (350g) lamb shank
9oz (250g) lamb neck fillet, cut into 1¾in (4cm) pieces
2 onions, coarsely chopped
2in (5cm) piece of ginger, peeled and chopped
5 garlic cloves, halved
1 tsp cumin seeds, dry-roasted (see p25)
½ tsp cloves
2 bay leaves

2in (5cm) cinnamon stick
8 green cardamoms, crushed
1 large brown cardamom, crushed
¼ tsp black peppercorns
1 blade mace
sea salt
1 tbsp vegetable oil
9oz (250g) button mushrooms, sliced
1 green chile, seeded and shredded
13oz (375g) ready-to-use puff pastry
1 egg, beaten

1 Pour the stock into a large pan with the lamb, onions, ginger, garlic, and spices. Season with salt and bring to a boil. Partially cover, then simmer for 2 hours or until the meat is tender and the broth reduced by one-third. Cool, then remove the lamb with a slotted spoon and cut into small pieces.

2 Strain the broth through a sieve into a clean pan, pressing the ingredients against the sides of the sieve to extract maximum flavor. Bring to a fast boil and season with salt. Meanwhile, heat the oil in a frying pan and cook the mushrooms and chile for 5 minutes or until just starting to color. Add to the broth, along with the lamb. If you're working a day ahead, set aside to cool, then chill in the refrigerator. Remove the fat from the surface the next day.

3 Preheat the oven to 425°F (220°C). Almost fill four ovenproof bowls with broth. Cut four circles—about 1in (2.5cm) wider than the bowls—from the pastry. Brush the lip and edge of the bowls with egg and cover with the pastry lids. Each should have an overhang—press this down the sides of the bowl to seal. Brush the top and sides of the lid with egg, make a small hole in the top of each one, and bake for 15–20 minutes, or until golden and crisp.

fruit

This is a soup that is easy to make in a hurry. All that's needed to bring out its fruity flavor is ample time to chill—and a perfectly ripe melon.

chilled melon and ginger soup

SERVES 4   **PREP** 15 MINS   **FREEZE** UP TO 1 MONTH
AT THE END OF STEP 3

1 ripe Galia melon peeled and seeded
1in (2.5cm) piece fresh ginger
1 tsp fennel seeds
7oz (200g) white seedless grapes
juice and grated zest of 1 lime
1 tsp dried mint
4 tbsp Greek yogurt, beaten
salt and freshly ground black pepper

for the garnish
2 tbsp fresh mint leaves
pinch of sugar
1oz (25g) crystallized ginger, finely chopped

1 Coarsely chop three quarters of the melon flesh into bite-sized chunks. Finely chop the remainder and set aside. Coarsely grate the ginger and squeeze any juice over the melon chunks. Discard the leftover ginger.

2 Heat a sturdy frying pan over low heat and lightly toast the fennel seeds for about 30 seconds, until you smell an anise-like aroma. Grind the seeds to a coarse powder using a mortar and pestle.

3 Put the ground fennel seeds into a blender with the chopped melon and ginger juice. Add the grapes, lime juice and zest, and dried mint. Process until smooth and push through a sieve to remove the skins.

4 Stir in the yogurt, season, and chill thoroughly—it's best to half-freeze this soup, then quickly whisk it just before serving. Spoon into bowls, adding a small pile of the reserved melon to each one. Shred the fresh mint with the sugar, mix with the crystallized ginger and scatter over the soup, then serve immediately.

This soup provides an unexpected, beautiful finale to a meal on a warm summer's day. It comes into its own when a ripe cantaloupe is used.

chilled melon and white wine soup

SERVES 6   **PREP** 10 MINS PLUS 1–2 HRS CHILLING TIME   **FREEZE** NOT SUITABLE

1 cantaloupe or other melon,
   weighing a generous 2¼lb (1kg)
⅔ cup sugar

1 cup dry white wine
lemon juice
⅔ cup crème fraîche

1 Discard the seeds and scoop the flesh from the melon. Ideally you should have 1½lb (750g) weight, but don't worry if you have more or less. The other quantities can be adjusted to your taste and this will depend more on the strength of the melon's flavor than on its bulk.

2 Dissolve the sugar in 2½ cups of water over low heat, then simmer for 4–5 minutes. Remove from the heat and let cool completely.

3 In a food processor or blender, process the melon with the wine until smooth, then gradually add the cool syrup. Stop when the mixture tastes just a little sweeter than you would ideally like it. Now mix in a few good squeezes of lemon juice and the crème fraîche. Serve chilled, with tiny almond cookies or meringues.

This unusual chilled soup is extraordinarily good, bursting with health and vitality, and is made in just a few minutes. What's not to like?

mango, cilantro, and pomegranate soup

SERVES 4 **PREP** 5 MINS **FREEZE** NOT SUITABLE

1 large or 2 small ripe mangoes
1 red chile, seeded and coarsely chopped
½in (1cm) piece fresh ginger, peeled and finely chopped
1 tbsp coarsely chopped cilantro leaves

juice of 1–1½ limes
sea salt
1¼ cups pomegranate or cranberry juice
coarsely chopped cilantro, to serve
a few pomegranate seeds, to serve (optional)

1 Peel the mango and cut off all the flesh. Add to a blender or food processor along with the chile, ginger, cilantro, lime juice, pomegranate juice, and a little salt and blend to a purée. Taste and add a little more salt if needed.

2 Pour into small bowls or shot glasses, top with a little more chopped cilantro and a few pomegranate seeds (if using), and serve at once.

PREPARING MANGO

Halve the mango, cutting slightly off-center to avoid the pit in the middle. Repeat on the other side.

Slice the flesh in a lattice, then push the cubes of fruit out, using a knife if necessary.

Alfonso mangoes, renowned for their fragrant flesh and creamy texture, have a short season in India from early April through May. Other varieties work well too.

mango and curry leaf soup

◎ SERVES 4   **🕐 PREP** 15 MINS **COOK** 20 MINS   **❄ FREEZE** UP TO 1 MONTH
AT THE END OF STEP 3

for the garnish
small handful of curry leaves
vegetable oil for deep frying

for the soup
4 ripe mangoes, Alfonso if in season,
   available from South Asian stores
2 tbsp vegetable oil
1 tsp black mustard seeds
handful of fresh curry leaves

1 red chile, seeded, finely chopped
2 tsp palm sugar or dark brown
   (muscovado) sugar
½ tsp turmeric
2 tsp rice flour
1¼–1¾ cups vegetable stock
1¼ cup coconut milk
juice of 1 lime, to taste
salt and freshly ground black pepper
2 tbsp chopped fresh cilantro

1 First make the garnish: deep-fry the curry leaves in hot oil until crisp—it only takes a few seconds. Drain on paper towels and set aside.

2 Coarsely chop the flesh of 3 mangoes into small pieces and finely dice the fourth. Set aside. Heat the oil in a medium pan and, when hot, fry the mustard seeds for a few seconds before adding the curry leaves and chile. Continue frying for 30 seconds, until the leaves stop sputtering.

3 Add the 3 chopped mangoes to the pan, reserving the diced mango. Turn the heat to low and simmer the fruit until softened. Stir in the sugar and cook until the mango begins to caramelize. Sprinkle over the turmeric and rice flour and cook for 30 seconds, stirring all the time. Pour over 1¼ cups of the stock and simmer for 10 minutes.

4 Add the coconut milk and simmer for 2–3 minutes. Sharpen with lime juice, season with salt and pepper, and stir in the cilantro and diced mango. If the soup is too thick, add a little hot vegetable stock. Divide the soup between the bowls and sprinkle with a few crisp-fried curry leaves.

in praise of...
berries

In the summer, freshly picked berries are ideal for making wonderful chilled soups in a matter of minutes. All you need is a little sugar, lemon, and a smoothing touch of yogurt or cream.

Rose hip soup is very popular in Scandinavia, where it is served both chilled and hot. Fresh rose hips are best, but you can make it with presoaked dried rose hips.

rose hip soup

SERVES 4 **PREP** 30 MINS **FREEZE** NOT SUITABLE
COOK 1 HR PLUS 1 HR CHILLING

CHILLED

1lb 2oz (500g) ripe rose hips, rinsed
1 vanilla pod, split lengthwise
superfine sugar to taste
½ cup heavy (whipping) cream
3 tbsp natural yogurt

2 tbsp lemon juice
1¾oz (50g) slivered almonds, toasted and
   sprinkled with sugar
Amaretti cookies, to serve

1 Put the rose hips in a large saucepan and pour in enough boiling water to cover generously. Add the vanilla pod. Simmer over low heat for about 20–30 minutes until soft. Strain over a bowl, but reserve and set aside the cooking liquid as well as the vanilla pod.

2 Place the sieve of rose hips over a second bowl. Press the rose hips to extract a purée and set aside. Add what's left in the sieve to the saucepan. Add the reserved cooking liquid and the vanilla pod. Return to a simmer and cook for 20 minutes. Strain enough of the mixture into the reserved purée to produce a smooth soup. Stir in sugar to taste. Chill for one hour or until ready to serve.

3 Just before serving, whisk together the cream and yogurt, and sweeten to taste. Stir the lemon juice into the chilled soup, and pour or spoon into glass bowls. Add a sprinkling of almonds, a dollop of whisked cream, and serve chilled with the Amaretti cookies on the side.

ROSE HIPS
Rich in vitamin C, rose hips have an excellent nutritional profile and a distinctive flavor. Make sure you forage for the wild rose hips that grow on shrubs, rather than picking those from the garden.

This Hungarian soup is meant to taste fresh rather than sweet. The ratio of lemon to sugar is a guideline only, depending on how ripe the cherries are.

cherry soup

SERVES 4   **PREP TIME** 5 MINS **COOK** 15 MINS   **FREEZE** UP TO 6 MONTHS

10oz (300g) cherries, fresh or canned
2 cups white wine
1 cup water

scant 2oz (55g) sugar
1 lemon, zest and juice
1¼ cups sour cream

1 Pit the cherries and reserve the fruit. Add the pits, stems, and any juice to the wine and water in a saucepan over medium heat. Bring to a boil. Simmer, uncovered, for 10 minutes.

2 Strain the liquid into a clean pan and add the reserved fruit, sugar, and lemon. Bring to a boil then, away from direct heat, whisk in the sour cream. Chill well before serving.

CHERRIES
Look for reddish-purple, sweet cherries that are firm but give a little when squeezed. If they are underripe, store them in a fruit bowl to allow them to ripen. When ripe, they can be stored in the refrigerator for a few days.

cheese

Rich and fragrant, this characterful soup should be served in small portions. Play around with the quantities of pear and Stilton to find the right balance for you.

pear and stilton soup

⊘ SERVES 4 **🕑 PREP** 10 MINS **COOK** 20 MINS **✺ FREEZE** UP TO 3 MONTHS
AT THE END OF STEP 1

1 onion, chopped
1 tbsp unsalted butter
4 ripe pears, cored, quartered, and chopped
3¼ cups chicken stock

salt and freshly ground black pepper
4½oz (125g) Stilton, crumbled
juice of ½–1 lemon, to taste
fresh chives, chopped, to serve

1 In a large pan, cook the onion gently in the butter without browning. Add the pears and the stock and season lightly with salt and pepper. Simmer until the pears are very tender. Pass through the fine blade of a mouli-legumes, or process in a blender until smooth. If making this soup in advance, cool it now and continue when you want to serve.

2 Return to the pan and reheat, without boiling. Add the Stilton and stir until melted. Sharpen with lemon juice to taste and adjust the seasoning. Sprinkle the chives over the top and serve.

STILTON
The smell of Stilton is strong, but it should still be pleasant. Try another organic blue cheese in place of Stilton, if you wish. Whatever blue you choose, it should be fresh and moist, but not wet. Cut off any rind before cooking.

Use well-flavored Cheddar and serve the soup with plenty of warm, crusty bread. Use blue cheese if you prefer, but crumble it rather than try to grate it!

cheddar and chive soup

⊘ SERVES 4   **⏱ PREP** 10 MINS   **❄ FREEZE** UP TO 3 MONTHS
COOK 30 MINS PLUS REHEATING   WITHOUT THE CRÈME FRAÎCHE

2–3 tbsp of butter
¼ small celeriac, chopped
1 onion, chopped
1 carrot, chopped
1 potato, chopped
3¼ cups vegetable or chicken stock

1 bay leaf
salt and freshly ground black pepper
small handful of fresh chive stalks
⅔ cup milk
4oz (115g) Cheddar cheese, grated
4 tbsp crème fraîche, plus extra to serve

1 Melt the butter in a large saucepan. Add the celeriac, onion, carrot, and potato, and cook gently, stirring, for 2 minutes, or until softened but not browned. Add the stock and bay leaf and season with salt and pepper. Bring to a boil, reduce the heat, cover, and simmer gently for 30 minutes. Remove the bay leaf, purée the soup in a blender or food processor, then return to the rinsed-out pan.

2 Reserving 4 chive stalks for garnish, chop the remainder finely. Add to the soup with the milk, cheese, and crème fraîche. Heat through gently, stirring, until the cheese melts and the soup is piping hot. Do not allow to boil.

3 Taste and adjust the seasoning, then ladle into warm, shallow soup bowls, adding a dollop of crème fraîche to each. Cut the reserved chive stalks in half and gently lay them, slightly crossed, on top.

German-style cheese soups are often flavored with beer, sometimes using lager or pilsner. This version uses wheat beer, and is thick and rich with a good blend of flavors.

emmental and beer soup

⊘ **SERVES** 6   🕐 **PREP** 10 MINS **COOK** 30 MINS   ❄ **FREEZE** NOT SUITABLE

2 tbsp butter
2 onions, finely chopped
1 clove garlic, chopped
⅓ cup flour
3¼ cups chicken stock

⅔ cup German wheat beer
5½oz (150g) Emmental, finely grated
5½oz (150g) Gruyère, finely grated
freshly ground white pepper
1 tbsp fresh thyme leaves, to serve

1 Melt the butter over low heat in a large, heavy pan. Add the onion and garlic and sauté for 10 minutes until soft but not colored. Gradually stir in the flour, then add the stock a little at a time, stirring constantly until smooth. Bring to a boil, then simmer for 10 minutes or until the liquid begins to thicken slightly. Stir regularly to be sure the mixture doesn't start to stick to the pan, then add the wheat beer and return to a gentle boil.

2 Remove from the heat and very gradually add the two cheeses, adding a handful at a time and stirring constantly. Season to taste with pepper, pour into warm soup bowls, and top with fresh thyme. Serve with German bread and beer.

A great way to use up any white-rinded soft cheese, even if it's strong-smelling. If you don't have celeriac, use a large potato and season with celery salt.

camembert and celeriac soup with cranberry swirl

SERVES 4 **PREP** 10 MINS **COOK** 25 MINS **FREEZE** UP TO 3 MONTHS
BEFORE CREAM IS ADDED

2–3 tbsp butter
1 onion, chopped
½ small celeriac, about 8oz (225g) prepared
  weight, coarsely diced
2 cups chicken or vegetable stock
1 bouquet garni
salt and freshly ground black pepper

2 cups milk
4oz (115g) ripe Camembert, diced
4 tbsp heavy cream
4 tsp cranberry sauce
4 tsp orange or cranberry juice
4 tsp sunflower oil

1 Melt the butter in a saucepan. Add the onion and cook gently, stirring, for 2 minutes, or until softened but not browned. Add the celeriac, stock, bouquet garni, a little salt, and lots of pepper. Bring to a boil, reduce the heat, cover, and simmer gently for 15 minutes, or until the celeriac is tender. Remove and discard the bouquet garni.

2 Purée the mixture in a blender or food processor, adding the milk and cheese. Return the soup to the rinsed-out pan, stir in the cream, and reheat, but do not boil. Taste and adjust the seasoning.

3 Meanwhile, whisk the cranberry sauce with the juice and oil until thoroughly blended. Ladle the soup into warm, shallow soup bowls. Whisk the cranberry mixture again and, using a teaspoon, swirl a little of the cranberry mixture in the center of each bowl and quickly draw a toothpick from the center to the edge all around to form a pinwheel-shaped design. Serve immediately.

breads

This basic white loaf is soft on the inside, with a light texture. If you have any left the day after you've baked it, use it for croûtons (see p39).

crusty white loaf

MAKES 1 LOAF **PREP** 35 MINS, PLUS RISING **COOK** 40 MINS   **FREEZE** UP TO 6 MONTHS

3 cups bread flour
1½ tsp instant yeast
1¼ tsp salt

1 tsp sugar
1 tbsp vegetable or olive oil
1⅔ cups tepid water, as needed

1 Stir the flour, yeast, salt, and sugar together in a large bowl. Make a well in the center and pour in the oil. Stir in as much of the water as needed to make a soft dough

2 Knead on a lightly floured work surface about 8 minutes, until smooth and elastic. Shape into a ball. Turn into a large oiled bowl, and turn to coat. Cover with plastic wrap. Let stand in a warm place about 1 hour, or until doubled in volume.

3 Oil and flour the inside of a 9 x 5in (23 x 13cm) loaf pan, and tap out the excess flour. Punch down the dough. Shape it into a rough rectangle to fit the pan and place in the pan. Cover with plastic wrap and let stand about 30 minutes, or until almost doubled in volume.

4 Preheat the oven to 425°F (220°C). Dust the top of the loaf with flour. Cut a shallow slash down the center of the loaf. Bake for 20 minutes. Reduce the oven temperature to 400°F (200°C) and bake for 20 minutes more until the loaf sounds hollow when removed from the pan and tapped on the bottom. Transfer to a wire rack and let cool.

The mix of white and wholemeal flours in this loaf makes it lighter and moister. If the recipe seems complicated, it is actually much easier and quicker than it sounds.

wholemeal loaf

MAKES 1 LOAF **PREP** 35 MINS, PLUS RISING
COOK 40 MINS   ❄ **FREEZE** UP TO 6 MONTHS

1⅔ cups bread flour, plus more for kneading
1⅔ cups whole wheat flour, plus
   more to dust
1½ tsp instant (fast-rising) yeast
1 tsp salt

¾ cup hot water
¾ cup whole milk
1 tbsp vegetable oil, plus more for the bowl
1 tbsp honey
1 large egg, beaten, to glaze

1 Mix the bread flour, whole wheat flour, yeast, and salt in a large bowl. Make a well in the center. Stir the hot water, milk, oil, and honey together and pour into the well. Mix to form a slightly sticky dough. Cover with plastic wrap and let stand for 10 minutes.

2 Knead the dough on a lightly floured work surface for 8–10 minutes, or until it is smooth and elastic. (The dough will remain slightly tacky—do no add too much flour.) Shape into a ball, place in a large oiled bowl, and turn to coat with oil. Cover loosely with plastic wrap and let stand in a warm place for 1 hour, or until doubled in size.

3 Oil and flour a 9 x 5in (23 x 13cm) loaf pan, and tap out the excess flour. Briefly knead the dough on the work surface. Press the dough into a rough rectangle and place in the pan. Cover loosely with oiled plastic wrap. Let stand in a warm place about for 30 minutes, or until doubled in size.

4 Preheat the oven to 425°F (220°C). Brush the egg over the loaf to glaze it, and sprinkle with a little whole wheat flour. Slash a few diagonal slits in the top of the loaf. Bake for 20 minutes. Reduce the oven temperature to 400°F (200°C) and bake for 20 minutes, or until the loaf sounds hollow when tapped on the bottom. Let cool on a wire rack for 10 minutes. Invert and unmold onto the rack and cool completely.

Use only a small amount of flour on your hands and work surface when you're kneading and shaping the dough for these rolls—too much will make it dry and stiff.

soft white rolls

◎ MAKES 16   **◷ PREP** 40 MINS, PLUS RISING   **❄ FREEZE** UP TO 6 MONTHS
COOK 20 MINS

3⅔ cups bread flour
one ¼oz (7g) envelope instant yeast
2 tsp light brown sugar

2 tsp salt
1 cup plus 2 tbsp tepid water

1 Combine the flour, yeast, brown sugar, and salt in a large bowl. Make a well in the center and pour in the water. Stir to make a soft dough. Knead well on a lightly floured work surface about 10 minutes, until smooth and elastic. Place in an oiled bowl and turn to coat. Cover with plastic wrap and let stand in a warm place for 1 hour, until doubled.

2 Punch down the dough. Divide into 16 pieces and shape into balls. Arrange 2in (5cm) apart on two lightly oiled baking sheets. Cover loosely with plastic wrap and let stand until puffy, about 30 minutes.

3 Preheat the oven to 400°F (200°F). Bake for 20 minutes, or until they are golden brown and sound hollow when tapped on the bottom.

These rolls are perfect with hearty soups. For a special occasion, you could roll each piece of dough into a long rope and then wind it in a spiral or tie it in a figure-of-eight knot.

wholemeal rolls

⊘ MAKES 16 **🕐 PREP** 20–25 MINS, PLUS RISING **❋ FREEZE** UP TO 6 MONTHS
COOK 15–20 MINS

1⅔ cups bread flour, plus more for kneading
1⅔ cups whole wheat flour
one ¼oz (7g) envelope instant yeast
1 tsp salt
¾ cup plus 2 tbsp tepid whole milk

⅔ cup tepid water
1 tbsp vegetable oil
1 tbsp honey
1 large egg, beaten, to glaze
rolled oats, to sprinkle

1 Mix the flours, yeast, and salt in a large bowl. Stir the milk, water, oil, and honey together, then pour into a well in the flours. Stir until slightly sticky. Cover with plastic wrap and leave for 10 minutes.

2 Knead the dough on a floured work surface for 8 minutes, until elastic. The dough will remain slightly sticky. Shape into a ball, place in an oiled bowl, and turn to coat. Cover and leave for 1 hour, until doubled.

3 Lightly oil a baking sheet. Punch down the dough and knead. Divide into 16 balls and place on the sheet. Cover with oiled plastic wrap and leave for 30 minutes.

4 Preheat the oven to 400°F (200°C). Brush the egg over the rolls and sprinkle with oats. Bake for 15–20 minutes. Cool on a wire rack.

These simple yeast-raised breads are cooked in a frying pan. If you would like to make them in advance, simply wrap them in foil, then reheat in the oven just before serving.

easy flatbreads

⊘ MAKES 8　　　**🕐 PREP** 10 MINS, PLUS RISING　　　　　**❄ FREEZE** UP TO 6 MONTHS
COOK 40 MINS

3⅔ cups bread flour
one ¼oz (7g) envelope instant yeast
2 tsp salt

1¼ cups tepid water
3 tbsp olive oil

1 Mix the flour, yeast, and salt in a bowl. Make a well in the center and add the water and oil. Stir to make a soft dough. Knead on a lightly floured work surface 8–10 minutes. Place in a lightly oiled bowl, turn to coat the dough with oil, and cover tightly with plastic wrap. Let stand in a warm place for 45 minutes, until doubled.

2 Briefly knead the dough on a lightly floured work surface. Cut into 8 equal pieces. Flatten each into a round about ½in (1cm). Use a rolling pin to make them a little thinner. Place on lightly floured baking sheets, cover with plastic wrap, and let stand about 10 minutes, until puffy.

3 Heat a large frying pan over medium heat. One at a time, add a flatbread. Cook about 3 minutes, until the underside is browned. Turn and cook about 2 minutes to brown the other side. Transfer to a wire rack to cool. Serve warm.

To give it a lighter texture, this yeast-free bread is made with buttermilk rather than plain milk. For brown soda bread, replace half or all the white flour with wholemeal flour.

soda bread

🌀 **MAKES** 6   🕐 **PREP** 10 MINS **COOK** 30–35 MINS   ❄ **FREEZE** UP TO 6 MONTHS

3¼ cups bread flour, plus extra
   for dusting
2 tsp baking soda
2 tsp cream of tartar

1 tsp salt
4 tbsp butter or lard, diced
1¼ cups buttermilk or 1¼ cups whole milk
   mixed with 1 tsp cider vinegar

1 Preheat the oven to 425°F (220°C). Dust a baking sheet with flour. Sift the flour, baking soda, cream of tartar, and salt together into a bowl. Add the butter and rub in with your fingertips to form fine crumbs.

2 Make a well in the center. Pour in the buttermilk and then mix to form a soft dough. Knead briefly on a lightly floured work surface. Shape into a ball, then roll on the work surface to smooth the surface.

3 Place on the baking sheet, and lightly flatten the top. Using a floured knife, cut into 6 equal wedges, without completely cutting all the way through the dough.

4 Bake for 30–35 minutes, or until golden brown and the bread sounds hollow when tapped on the bottom. Transfer to a wire rack and let cool.

Wholesome and healthy, this chewy bread is made from oats, millet, polenta, quinoa, rice, rye, and bulgur. If you don't have one of these, replace it with one of the others.

seven-grain bread

MAKES 2 LOAVES **PREP** 20 MINS, PLUS 1½ HRS RISING **COOK** 35–40 MINS **FREEZE** UP TO 3 MONTHS

½ cup bulgur (cracked) wheat
⅓ cup polenta
¼ cup millet
¼ cup quinoa
1¾ cups boiling water
1¼ cups whole milk
¼ cup honey
½ cup cold water
2 tsp salt

2 tbsp vegetable oil, plus more for the bowl and for brushing
3¼ cups bread flour
⅔ cup old-fashioned (rolled) oats
⅔ cup rye, wheat, barley, or triticale flakes
two ¼oz (7g) envelopes instant yeast
1¾ cups whole wheat flour, as needed, plus more for kneading
⅓ cup cooked rice

1 Combine the first four ingredients in a bowl. Stir in the boiling water, then let stand, stirring often, for 20 minutes. Add the milk, honey, cold water, salt, and oil. Stir in the bread flour, oats, rye flakes, and yeast. Stir in enough of the whole wheat flour to make a heavy, sticky dough. Dust a work surface with flour and knead the dough for 5 minutes. Add the rice, and knead 5 minutes more or until the dough is supple. Shape the dough into a ball, and roll it around in an oiled bowl, to coat. Cover the bowl with plastic wrap, and let stand in a warm place for 1 hour, or until doubled in volume.

2 Oil two 9 x 5in (23 x 13cm) loaf pans. Knead the dough for 1 minute, cut into two pieces, and form each into a ball. Use a floured rolling pin to roll into 9 x 10in (23 x 26cm) rectangles. Starting at a short side, roll these up, and pinch the long seams to seal. Press into the pans, seam side down, to fill the pans with dough. Cover with a kitchen towel and let rise for 30 minutes.

3 Preheat the oven to 425°F (220°C). Brush the tops of the loaves with oil and bake for 10 minutes. Reduce the heat to 375°F (190°C) and bake for 25–30 minutes or until the unmolded loaves sound hollow when tapped on the bottom. Cool briefly, then turn out onto wire racks to cool completely.

Despite the need for forward planning, this loaf is relatively straightforward to make. The sourdough "starter" gives the bread an agreeably tangy flavor.

rye bread

⏲ **MAKES** 1 LOAF   🕐 **PREP** 25 MINS PLUS RISING   ❄ **FREEZE** UP TO 3 MONTHS
COOK 50 MINS

for the starter
1 cup tepid water
1 cup rye flour
¾ cup plain yogurt
1 tbsp unsulfured molasses
1 tsp instant yeast
1 tsp caraway seeds, lightly crushed

for the dough
1 cup rye flour
2 tsp salt
1¾ cups bread flour, as needed
1 large egg, beaten, to glaze
1 tsp caraway seeds, for the crust

1 Whisk the starter ingredients together in a medium bowl. Cover with plastic wrap and let stand for 8–12 hours, until bubbly.

2 Transfer to a large bowl. Stir in the rye flour and salt. Stir in enough of the bread flour to make a stiff dough. Knead on a lightly floured work surface, adding more flour as needed, about 8 minutes, until the dough is smooth and elastic, but slightly sticky—do not add too much flour. Shape the dough into a ball, and turn in an oiled bowl. Cover with plastic wrap and let stand in a warm place until the dough doubles, about 1 hour.

3 Punch down the dough and form into a 9in (23cm) long football shape. Transfer to a floured baking sheet, cover with plastic wrap, and let stand until almost doubled, about 30 minutes.

4 Preheat the oven to 425°F (220°C). Brush the loaf with beaten egg and sprinkle with caraway seeds. Cut a shallow slash down the center of the loaf. Bake for 20 minutes. Reduce the oven temperature to 400°F (200°C) and continue baking until the dough sounds hollow when tapped on the bottom. Cool on a wire rack.

Favorites in the South, these biscuits are a bit like English scones. They are delicious with soup and are best served straight from the oven.

buttermilk biscuits

MAKES 12   **PREP** 12 MINS **COOK** 15 MINS   **FREEZE** UP TO 6 MONTHS

2⅓ cups all-purpose flour, plus more
  for kneading
1½ tbsp sugar
2 tsp baking powder
¾ tsp baking soda

¾ tsp salt
6 tbsp butter chilled, cut into
  thin slices
1 cup plus 2 tbsp buttermilk, plus more
  for glazing the tops

1 Preheat the oven to 425°F (220°C). Have an unbuttered 10in (25cm) round cake pan ready.

2 Sift the flour, sugar, baking powder, baking soda, and salt into a large bowl. Use your fingertips to rub in the butter until the mixture resembles fine crumbs (or cut in the butter with two knives). Add the buttermilk and stir, adding a little more buttermilk if needed, to make a soft dough.

3 Turn the dough out onto a lightly floured work surface. Knead once or twice, then gently shape into a rectangle about 1in (2.5cm) thick. Using a 2½in (6cm) round cookie cutter, cut out the biscuits and place them in the cake pan with the sides of the biscuits touching. Gather up the scraps, knead together gently, and cut out the remaining biscuits, discarding any scraps.

4 Brush the tops with buttermilk. Bake for 15–20 minutes, or until the biscuits are risen and the tops are golden. Transfer to a wire rack to cool for a few moments before serving hot.

A golden quick bread that is delicious straight from the oven. To ring the changes, add a couple of crushed cloves of garlic, a diced chili, or some grated Cheddar to the batter.

cornbread

MAKES 1 LOAF   **PREP** 5 MINS **COOK** 30 MINS   **FREEZE** UP TO 6 MONTHS

vegetable oil, for the pan
1¼ cups yellow cornmeal
½ cup all-purpose flour
1½ tbsp sugar
1 tsp baking powder

1 tsp salt
1¼ cups whole milk
2 tbsp butter, melted
1 large egg, beaten

1 Preheat the oven to 375°F (190°C). Lightly oil the insides of an 8in (20cm) square baking pan.

2 Whisk the cornmeal, flour, sugar, baking powder, and salt in a large bowl. Make a well in the center. Pour in the milk, butter, and egg to the well and stir with a wooden spoon just until combined. Do not overmix. Spread the cornbread mixture evenly in the pan.

3 Bake for 25–30 minutes, or until the cornbread is browned around the edges. To test if it is cooked, insert a wooden toothpick into the center—it should come out clean. Cut into squares and serve warm.

index

acknowledgments

Dorling Kindersley would like to thank:
Editorial: Susannah Marriot, Diana Vowles,
Constance Novis, Lucy Bannell

Recipe testing: Anna Burges-Lumsden, Richard Harris,
Lisa Harrison, Rachel Wood

Consultant: Carolyn Humphries

Prop stylist: Sue Rowlands
Food stylist: Jane Lawrie, Annie Rigg
Art Director for Photoshoot: Nicky Collings

Index: Hilary Bird

Useful websites
American Food and Wine Festival **www.awff.org**

Blue Hill **www.bluehillfarm.com**

Chez Panisse **www.chezpanisse.com**

The Cookbook Store **www.cook-book.com**

The Culinary Institute of America **www.ciachef.edu**

Honeybrook Organic Farm **www.honeybrookorganicfarm.com**

Local Harvest **www.localharvest.org**

Merridee's Bread Basket **www.merridees.com**

Organic Consumers Association **www.organicconsumers.org**

The Soup Box **www.thesoupbox.com**

Worldwide Opportunities on Organic Farms **www.wwoofusa.org**